JOURNAL FOR THE STUDY OF THE OLD TESTAMENT
SUPPLEMENT SERIES
321

Sheffield Academic Press

Signs of Weakness

Juxtaposing Irish Tales and the Bible

Varese Layzer

Journal for the Study of the Old Testament
Supplement Series 321

For my parents

Copyright © 2001 Sheffield Academic Press

Published by
Sheffield Academic Press Ltd
Mansion House
19 Kingfield Road
Sheffield S11 9AS
England

www.SheffieldAcademicPress.com

Typeset by Sheffield Academic Press
and
Printed on acid-free paper in Great Britain
by Bookcraft Ltd
Midsomer Norton, Somerset

British Library Cataloguing-in-Publication Data

A catalogue record for this book is available
from the British Library

ISBN 1-84127-172-1

CONTENTS

ACKNOWLEDGMENTS

I thank the Committee of the Vice-Chancellors and Principals of the Universities of the UK for their Overseas Research Students Award.

ABBREVIATIONS

AB	Anchor Bible
Ad VC	*Adomnán's Vita Columbae* (Life of Columba)
AOA	*Aided Óenfir Aífe* (The Death of Aífe's Only Son) (in A.G. van Hamel [ed.], *Compert Con Culainn and Other Stories* [repr. Dublin: DIAS, 1978 (1933)])
BCC	*Betha Colaim Chille; Life of St Colum Cille* (ed. and trans. A. O'Kelleher and G. Schepperle; Urbana: University of Illinois, under the auspices of the graduate schools 1918)
BDD	*Togail Bruidne Da Derga* (The Destruction of Da Derga's Hostel) (ed. and trans. W. Stokes), in *RC* 22 (1902), pp. 9-61, 165-215, 282-83, 390-437.
BJRL	*Bulletin of the John Rylands University Library of Manchester*
CBQ	*Catholic Biblical Quarterly*
CMCS	*Cambrian Medieval Celtic Studies*
DIAS	Dublin Institute for Advanced Studies
DIL	*Dictionary of the Irish Language* (compact edn; Dublin: RIA, 1990)
Froech	*Táin Bó Fraích* (The Cattle-Raid of Froech) (ed. and trans. W. Meid; Dublin: DIAS, 1900)
GCT	Gender, Culture, Theory
GKC	*Gesenius' Hebrew Grammar* (ed. E. Kautzsch; revised and trans. A.E. Cowley; Oxford: Clarendon Press, 1910)
HR	*History of Religions*
ICCS	International Congress of Celtic Studies
Int	*Interpretation*
JBL	*Journal of Biblical Literature*
JCS	*Journal of Celtic Studies*
JQR	*Jewish Quarterly Review*
JSOT	*Journal for the Study of the Old Testament*
JSOTSup	*Journal for the Study of the Old Testament*, Supplement Series
Lg	*Longes Mac n-Uislenn: The Exile of the Sons of Uisliu* (ed. and trans. V. Hall; New York: Modern Language Association of America, 1949)
RC	*Revue Celtique*
RIA	Royal Irish Academy

SC	*Serglige Con Culainn* (The Wasting-Sickness of Cú Chulainn) (ed. and trans. M. Dillon; Dublin: DIAS, 1953)
ScrB	*Scripture Bulletin*
Táin	*Táin Bó Cuailnge* (The Cattle-Raid of Cooley) (ed. and trans. C. O'Rahilly; Dublin: DIAS, 1976).
TBec	*Tochmarc Becfhola* (The Wooing of Becfhola) (ed. and trans. M. Bhreathnach), in 'A New Edition of *Toch Marc Becfhola*', *Ériu* 35 (1984), pp. 59-92.
TCD	Trinity College, Dublin
TEm	*Tochmarc Emire* (The Wooing of Emer) (in A.G. van Hamel [ed.], *Compert Cu Culainn and Other Stories* [repr. Dublin: DIAS, 1978 (1933)], pp. 20-68.
TAPA	*Transactions of the American Philological Association*
TZ	*Theologische Zeitschrift*
VT	*Vetus Testamentum*
ZCP	*Zeitschrift für celtische Philologie*

INTRODUCTION

What could early Irish literature of the sixth to twelfth centuries have in common with the Hebrew Bible? One answer is that literacy came to Ireland with Christianity, and thus the Bible had a special place in the mind of any early Irishman who could write. This does not mean that verbal culture in Ireland began one day in 432, however, nor that all early Irish literature is biblically rooted:

> It does not follow from the fact that literacy reached Ireland through Christian-Latin channels that the entire vernacular literature that resulted was bound, whatever the genre, to be permeated by biblical and classical influences.[1]

What it does mean is that the early Irish scribal and ecclesiastical communities had a special relationship with the Bible, as has been thoroughly explored by Fournier, Kottje, Richter, and others.[2] The question remains, however, to what extent this special relationship emerges not only in ecclesiastical texts, but in secular literature. That such influence does indeed permeate other genres of early Irish literature is maintained vigorously by others such as Kim McCone (whose *Pagan Past and Christian Present* Sims-Williams is critiquing in the above quote). For McCone, the history of Christianity in Ireland is the appropriate framework from which to understand and appreciate the interplay of the Bible with early Irish literature.

Valuable work like McCone's does not, however, help with the task here, although it gives it legitimacy (by its own terms). By writing literary criticism I hope to reveal themes and patterns shared by some early Irish vernacular and ecclesiastical texts with certain biblical texts

---

1. P. Sims-Williams, review of Kim McCone, *Pagan Past and Christian Present*, in *Éigse* 29 (1996), pp. 181-96 (189).

2. See, for example, P. Fournier, 'Le *Liber ex Lege Moysi* et les tendences bibliques du droit canonique irlandais', *RC* 30 (1909), pp. 221-34; R. Kottje, *Studien zum Einfluss des Alten Testamentes auf Recht und Liturgie des frühen Mittelalters* (Bonn: Röhrscheid, 1970).

on a literary level.[3] My work operates independently of historians' work because I am not concerned with the question of whether a trait shared by two texts is the result of one's influence over the other—if this is indeed to be proved at all. Jackson wrote that no such theory 'should even be advanced until one has made sure that the motif one is studying is not an international one'.[4] For example, in Chapter 4 I explore a close analogy between the book of Jonah and an anecdote from *Adomnán's Vita Columbae* (Life of Columba) (*Ad VC*),[5] and yet some of the same details can be found in one of Aesop's fables. The question of who copied whom, and when, becomes fraught.

It is, however, the methodological difficulty of proving influence that has created a need for a supplement to historical approaches to early Irish literature. With reference to a possible parallel between the Absalom/Tamar episode of 2 Samuel 13 and *Tochmarc Étaíne* (The Wooing of Étaín), McCone observes, 'Proof can hardly be supplied in such a case, but a creative interplay of native and biblical models does look like a distinct possibility'.[6] This should be subject to Jackson's reminder: can we be sure that this motif is not also found somewhere other than where we would like it to be? But more pertinently, what does 'it looks like' mean to another reader when, as McCone writes, no proof is supplied?

Far from suggesting that this and other parallels should be ignored, I should like to see those proofs created. Sims-Williams has pointed out the complexity of such apparently simple designations, stating that such a comparison demands as much investigation as an apparent linguistic similarity (thus putting it in McCone's own terms).[7] This does not discount borrowings from Deuteronomic and other biblical laws in early Irish law texts, where wording can be compared successfully

---

3.   Throughout this thesis I use 'biblical' and 'Bible' to refer to the Hebrew Bible.

4.   Kenneth Jackson, *The International Popular Tale and Early Welsh Tradition* (Cardiff: University of Wales Press, 1961), p. 129, cited in R. Mark Scowcroft, 'Abstract Narrative in Ireland', *Ériu* 46 (1995), pp. 121-58 (155).

5.   I use italics when referring to Irish tale names, regardless of whether they are titles of volumes or tales within volumes, as opposed to standard conventions of notation in English.

6.   Kim McCone, *Pagan Past and Christian Present* (Maynooth: An Sagart, 1990), p. 34.

7.   Sims-Williams, review of *Pagan Past*, pp. 181-96.

down to the numbers of sheep or wives.[8] Nor do I question the validity of a great number of McCone's other examples, for which he does indeed offer convincing evidence. The problem is that all of these observed similarities deserve to be explained: it is not enough to suggest and dismiss likeness in a phrase. What if McCone's interpretation of Absalom—for he is implicitly interpreting the story—is not the same one adopted by the early Irish ecclesiastical community, or by the author himself? Is it not possible that these are different? In that case the author would not have had that biblical model in mind, and quite another one instead, or none at all, or one we cannot know.

The idea that all people do not read the same text the same way lies at the core of much of the literary theory of the twentieth century, an idea sometimes exaggerated by 'Theory's' proponents, but one which is however especially valid when dealing with an ancient text. McCone, as a twentieth-century Christian Englishman, supposes he has the same Bible in mind as would a seventh-century Irishman whose grandfather still worshipped the Dagda. Certainly no one would argue that Christianity has not changed in that time, and James Mackey has criticized McCone's book on these grounds.[9] The way to address the subtleties of comparison is to acknowledge assumptions and interpretations, and to examine the 'first' text—in this case, the Bible—as scrupulously as the early Irish text. 'Only examination of the texts themselves with the methods of comparative literature can prove such influence'.[10]

The label 'influence' is thus always subjective and finally inconclusive. Whatever we may want to believe, we will never know whether our scribe had 2 Samuel open on the desk in front of him as he wrote. Instead, we can propose to look systematically at the differences between two texts. Having seen a pattern in both places, we can ask what that pattern is composed of, and what we know about the variations on that pattern. Alan Dundes has written analogously with reference to the moment of determining a European source for a native American tale: 'The statement that it is a European tale does not answer such questions

8.   See, for example, Donnchadh Ó Corráin, 'Irish Vernacular Law and the Old Testament', in Próinséas Ní Chatháin and Michael Richter (eds.), *Irland und die Christenheit: Bibelstudien und Mission* (Stuttgart: Klett-Cotta, 1987), pp. 284-307.
9.   J. Mackey, 'Christian Past and Primal Present', in *Etudes Celtiques 9th CIEC 1991* (Paris: CNRS, 1993), pp. 285-98.
10.   Sims-Williams, review of *Pagan Past*, p. 189 (his italics).

as what have the Potawatomi done with the tale?—how have they changed it, and how do these changes tell us something ...?'[11]

McCone's work is nevertheless groundbreaking, and it would take many theses to pursue all the valuable leads he has provided in *Pagan Past and Christian Present* and elsewhere.[12] There are books to be written on the exact ways early Irish law borrows from the Torah [Pentateuch], and what that devotion reveals about early Irish legal and social culture. There are books to be written on the biblical and early Irish tendency towards genealogical lists, wisdom literature, and their views on kingship—to name just a few—to which research others, like Donnchadh Ó Corráin, have paved the way. My work covers a corner of this field by using methods of literary criticism on texts involving narrative depictions of such qualities as mercy, folly, power, courtship and, ultimately, weakness.

Patrick Ford wrote in 1981 that there have been 'very few attempts to give an extended account and analysis of the levels of meaning in medi-aeval Celtic literatures that venture beyond the historical approach'.[13] The literary-critical approach is still finding its feet in early Irish studies. (I outline its progress in the next chapter.) I will build on the work of scholars like Ford who believe that early Irish literature is not too fragile or too full of scribal errors to 'endure' literary criticism. Difficulties of textual transmission, while significant, do not make it impossible to examine one text as a single unit. Instead of asking and an-swering questions of historical criticism, I would ask with Ann Dooley

> What happens when a modern reader attempts to break through the bar-riers of textual difficulties, of faulty manuscript transmission and of cul-tural distance in order to arrive at the point where he is actually reading the text itself as it has survived?[14]

I have chosen three rather different kinds of protagonist to study from different sections of the Bible and different parts of early Irish litera-

---

11. A. Dundes, *Analytic Essays in Folklore* (The Hague: Mouton, 1975), p. 33.

12. See also, for example, K. McCone, 'A Tale of Two Ditties: Poet and Satirist in Cath Maige Tuired', in D. Ó Corráin, Liam Breatnach and Kim McCone (eds.), *Sages, Saints, and Storytellers* (Maynooth: An Sagart, 1989), pp. 122-43.

13. P. Ford, 'Prolegomena to a Reading of the Mabinogi', *Studia Celtica* 16/17 (1981–82), pp. 110-25 (110).

14. A. Dooley, 'The Heroic Word: The Reading of Early Irish Sagas' in R. O'Driscoll (ed.), *The Celtic Consciousness* (New York: Braziller, 1982), pp. 155-59 (155).

ture. First I will compare Jonah with Columba's disciples in episodes from *Ad VC*, 'The Irish Life of Colum Cille', and Manus O'Donnell's *Betha Colaim Chille* (Life of Colam Cille) (*BCC*). Then I look at Samson in Judges 13–16 and Cú Chulainn in *Tochmarc Emire* (The Wooing of Emer) (*TEm*). *Aided Óenfir Aífe* (The Death of Aífe's Only Son) (*AOA*), and *Serglige Con Culainn* (The Wasting-Sickness of Cú Chulainn) (*SC*). Finally I will compare Ahasuerus and Esther in the book of Esther with Díarmait and Becfhola in *Tochmarc Becfhola*.

After illustrating different patterns and themes within the narrative of each pair, I conclude that each episode includes a character whose weakness is central to that episode. I do not propose that this distilled theme of weakness has 'provoked' the creation of the early Irish analogue in the first place, but that in the final analysis, perhaps by different means, this theme emerges. In the first two chapters I describe my own methodology in this process with reference to existing criticism of early Irish and biblical texts.

Each chapter represents one of the first examples of such criticism about the particular text or group of texts. If nothing else, I hope to have reconfirmed that such an experiment is valid, whether conclusive or not in its results. Each kind of criticism I use is matched to the issues the particular text raises. (This approach can be compared with several such experimental works in biblical criticism, as well as ones within Celtic studies.)[15]

Thus, I want to cast some light on individual characters and the signs of weakness in these texts, but also to explore each of the texts at length in its own terms. Weakness is central to each text discussed, but they are different kinds of weakness which work as literary devices in the texts in different ways. Ultimately such exploration is more important in itself than the insistence on a theme or pattern.

---

15. For example, David Clines applies five different 'reading strategies' to the book of Esther in 'Reading Esther from Left to Right: Contemporary Strategies for Reading a Biblical Text', in D.J.A. Clines, S.E. Fowl and S.E. Porter (eds.), *The Bible in Three Dimensions* (JSOTSup, 87; Sheffield: JSOT Press, 1990), pp. 31-52. In 'Prolegomena to a Reading of the Mabinogi' Patrick Ford sets out to 'examine the tales as closely as [he] can, eschewing any one methodology for an eclectic approach' (p. 111).

Chapter 1

PROLEGOMENA TO A READING
OF THE CRITICISM OF EARLY IRISH TEXTS

When did the criticism of early Irish texts begin? Was it twenty-five years ago when historical and form criticism began to give way to a few structuralist assessments? Or was it only in the 1990s, with the publication of *Aspects of the Táin* and *Ulidia*,[1] when other approaches to literature like feminist criticism began to demand an audience? These new approaches examined the texts for their narration, for style, and not for their structure alone.

Perhaps criticism of early Irish literature began only 1996 with Morgan Thomas Davies' article 'Protocols of Reading in Early Irish Literature'.[2] His is the first article to acknowledge the history of early Irish criticism, then to assess it, and to carry it a step further into the late twentieth century.

Why has early Irish literature so long resisted interpretation? It may be because it seemed to so many scholars grounded in the 'classical' tradition of early Irish studies, begun by Rudolf Thurneysen and others, that to stray from a linguistic or historical explanation for literature was inappropriate to the text.[3] Could texts from the early Middle Ages

1. J.P. Mallory, (ed.), *Aspects of the Táin* (Belfast: December Publications, 1992); J.P. Mallory and G. Stockman (eds.), *Ulidia: Proceedings of the First International Conference on the Ulster Cycle of Tales* (Belfast: December Publications, 1994).

2. M. Davies, 'Protocols of Reading in Early Irish Literature: Notes on Some Notes to "Orgain Denna Ríg" and "Amra Coluim Cille" ', *CMCS* 32 (Winter 1996), pp. 1-23.

3. Tomás Ó Cathasaigh summarizes the history of the field in his 'Early Irish Narrative Literature', in Kim McCone and Katherine Simms (eds.), *Progress in Medieval Irish Studies* (Maynooth: Department of Old Irish, Saint Patrick's College, 1996), pp. 55-64.

be examined with the same kinds of methods used on more modern literatures?

The answer seems to be yes. Just as surely as English literary scholarship has found more than a political importance to *Richard III*, so does the great body of early Irish texts—which form the largest vernacular literature of mediaeval Europe—deserve to have more attention paid to what may lie beneath their surfaces.

It is perhaps astonishing that there have been so few articles and books published in this area although, as Tomás Ó Cathasaigh notes, that is changing.[4] While literary articles do appear in Celtic journals with increasing frequency, there are few, if any, full-length literary studies of early Irish texts. J.F. Nagy's *Wisdom of the Outlaw*—a structural anthropological account of elements of the 'Fenian Cycle'—and Ó Cathasaigh's *Heroic Biography of Cormac Mac Airt*[5] (also a structuralist study) might be considered exceptions; they are indeed thorough investigations of certain early Irish texts. While these are neither linguistic nor historical analyses, neither can they accurately be called literary criticism or theory.

Two recently published volumes include a large proportion of literary articles, namely *Aspects of the Táin* in 1992, and *Ulidia* (the Proceedings of the First International Conference on the Ulster Cycle of Tales) in 1994. The collected scholarly essays in these acknowledge the importance of a literary approach to the tales, alongside archaeological, historical, and linguistic investigations. *Ulidia* in particular illustrates a new enthusiasm in Celtic studies for thinking not necessarily grounded in political or geographical fact, for which credit is due to its editor and that of *Aspects*, J.P. Mallory, as well as to individual scholars. Some of these articles will be alluded to in this chapter.

The difficulty of Old and Middle Irish as languages, and the small number of scholars working on processing (editing, translating, etc.) manuscripts at any given time are other good reasons for the delayed entry of this corpus onto the literary scene. In one sense, Celtic studies can be compared wih no other discipline because there are so few scholars with so much work on their hands. Some editions demand nearly a lifetime of work, such as the six-volume Book of Leinster edited by

---

4.   Ó Cathasaigh, 'Early Irish Narrative Literature'.

5.   J.F. Nagy, *The Wisdom of the Outlaw: The Boyhood Deeds of Finn in Gaelic Narrative Tradition* (Berkeley: University of California Press, 1985); T. Ó Cathasaigh, *The Heroic Biography of Cormac Mac Airt* (Dublin: DIAS, 1977).

Best, Bergin, O'Brien, and O'Sullivan, of which no full translation has yet been published.[6] It necessarily takes a generation to move from translation to commentary, and another to move from commentary to interpretation, to poetics and readings.

What has happened in the last five—or twenty-five—years is that more and more scholars of early Irish literature have begun to jettison the critical techniques made popular in the nineteenth century in favour of some of the critical and analytic tools of the twentieth and twenty-first centuries. This new and, some might say, improved language of literary studies and its analytic tools have done a great deal for early Irish studies, and can do still more.

Literary studies, or critical theory, may employ a jargon that sounds exclusive, but that language grapples with phenomena which are familiar to a larger international and interdisciplinary community. It is also a language that came about partly to make literature *more* approachable to more kinds of people. Therefore, its use can serve as an invitation to scholars from other disciplines to compare other ancient and modern literatures with early Irish's much as Georges Dumézil was inspired to include early Irish mythology in his creation of a paradigm of Indo-European mythology. His conclusions are necessarily based on what material he had access to, those translations that were available to him at the time he was writing—and only to this extent can any aspect of early Irish literature be accessible to a scholar outside Celtic studies. Thus, new models for criticism, far from detracting attention from the need for translations and editions of texts—the foundations of this discipline—actually call attention to that need.

Scholars of other mediaeval literatures have availed themselves of the use of these tools decades ago. This may be because much of that literature comes from periods many hundreds of years after the earliest early Irish works, and thus the literature may be considered somehow nearer, less 'strange', more 'attractive' for its themes' having obvious parallels in contemporary literature. It is also the case that, for these and other reasons, there are simply more translators available for Old French than for Old Irish; it may not be a fair comparison for these numerical reasons alone. Literary criticism and theory, such as it has been used by larger disciplines to understand other mediaeval literatures can serve as a model for application to early Irish texts.

6.   *The Book of Leinster* (6 vols.; Dublin: DIAS, 1934–83).

In 1979, an issue of *New Literary History* was devoted to literary criticism of mediaeval literature. In this issue, Morton Bloomfield wrote, 'We are deep in an age of theory and do not in mediaevalist studies wish to spend too much time on the history of Germanic sound changes. The age of positivist scholarship seems to be past'.[7] (Where positivism is 'not interested in the features of the literary texts itself except from a philological and historical viewpoint … as if they were indistinguishable from other sorts of historical document'.)[8]

Thus, while criticism of early Irish texts is not in a race to keep up with criticism of other mediaeval literature, Bloomfield's quote is revealing as to the state of the art. R. Mark Scowcroft wrote of early Irish literature in similar terms in 1995 more simply, 'Source criticism cannot afford to ignore literary aesthetics'.[9] It may have taken twenty-five years for the term 'positivism' even to be articulated in early Irish studies, but it will not take as long to progress beyond it.

In his article Davies explains a number of assumptions involved in the positivist approach underlying the writing of many decades of scholarship in early Irish studies. Assumptions inform any decision, of course, but when these remain unchallenged for generation after generation they need to be redefined and articulated. They need to have relevance to the needs of a contemporary scholar, or be rejected.

Myles Dillon's *Early Irish Literature* was an important achievement in the history of early Irish studies, and it is still important.[10] It is, however, inadequate that a reprint of 1940s blurbs and commentary should be the only critical text available to, a class of 2001 on Irish saga literature. Those same students will have been exposed to contemporary theory elsewhere and may want to apply it to early Irish literature—and so may their lecturers! Dillon's work and that of others of his generation might best be used as the beginning of a whole range of possible views.

These are the intentionalist points that Davies highlights, citing in particular a paragraph by David Greene:

7. M.W. Bloomfield, 'Continuities and Discontinuities', *New Literary History* 10/2 (Winter 1979), pp. 409-15 (410).

8. Ann Jefferson and David Robey, 'Introduction', in *idem* (eds.), *Modern Literary Theory* (London: B.T. Batsford, 1986), pp. 7-23 (9).

9. Scowcroft, 'Abstract Narrative', p. 158.

10. Myles Dillon, *Early Irish Literature* (Dublin: Four Courts Press, 1994).

[One] that there is something we can call an original text or reading; (2) that the meaning of this original text or reading is to be equated with the original intentions that lie behind it; (3) that both the text or reading on the one hand and the intentions behind it on the other hand are likely to have been obscured through a process of scribal or editorial interference, intentional or otherwise… referred to as 'corruption'; and (4) that interpreting the text or reading is a matter of clearing away that obstruction and arriving at the unique, correct meaning of the text or reading—a meaning that presumably coincides with the intention of the original author.[11]

In other words, the premises he locates are:

1.   There is an original text (this is not it).
2.   Its meaning = what it was written to do (and nothing else).
3.   This is not the original (it has been interfered with).
4.   Its meaning = this minus the interference = what the author really wanted.

By simply isolating and articulating points like these, attention is drawn to the fact that a choice is being made at every step, and a reasoning being used: Greene is not simply holding up a mirror to the texts, as it might seem. Davies goes on to show the theoretical and practical difficulties of these presumptions.

Another example of unwritten assumptions occurs in a work by a distinguished historian who writes, 'The Irish audience did not ask, as we do, "Is this story true?" meaning "Is it literal fact?" They wanted to be amused.' Here the (implicit and explicit) premises about the 'story' include:

1.   Its meaning = what it was written to do (and nothing else).
2.   Its meaning = what the audience wanted to hear.
3.   The audience ≠ the present reader where
4.   the present reader is all possible readers of this book, and they locate the same meaning as the author and
5.   read for the same reasons she states.
6.   Amusement ≠ knowing a story is true.

Again, the articulation of the presumptions reveals the historian's view of early Irish literature.

11. Davies, 'Protocols of Reading', pp. 3-4.

One particular problem Davies locates is the attempt to estimate a text's creation: '[T]he very notion of "original intention" is problematic from a simple practical perspective. It is also problematic from a theoretical perspective.'[12] Some theorists writing as long ago as the 1920s saw the problems with this as well. Summarizing the work of Mikhail Bakhtin, Simon Dentith writes, 'The scholarly fantasy of reconstructing the original moment of a text's reception as a way of discovering the truth of the text is not only a fantasy but a disabling one ...'[13]

Northrop Frye was reacting to similar assumptions in scholarship generally some forty years before Davies when he wrote:

> The failure to make ... the distinction between ... imaginative and discursive writing produces what in criticism has been called the 'intentional fallacy', the notion that the poet has a primary intention of conveying meaning to a reader, and that the first duty of a critic is to recapture that intention.[14]

He adds: 'If the author has been dead for centuries, such speculation cannot get us very far, however irresistibly it may suggest itself'.[15]

Literary theory may have moved on from the label 'intentional fallacy' and parsed the author–reader–text relationship even further than Frye could have anticipated. However, since the criticism of early Irish texts is still reacting to textual criticism and positivism, it may be appropriate to use the language of literary criticism as it was used by its original advocates in reaction against those schools in their day.

Not being able to establish the 'original' meaning does not mean that a text is without meaning. It is in no way a contradiction of the text to locate meaning in it. Furthermore, as Davies and others have written, there is no reason to assume that the early Irish were incapable of creating intricate meanings on the kinds of levels a modern reader might locate. We may not be able to find the blueprints of composition, but we can try to read as best we are able. Some of the many scholars of early Irish writing who have pursued this course are discussed below.

Davies is not the only one to articulate some protocols of early Irish reading, and the scholars who have written in this direction before him deserve to be acknowledged in this context. Patrick Ford writes,

12. Davies, 'Protocols of Reading', pp. 22.
13. S. Dentith, *Bakhtinian Thought* (London: Routledge, 1995), pp. 98-99.
14. N. Frye, *Anatomy of Criticism* (London: Penguin, 1990), p. 86.
15. Frye, *Anatomy of Criticism*, p. 87.

> The basic assumption about the tales must be … that they did have a meaning for the scribe as well as for his audience, whoever and whatever that was. It is the only assumption, in fact, that in any way justifies our own excursions into their inner and outer meanings.[16]

Ford also mentions the burden of the seemingly intentionally limiting language of previous scholars, which 'formulations of despair are likely to discourage students and scholars alike from seeking new approaches to meaning in the tales'.[17] In this article he argues that the texts deserve consideration in their current form, that early mediaeval people could be a capable audience (as well as being capable narrators) and, crucially, he argues that there are meanings in the texts that he cannot anticipate, let alone justifiably condemn.

Daniel Melia is another scholar who wrote of the prejudices of previous critics, some twenty-five years before Davies' article: 'We cannot judge someone else's aesthetics on the basis of our own, and in a real sense it is impossible to recreate a sensibility completely—especially one as seemingly distant as that of mediaeval Ireland.'[18] Calling something a corruption is either an unjustified or unexplained aesthetic judgment based on the understanding that there is a clear original of the text in question. When there is no original, designating some passage a corruption is just one of many possible interpretations and could profit by being labelled as such, with the rationale behind the label explained.

Scowcroft's article features this kind of deconstruction as part of its agenda. He takes it further: if we try not to judge early Irish aesthetics on the basis of our own, what are some features of early Irish narrative (i.e. not 'what it was' before being written, or what it 'ought' to be like)? He locates literary intentions and devices on the part of the early Irish narrator, writing that the composition was not an imitation of another lost text (like *The Aeneid* or the Bible), a transcription of an oral narrative, or a testimony to political events alone. He does not deny the possibility of their relevance, but chooses to focus on narrative composition instead. Specifically, he explores 'abstract narrative' which he defines here as

---

16. Ford, 'Prolegomena', p. 113.
17. Ford, 'Prolegomena', p. 113.
18. D. Melia, 'Narrative Structure in Irish Saga' (Unpublished PhD dissertation, Harvard University, 1972), p. 10.

elements of the medium itself—story-patterns, motifs, principles, themes, metaphors and other verbal associations, literal and metaphorical meanings coming together ... The narrative itself acts out and literalises the multiple meanings of the words.[19]

(See Nagy in this chapter for more examples of this kind of thinking.)

Far from pointing out 'sloppy' scribal work, Scowcroft credits the early Irish literati with 'a corpus of hidden learning and "implicit metaphor" as compelling and useful as classical mythology for the rest of mediaeval Christendom'.[20] The abstract narrative of Scowcroft fits well with the work of several recent scholars who credit the early Irish with a consciousness of composition.

Ó Cathasaigh is another such scholar, one who has been urging the reappraisal of the importance of early Irish texts for twenty-five years. Of the *Táin Bó Cuailnge* (*Táin*) he declares that 'its primary claim to our attention must be as a work of literature.'[21] Like the critics mentioned above, Ó Cathasaigh is keen to dismantle the positivism of a generation, not in order to pursue a literary approach alone, but to acknowledge that a literary approach should always be included in a discussion of an early Irish text.

> There has been a tendency to discredit the literary status of early Irish narrative texts, to see them not as works in their own right, but rather in relation to myth or history or oral tradition... All that I am saying is that we should always bear in mind what it is that we are dealing with.[22]

In so writing, he is doing much of the work to shift the attention of philologists and mythologists—among whom he is a leader also—to other dimensions of early Irish literature, and the *Táin* in particular. Again, he is not denying the place of the other disciplines, but advising on the use of their methods. His words are a caution for those who would see only one aspect of the literature.

Ó Cathasaigh's own work has changed significantly in the time he has been writing. Over the years he has come to show how texts can be not only a good vessel for myth, but how their 'literature casing' is at least as deserving of structural analysis. In 1982—ten years before the

---

19. Scowcroft, 'Abstract Narrative', pp. 123, 129.
20. Scowcroft, 'Abstract Narrative', p. 157.
21. T. Ó Cathasaigh, 'Mythology in Táin Bó Cuailnge' in H.L.C. Tristram (ed.), *Studien zur Táin Bó Cuailnge* (Tübingen: G. Narr, 1993), pp. 114-32 (115).
22. Ó Cathasaigh, 'Mythology', p. 115.

above quote—he writes that 'a central task of criticism must be to un-cover and to restate in abstract terms the configuration of the mytho-logical patterns which underlie the myths.'[23] He writes with reference to the work of the structural mythologist Georges Dumézil. But such an assertion still leaves room for the question whether the primary impor-tance of a text is to furnish further evidence for a ternary ideology, or whether that is only one possible importance.

Ó Cathasaigh has come to include and address those new kinds of questions. In a 1995 article, 'Reflections on *Compert Conchubuir* and *Serglige Con Culainn*', Ó Cathasaigh shifts his focus to the very literary terms of story and discourse, offering a 'compositional study'.[24] This kind of structuralism (based on the work of Seymour Chatman) looks not only at what is told, but the ways of telling, and the tension between these two factors.

Philip O'Leary is another to have brought literary attention to early Irish texts over many years. O'Leary implicitly acknowledges the rich-ness of early Irish writing by his pursuit of an understanding of the honour code of early Irish society as seen through that literature. His position has led him to see the texts as sociological tracts, refuting a literary approach inasmuch as he does not try to distinguish imaginative from discursive writing.

O'Leary has focused on specific behavioural and emotional responses of characters within early Irish society *as presented in the literature*.[25] But if that italicized phrase is removed, the argument turns positivist. Conclusions about the early Irish heroic code—like that generosity is a means of asserting power—are based on a certain text or another and are carefully wrought statements about that text. While these statements are logically consistent, the posited relationship between the text and the larger social world of pre-Christian Ireland in which the observa-tions are rooted needs explanation.

Scowcroft warns, 'Those who seek a picture of Irish society or nor-mative ethics in such texts have as much reason for caution as the

23. T. Ó Cathasaigh, 'Between God and Man: The Hero of Irish Tradition' in M.P. Hederman and R. Kearney (eds.), *The Crane Bag Book of Irish Studies*, I (Dublin: Blackwater Press, 1982), pp. 220-27 (220).

24. T. Ó Cathasaigh, 'Reflections on *Compert Conchubuir* and *Serglige Con Culainn*', in Mallory and Stockman (eds.), *Ulidia*, pp. 85-90.

25. See, for example, P. O'Leary, 'Magnanimous Conduct in Irish Heroic Lit-erature', *Éigse* 25 (1991), pp. 28-44.

students of Irish or Indo-European paganism. Early Irish literature is a great deal more than the sum of its parts.'[26] That is, there may be a temptation to draw sociological conclusions from the early Irish tales, but that approach implicitly eliminates the possibility that they are imaginative discourse. Increased clarity might require no more than a different choice of words. Instead of discovering 'evidence' from the tales, Joanne Findon describes 'the heroic code of honour, which seems to have existed—at least in the literary world of the texts—alongside the laws.'[27] Findon's words make the context of such an observation textually based entirely, and therefore verifiable. I will rely greatly on Findon's work in Chapter 4.

On a practical level, since we cannot know if it is the society of pre-Christian Ireland or the Ireland of hundreds of years later whose virtues are meant to be the stories' variables, it is hard to make any such judgment. Scowcroft's warning and Findon's carefulness on this point work very well with Davies's article. By separating the two notions of historical and literary interest, they pave the way for a study of character development or other literary approaches, independent of any anthropological investigations.

O'Leary's work here can be considered in another light, however, and one which attributes less of a positivist stand to him. A literary attempt to understand motives for characters' actions is called psychoanalytic criticism. Since his work is based on fiction, his articles may be read as literary critiques of those fictional texts. If his work is read as such, he sets a precedent for other psychoanalytic critiques of early Irish literature.

In later articles O'Leary continues to provide useful insights into early Irish literature, now with the intention of redrawing the frames around his arguments. Those psychological, cultural, and sociological levels he observes are part of 'early Irish literature' and not the 'early Irish world', moving from the position of 'the literature tells us what the early Irish heroic code involved' to 'the redactor plays with the presentation of a heroic code in early Irish literature'.

It has been shown how it is not Davies alone who has suggested the possibility of seeing early Irish texts as literature. At the disposal of the scholar of early Irish literature are also the works of Ó Cathasaigh,

---

26. Scowcroft, 'Abstract Narrative', p. 158.

27. J. Findon, 'A Woman's Words: Emer versus Cú Chulainn in Aided Óenfir Aífe', in Mallory and Stockman (eds.), *Ulidia*, pp. 139-48 (145).

O'Leary, Melia and others, like Ann Dooley and John Carey. Davies has in turn given permission, in a sense, to subsequent scholars to answer the questions that texts and other critics' work pose. It may be that he has provided a forum for the discussion of the criticism of early Irish literature.

From here it can now be asked how critics have located meaning in the tales. In the preceding section some of those meanings have been touched on. Many more scholars have continued on, pursuing various ideas. Davies deserves to be mentioned again in this context because of the affirmation he gives to the possibility of multiple meanings.

This point is spun from the concept stated above that the early Irish were capable of reading and writing creatively. Their glosses and 'interpolations' can be seen as converging opinions and possibilities, each with an equal claim to being 'true', although not necessarily in the same way. Therefore, according to Davies, the running multidimensional commentary of the early Irish glossator should serve not as embarrassment to the contemporary scholar of early Irish, but as an example.

How can this ancient reading strategy, as he sees it, make so many years' worth of early Irish scholarship seem old-fashioned themselves? It is because of scholars' very unwillingness to acknowledge differences of perspective, Davies implies. His article is singular, not for his awareness of this limitation, but because he addresses the terms of that 'old-fashioned' scholarship and argues from that position, leading away from it without apologizing for doing so.

The period before Davies may fruitfully be considered as being divided into different eras of action and reaction, as a few examples should reveal.

In 'The Happy Otherworld' (1895), Alfred Nutt writes:

> It might be thought that the less or greater admixture of the non-Christian element supplied a sure indication of the age of these stories. But this is not so. In this, as in other things, the Viking period is a disturbing cause, the full effects of which are by no means clearly defined. On their arrival in Ireland, and for a century and a half after, the mass of the invaders were not only pagan, but aggressively and ferociously anti-Christian. It is more than likely that their advent must have fanned whatever fires may have been slumbering in the ashes of Irish paganism...[28]

28. A. Nutt, 'The Happy Otherworld in the Mythico-Romantic Literature of the Irish', in Kuno Meyer (ed.), *The Voyage of Bran*, I (London: D. Nutt, 1895), pp. 105-331 (127-28).

A hundred years later, Ann Dooley grapples with influence from the other side:

> I want to use feminist critical ways of reading, to suggest a conscious-
> ness of vulnerability in the splendid world of male heroic action, whether
> of twelfth-century anxiety about the political other, in the midlands, or
> more fundamental gender unease in the fiction of the heroic male him-
> self—a fiction, it must be remembered, endorsed and manipulated by the
> ecclesiastical authors/handlers of the *Táin* texts.[29]

The difference between these two quotations can be stated as a question of which external force is being targeted as a threat to the early Irish text (although Dooley is prepared to prove her point). Both schol-ars demand that attention be paid to the truth beyond that oppression. This tone may also be heard in Kim McCone's arguments (where the threat is 'nativists') as well as Greene's, and others.

In fact, each group has much to offer and has shed light on another corner of early Irish studies. Furthermore, they share a motivation which may be less common in other fields, namely a desire to understand and even enjoy this literature. Davies may have provided a sound logi-cal framework from which differing points of views can continue to develop.

One of the schools of theory that has attracted a large number of early Irish scholars is semiotics. Another is structuralism, as well as more specific schools thereof like comparative structuralism (often asso-ciated in Celtic studies with Dumézil) and structuralist anthropology (associated with Claude Lévi-Strauss).

Structuralism has been defined by Lévi-Strauss as 'the quest for the invariant, or for the invariant elements among superficial differences'.[30] (Although there are variations within the broad label 'structuralism', Lévi-Strauss's definition is non-specific enough to be inclusive.) This approach might be especially attractive as a reaction against a long period of traditional scholarship that consigned no consistency, no inherent logic whatever to early Irish texts.

On the other hand, structuralism has built into it a reason why it would be unattractive to Celtic scholars. Lévi-Strauss invites scholars to view with equal attention all versions and recensions of a myth along

29. A. Dooley, 'The Invention of Women in the Táin', in Mallory and Stock-man (eds.), *Ulidia*, pp. 123-33 (123).

30. C. Lévi-Strauss, *Myth and Meaning: Cracking the Code of Culture* (New York: Schocken Books, 1995), p. 30.

with its first available recension. He famously legitimized all retellings of the Oedipus myth, from Sophocles to Freud, in order to render visible the underlying structure of that myth. In early Irish literature this would mean considering Yeats's 'Cuchulainn Cycle' alongside the various recensions of the *Táin*, for example.

Applications and interpretations of structuralism in this discipline vary, often to the extent that they defy easy categorization. Each attempt is necessarily the first of its kind, and each critic is faced with the excruciating task of redefining a school of theory in a way that makes sense for early Irish studies.

One of the earliest such applications following the work of Melia and Ó Cathasaigh (above) was an article in *The Celtic Consciousness* by Ann Dooley in 1981.[31] There she analyses the power of words in the Deirdre story 'in fairly simple, quasi-structuralist terms' stating that 'in [Deirdre's] society women function primarily as signs, not users of signs'.[32]

Dooley's language reveals an acute awareness of different schools of theory, even though the only theorist she mentions by name is the semiotician Roland Barthes. She then tackles the significant task of customizing that school's language for the early Irish text she is addressing, *Longes mac n-Uislenn*.[33] To my knowledge, there is nothing so adventuresome in early Irish criticism for fifteen years afterwards. In fact, because her article does not wait for the criticism of early Irish texts to have caught up with it, it may have been impossible for an uninitiated scholar to follow its lead for all those years.

Melia has provided a thorough structuralist analysis to some of the Ulster Tales in his unpublished PhD dissertation, 'Narrative Structure in Irish Saga',[34] and in subsequent articles built around that work.[35] He accepts the integrity of the tales and argues that they are far more complex and coherent structurally than had been assumed. He stops short of

31. Dooley, 'Heroic Word', pp. 155-59.
32. Dooley, 'Heroic Word', pp. 155-56.
33. V. Hull (ed.), *Longes Mac n-Uislenn: The Exile of the Sons of Uisliu* (New York: Modern Language Association of America, 1949).
34. Harvard University, 1972.
35. 'Parallel Versions of "The Boyhood Deeds of Cuchulainn"', in J.J. Duggan (ed.), *Oral Literature* (New York: Barnes & Noble Books, 1975), pp. 25-40; 'Remarks on the Structure and Composition of the Ulster Death Tales', *Studia Hibernica* 17/18 (1977–78), pp. 36-57.

allowing the possibility of other readings, however, asserting, for example, that 'Motivation is a legal triggering mechanism, not a signal of personal psychological reaction.'[36] Like Ó Cathasaigh in his early writing, Melia seems to insist that there is nothing about the early Irish text that structuralism cannot assess. While his work is a crucial step toward an understanding of the levels of early Irish texts (some of the tales he works with have not received critical attention before or since) it also implies there is simply not a lot more to be done.

Nagy consistently produces succinct and insightful articles on various early Irish texts, focusing mainly on the Fenian Cycle. While he also seems to be working as a semiotician or a structuralist, his writing usually defies categorization. An article like 'Liminality and Knowledge in Irish Tradition'[37] is clearly in the structural anthropologist mode, including things both raw and cooked. In other articles, however, his pursuit of the liminal leads him into the ultimate liminality, that of textual compositional 'worlds', and the tension that he locates between oral and written narrative within those worlds.

An example from a later work reveals another progression, where he employs a technique that anticipates and surpasses the work of Scowcroft, below. In 'Compositional Concerns in the *Acallam na Senórach*'[38] (discussed in Chapter 5) Nagy comments on that story which involves a meeting of characters—Saint Patrick and the last of the Fíanna—from different times (the Christian and pre-Christian). He argues that the narrative itself echoes the tension of their meeting. The form suggests to Nagy that it could begin and end anywhere, defying conclusion. This he considers a metafiction for the meeting of worlds, and for what he sees as the community-friendly continuity of pre-Christian traditions within the Christian time. In that context the form 'represents almost despite itself a triumph over closure of various kinds'.[39]

Such an enterprise necessarily involves a certain dimension of positivism (the texts are to be understood as historical documents). Nagy, however, employs a language entirely more playful and innovative than

36. Melia, *Narrative*, p. 118.

37. *Studia Celtica* 16/17 (1981–82), pp. 135-42.

38. In Donnchadh Ó Corráin, Liam Breatnach and Kim McCone (eds.), *Sages, Saints and Storytellers* (Maynooth: An Sagart, 1989), pp. 149-58.

39. J.F. Nagy, 'Compositional Concerns in the Acallam na Senórach', in Ó Corráin, Breatnach and McCone (eds.), *Sages*, p. 150.

that term implies. We are invited to think that he is neither rejecting positivism nor accepting it, but locating meaning in the very ambiguity!

Is he arguing a kind of Marxist reading where the text reflects the political content of its time at the level of narrative (an Ireland where Christian tradition is becoming a material reality invading a pre-existing system)? Or is he arguing that the text is historically useful, rooted in time and presenting that time like a mirror? (A major distinction between these two possible understandings of his work is that the first acknowledges the author, and the second would deny his or her role in composition.)

Is Nagy evoking a definition of allegory without mentioning it (where allegory is when 'the characters and actions that are signified literally in turn signify ... historical personages and events')?[40]

In another article he deals with the same theme and locates 'the most perilous of all their journeys between worlds—that from an oral tradition into a literary tradition'.[41] Is the literary passage to the Otherworld meant to stand for the political passage from an oral to a literary tradition in early Christian Ireland? If he is crediting the narrator with such compositional prowess, then he writes in the same vein as Scowcroft does in 1995. If he is saying that the text is a reflex of Christianity's oppression (and the remark intended as a kind of aside), then he is writing in the same vein as Nutt in 1895: 'Finally, if the sanctity of the fairy world be a product of the confusion of the introduction of Christianity, why... should it have assumed this special form?'[42]

Other scholars look for meaning in this twilight zone of overlapping traditions, and what possible role it may have played in creating the tales as we have them. O'Leary writes, 'The introduction of Christianity to Ireland produced in the native literature a fascinatingly hybrid morality in which the old and the new standards could at one time exist peacefully if not necessarily consistently.'[43] O'Leary's statement leaves little room for a label of allegory, however: a designation of 'hybrid

40. M.H. Abrams, *A Glossary of Literary Terms* (New York: Holt, Rinehart & Winston, 5th edn, 1988), p. 5.

41. J.F. Nagy, 'Close Encounters of the Traditional Kind', in Patrick Ford (ed.), *Celtic Folklore and Christianity* (Santa Barbara, CA: McNally & Loftin, 1983), pp. 129-49 (149).

42. Nutt, 'Otherworld', p. 178.

43. P. O'Leary, '*Fír Fer*: An Internalized Ethical Concept in Early Irish Literature?', *Éigse* 22 (1987), pp. 1-14 (13-14).

morality' demands an (unknowable?) knowledge of the pagan moral code as well as the eighth-century Irish Christian code. This is, however, the same echo of traditions as Nagy hears and the same one for which McCone is listening, albeit using different methods of detection.

The criticism of the last five to ten years marks a great advance in the variety of readings of early Irish texts, diverging into such schools as feminist literary criticism and speech act theory. Many of *Ulidia*'s articles address questions that can be said to have been posed in Davies's article. The last sentence of 'Protocols' is a *sin scéal eile*[44] ending: 'We should also, perhaps, be thinking of what such texts might mean for us; but that would be a topic for another paper.'[45]

How can the alterity of ancient texts be conquered and made meaningful today? One school would say this is no more complex than any other process of reading. 'Historical distance is thus only an extreme case of the distance that always divides reader from text, and this distance is the condition for meaningfulness.'[46]

Perhaps that school of literary theory which had the largest number of adherents (which is to say about half a dozen!) at both the 10th International Congress of Celtic Studies (July, 1995) and in *Ulidia* is that of feminist literary criticism.

Feminist Toril Moi might condemn the classification of this school with the others because it is

> a specific kind of political discourse: a critical and theoretical practice committed to the struggle against patriarchy and sexism, not simply a concern for gender in literature.... It is my view that, provided they are compatible with her politics, a feminist critic can use whichever methods or theories she likes.[47]

(Or he likes perhaps.) Allen Frantzen writes of the potential of (first-generation) feminist discourse in mediaeval studies:

> Restructuring of thought does not mean the facile inclusion of women in a male-designed and long-established system. It means a changing of that system, and a questioning of all the apparently neutral choices that led to its formulation.[48]

44. 'That's another story' (to be told another time).
45. Davies, 'Protocols of Reading', p. 23.
46. Dentith, *Thought*, pp. 98-99.
47. T. Moi, 'Feminist Literary Criticism', in Jefferson and Robey, *Modern Literary Theory*, p. 204.
48. A.J. Frantzen, 'When Women Aren't Enough', in Nancy Partner (ed.), *Study-*

Furthermore, feminist criticism does not necessarily signal the end of traditionalist studies. 'Feminists who work in mediaeval subjects need to account for the dates and material details of manuscripts, and traditionalists need to account for the social logic of sex that gender ideologies express in the Middle Ages.'[49]

It could be argued that a more extreme and recent form of feminist criticism (such as the one Moi advocates) would relieve feminists of even that obligation if an argument were put that it is not part of a feminine ideology to acknowledge the importance of material details of manuscripts. In two senses, anyway, existing feminist criticism of early Irish texts has been fairly conservative. It is uninterested in reappraising the place of gender unless it leads to an articulation of the feminine, and it continues to respect the largely male-populated institution of early Irish studies.

Much as it was shown to be appropriate to refer to Northrop Frye and his reaction against the 'intentional fallacy' in the general discussion of literary criticism of early Irish texts (despite the 'old-fashionedness' of this idea), so can the progress of feminist criticism be described gradually, as it relates to early Irish texts.

There have been strong proponents of feminist views in early Irish studies. Máire Herbert's critical oeuvre has stressed the importance of a literary approach generally and has articulated a concern for an awareness of gender in that developing approach. Próinséas Ní Cátháin rejects the label 'feminist' but in offering courses in women in early Irish society she has supported feminists by giving them the benefit of her vast knowledge. These two scholars deserve special mention because of the breadth of their 'traditional' work and the unusual flexibility they have shown in their willingness to embrace new tools of the trade. The fruit of both phases of their careers are core parts of early Irish studies.

Other scholars in their searches for the feminine have made strides in their way. Erica Sessle's article in *Ulidia* seeks to explain Medb's language and behaviour 'within the context of its own gender'.[50] Muireann Ní Bhrolcháin's article also parses Medb's identity. She does not take

ing Medieval Women: Sex, Gender, Feminism (Cambridge, MA: Medieval Academy of America, 1993), pp. 1-15 (14).

49. Frantzen, 'Women Aren't Enough', p. 14.

50. E. Sessle, 'Misogyny and Medb: Approaching Medb with Feminist Criticism', in Mallory and Stockman (eds.), *Ulidia*, pp. 135-38 (136).

advantage of the full political arsenal available to her as a feminist (according to Moi), but she does base her article on two unexplained premises: (1) That Medb is a sovereignty goddess within a Celtic 'pantheon' and (2) that there is a single definition of 'Christianity' whereby 'sexuality must have offended their [*sic*] sensibilities'.[51] This article is the inverse of James Carney's (discussed below), featuring 'suppressed goddesses' instead of 'suppressed miracles'.

Moi's invitation to the feminist to use whatever literary methods 'she' may have at her disposal may seem to sit oddly with the criticism of early Irish texts, which, according to McCone, is still emerging from a 'troglodyte' phase. It is positivist and not feminist to extract 'information' about men and women in early Irish society from a literary tale. It is still difficult to locate 'the original intention' of a tale, whether it be in order to establish monastic devotion or rebellion. So as not to be confused with such positivism, all feminist critics need to be as clear as Dooley is in their political and literary language, or they open themselves to attack. (Cf. Caoimhín Breatnach's critique of Joanne Findon's *Ulidia* article on what should be irrelevant historical grounds.)[52]

Dooley's article in *Ulidia* examines the possibility that 'one might find a form of discourse approaching the status of a distinct feminine rhetoric shared between women'.[53] Findon's work about Emer in *Ulidia* is also important. That article, 'A Woman's Words: Emer versus Cú Chulainn in Aided Óenfir Aífe', is based on part of Findon's unpublished PhD thesis,[54] the only work of its scale and kind, of female or male characters in any 'Cycle'.

One important aspect of these articles is the authors' awareness that they are working within a growing community (even if that community may be seen by some to be at odds politically with the larger early Irish scholarly community). Dooley acknowledges this current and implicitly encourages it as she writes, 'I should like to join my work to the other recent re-evaluations of the presence of the feminine in Irish saga

51. M. Ní Bhrolcháin, 'Re Tóin Mná: In Pursuit of Troublesome Women', in Mallory and Stockman (eds.), *Ulidia*, pp. 115-21 (115).

52. C. Breatnach, review of *Ulidia*, in *Éigse* 29 (1996), pp. 200-208 (208).

53. Dooley, 'Invention', pp. 128-29.

54. J. Findon, 'Emer and the Roles of Female Characters in the Medieval Irish Ulster Cycle' (Unpublished PhD thesis, University of Toronto, 1994). See also J. Findon, *A Woman's Words: Emer and Female Speech in the Ulster Cycle* (Toronto: University of Toronto Press, 1997).

literature.'[55] She mentions Máire Herbert, Patricia Kelly, and Findon, as well as theorists outside early Irish studies like Moi, Irigaray, and Kristeva. This remark also anticipates cooperation in the future and commemorates a sense of hope which may have been lacking previously.

One of the results of all these varied approaches is that the texts are rendered more open to comparison. What is particularly relevant to the present work is the potential for comparison with the Bible.

Necessarily, those early Irish scholars who are not interested in establishing a Christian basis for early Irish literature do not mention this 'potential' at all. Although even Dumézil himself attempted to find evidence of his Indo-European ternary paradigm in the Bible, a comparative structuralist approach to an early Irish text and the Bible has not attracted any of the capable structuralists in early Irish studies. If the Bible is viewed as a collection of Near Eastern and 'international' mythological motifs—as it is by many scholars—then it could offer insight into early Irish mythology. That would be one way scholars could avail themselves of the Bible's potential for comparison with early Irish texts.

Several scholars of early Irish ecclesiastical and secular texts have indeed argued for a literary approach in order to establish in literary terms what they have already explored in historical or philological terms, namely 'proof' of biblical 'influence'. Martin McNamara has written that among the tasks of scholarship that need to be done are 'an examination of the use of biblical citations and allusions in Irish (Hiberno-Latin and vernacular) literary sources. A list of such sources will need to be drawn up and each one systematically studied and the evidence recorded.'[56]

Such a study, or something of its ilk, is indeed called for. Previous studies have attempted so wide a scope that consistent literary arguments tended to fall by the wayside in pursuit of success in the use of other methods. These attempts are usually part of the artillery in a battle with 'nativists'. Instead of giving a play-by-play account of that war it is worth citing a typical example from the 1950s, which, it is hoped, illustrates the need for a new language, if not a new trajectory.

55. Dooley, 'Invention', p. 123.
56. M. McNamara, 'The Text of the Latin Bible in the Early Irish Church. Some Data and Desiderata', in Ní Chatháin and Richter (eds.), *Irland*, pp. 7-55 (54).

In 1956, Carney wrote 'The Ecclesiastical Background to Irish Saga' with reference to one (secular) tale, *Táin Bó Fraích* (The Cattle-Raid of Froech).[57] He argues that phrases, moods, and certain words in *Froech* are calques or copies of biblical or hagiographic motifs. That is, the early mediaeval author is seen to be at pains to transcribe a pre-Christian tale, but finds himself 'drawn into' 'Christian' idiom again and again, thus establishing 'unequivocally' the reality of his Christian milieu. The points in the text where the mediaeval author cannot bring himself to recreate the 'original' ecclesiastical gist Carney calls 'suppressed miracles'.[58] This rubric sustains him even when the opposite occurs: 'It is quite clear that the religious tale was the model and we can see the author's particular difficulty in adapting it.' That is, 'This is its model because it doesn't look like it.' 'It is quite clear' and 'we can see' also beg definition. Here, said clarity depends entirely on Carney's own argument up until this point.

When in *Froech* Findabair 'takes her clothes off and plunges into the water', this is for Carney a clear imitation of no other aquatic moment in all of early literature but one such in *Ad VC* where the saint orders someone to plunge into the water (after removing his clothes). 'If the author of the saga had not been following a model the heroine, seeing her lover in such dire straits, would have been made go to the rescue without waiting to undress.'[59] Do all lovers keep their clothes on while diving? It is by no means the universal principle that Carney implies it is.

Carney himself later commented with reference to *Studies in Irish Literature and History* (in which a version of the *Froech* article appears) that it was 'perhaps overstrong rebellion against ... entrenched orthodoxies'.[60]

Carney had to do two jobs: study the early Irish both in history and in literature. It may be that his drive to pursue the first weakened his arguments about the second. However, he established a precedent for an investigation of the historical connection of early Ireland to Chris-

---

57. J. Carney, 'The Ecclesiastical Background to Irish Saga', *Artica, Studia Ethnographica Upsaliensia* 11 (1956), pp. 221-27.

58. Carney, 'Background', p. 221.

59. Carney, 'Background', p. 223.

60. J. Carney, in a lecture at the Congress of Celtic Studies, quoted in Ó Cathasaigh, 'Early Irish Narrative Literature', p. 62.

tianity and the Bible, one which has indeed proved crucial to the understanding of early Irish literature. With this idea's acceptance, literary scholars can pursue avenues of comparison without having to assert historical arguments for their relevance.

As it is often appropriate to leave aside the historical transmission of a text while analysing it as literature, so is it worthwhile to move on from the history of Christianity in Ireland to focus on the Bible and early Irish texts as literature. Additionally, such an attempt at historical neutrality leads the concept of 'influence' to be put aside in favour of 'comparison' (which implies divergence as well as identity).

For this reason a detailed description of the scholarship that surrounds the history of Christianity in Ireland would be misplaced in the present work, but a brief summary may be helpful. Any such sketch of the scholarship would include the work of scholars of Latin and historians of the early mediaeval period who, working from the bulk of early Irish material written in that language, have done much to establish a picture of the ecclesiastical early Irish. Kim McCone, Donnchadh Ó Corráin and Dáibhí Ó Cróinín are among the scholars working in this area.

Fournier was the first scholar to explore this field with his 'Le *Liber ex Lege Moysi* et les tendences bibliques du droit canonique irlandais'.[61] Raymund Kottje has written perhaps the most thorough assessment of the liturgical, legal and other practices of the early Irish in his *Studien zum Einfluss des Alten Testamentes*. In his exploration of the material he locates a predilection on the part of the early Irish for the Hebrew Bible and its collection of laws (especially in the books of Moses). Why one law-revering people seems to have had such an affinity for the laws of the other can only be a matter for speculation: 'It begs the question: how can we explain this Irish predilection for the Old Testament? But the question can only ... be asked here'.[62]

Building away from this strong historical base then, what different approaches can be used to understand the literary relationships between the two literatures?

McCone has been the most outspoken proponent of the 'anti-nativist' cause since Carney's time, drawing attention not to the patently ecclesi-

---

61. Fournier, 'Le *Liber ex Lege Moysi*', pp. 221-34.

62. 'Es drängt sich wohl die Frage auf, wie die Offenheit des Iren für das Alten Testamentes gerade zu erklären ist. Die Frage kann aber hier nur gestellt...werden' (Kottje, *Studien*, p. 109).

astical material but specifically to the saga material written in Irish. This is the material most often associated with the primordial past of Ireland, although it reaches written form through the hands of the monastically educated. McCone asserts with finality in the beginning of his monumental *Pagan Past and Christian Present*, 'It can now be regarded as axiomatic that, assumed origins for some of its constituents notwithstanding, the proper frame of reference for early Irish literature is early Christian Ireland rather than the preceding pagan period.'[63]

This book contains a summary of both sides of that debate if perhaps featuring a more sympathetic description of the 'anti-nativist' position. In subsequent chapters McCone focuses on specific episodes in tales which, he argues, evidence the presence of, and even influence of, monastic learning.

McCone has assembled all imaginable historical information to show the influence of ecclesiastical or biblical scholarship on early Irish letters. He does not, however, argue his points with the 'overstrong rebelliousness' of Carney, but rather states that he has no intention of asserting that the early Irish practised 'slavish imitation of Old Testament models'.[64] Instead, he has sought to establish more indefinitely— at this theoretical stage, anyway—'the judicious application of appropriate themes'.[65] As such 'thematic application' is best identified by a literary approach, it is literary observations which McCone provides (along with philological, sociological and historical).

He does not, however, consistently provide literary arguments for his literary observations. Nor is that specifically what he has set out to do; indeed, it would take many more volumes to trawl the myriad literary parallels he evokes and provide consistent literary explanations to support them.

One of the chief limitations of McCone's approach, as I have stated above, is that it dismisses the possibility of a multiplicity of meanings, both in the early Irish texts and in the Bible. It assumes that there is only one possible meaning at each juncture, that that meaning is explicit, that he has grasped it, and that it is plain to the reader. Meanings can exist for McCone only inasmuch as they move in the direction of 'proving influence'. This limits unjustifiably the scope of both the

63. McCone, *Pagan*, p. 4.
64. McCone, *Pagan*, p. 133.
65. McCone, *Pagan*, p. 133.

Bible and early Irish literature, as putting logical stress on the 'influence' rubric, inviting its reassessment.

Is there a neutral way to approach comparison, that is, with less of a political agenda? It is argued here that the two texts can sustain just such a comparison, without having to rely on proof of historical contact.

> A weakness of both nativist and revisionist positions is that, ultimately, both sets of conclusions about the nature of early Irish tales are founded more on extra-textual considerations than on systematic examination of the texts themselves.[66]

For this a new rationale is needed, and until a quotation from Plato is found that will serve my purpose as well as Davies's served his, I offer the following metaphor. Here Seurat's post-impressionist painting *A Sunday Afternoon on the Island of La Grande Jatte* (1884–86) is the early Irish text to be read.

If it is known that Seurat used a model for a figure in the painting's foreground, and we wish to know the relationship between painting and hypothesized model—call her 'Dot'—then one tactic might be to trace Dot's actions in 1880s Paris, see where she lived and whether that was near Seurat's studio.[67] Let it be supposed then that she did indeed live nearby, and is known to have made frequent visits to Seurat's studio. Even then, it cannot be asserted with certainty that it was she Seurat used as the model for the figure in the foreground with the monkey.

At this point, the investigation of the painting in these terms seems unreliable. While much may have been learned about an aspect of Dot's life, and a corner of Seurat's, little or nothing has been revealed about the painting. The next step is to look at the painting itself, and at (a photograph of) Dot and see if there is some level on which they may be successfully compared. (These visual images are referred to because the question is one of conveying a visual image.)

What levels can be found in the painting? Use of light, colour, shade, design, tone? Can any of these be located in Dot's appearance? By searching for a common field, we recast the original question. Trying to

66. M. Herbert, 'The Universe of Male and Female: A Reading of the Deirdre Story', in C.J. Byrne, M. Harry and P. Ó Siadhail (eds.), *Celtic Languages and Celtic People: Proceedings of the Second North American Congress of Celtic Studies* (Halifax, Nova Scotia: D'Arcy McGee Chair of Irish Studies, St Mary's University, 1992), p. 53.

67. The name Dot for Seurat's model is borrowed respectfully from Stephen Sondheim's 1984 musical *Sunday in the Park with George*.

fit the photograph into the total picture of the painting has only diminished the relevant aspects of Dot *and* the painting, while leaving the question about their relationship unanswered. What has happened instead is a revaluation of the terms of comparison: what can be learned by such an investigation is *about* light, colour, shade, design, tone. We are left with an understanding of what the painting is, as much as what the painting is like.

That is, it is by investigating as many possible meanings or approaches to meaning in early Irish literature and the Bible that an interest in literary comparison can best be served. This multiplicity evokes Davies's theme again: 'I suspect also that the prescriptive, intentionalist approach to literary meaning... would have struck [early Irish readers] as rather curious and unfortunate foreclosures on valid (and valuable) interpretative possibilities.'[68]

This kind of critical thinking itself suggests a parallel with certain kinds of biblical criticism. Specifically, it is reminiscent of rabbinical commentary. Christian biblical criticism has taken a similar path to the criticism of early Irish texts and only now, in articles in *Semeia* and elsewhere, have critics begun to embrace the methodology of both contemporary theorists and those of the rabbis (discussed in the next chapter).

The rabbis read with an acknowledgment of the potential polysemy of any scriptural word and enjoyed that ambiguity in a way that was not matched for hundreds of years since in secular or biblical criticism and theory. (Some might say that it has not been matched at all by secular theory because its proponents do not seem to be enjoying themselves.) The parallel of very contemporary literary theory and certain midrashic commentaries has been demonstrated by several scholars, including deconstructionist Jacques Derrida.[69]

A brief example from both may suggest this parallel. Osborn Bergin has supplied an English language (parody) version of a typical early Irish gloss. His is based on the Shakespearean line 'Darraign your battle' which means 'Dispose your troops in battle array': '*Darraign,* that is *do ruin*, from its destructiveness; or *die ere you run*, that is, they

---

68. Davies, 'Protocols', p. 23.

69. Cf. J. Derrida, 'Shibboleth', in Geoffrey H. Hartman and Sanford Budick (eds.), *Midrash and Literature* (New Haven: Yale University Press, 1986), pp. 3-34; K. Dauber, 'The Bible as Literature: Reading like the Rabbis', *Semeia* 31 (1985), pp. 27-48.

must not retreat; or *dare in*, because they are brave; or *tear around*, from their activity; or *dear rain*, from the showers of blood.'[70]

The following example is a translation (and not a parody) of part of Rashi's commentary (eleventh century) on Talmud:

> The School of Ishmael taught: Scripture says, *So shall it be rendered* (lit., 'given') *to him again* (Lev. 24.19). Now the word 'to give' can apply only to monetary compensation. Objection: Would the words *as he hath maimed* (lit., 'given a blemish to') *a man* also refer to money?... So why do we need a repetition of the law with the words, *so shall it be rendered* (given) *unto him*? It must therefore come to teach that it refers to monetary compensation... The School of Hiyya taught: Scripture says, *hand for* (lit., 'in') *hand*. This implies something that is given from hand to hand. What is that? Money.[71]

The conclusion that Davies reaches—justifiably, I think—is that there is a multiplicity of meanings in any text. This applies both to early Irish texts alone and to comparative studies involving early Irish texts. The rabbis knew that their text could not be so fragile and limited as to offer only one possibility to every reader and, according to Davies, so did the early Irish know that. This one premise seems necessary if even an attempt is to be made to understand either literature in its own terms, and together with the other's.

---

70. Cited in K. Hughes, *Early Christian Ireland: Introduction to the Sources* (Ithaca, NY: Cornell University Press, 1972), p. 46.

71. From commentary on Gemara, *B. Qam.* 83bff, as cited in (and translated by) Chaim Pearl, *Rashi* (New York: Grove Press, 1988), p. 85.

Chapter 2

BOOKS OF MARGINS: READING BIBLICAL CRITICISM,
LITERARY THEORY AND EARLY IRISH TEXTS

> To decide how a text works means to decide which one of its various aspects is or can become relevant or pertinent for a coherent interpretation of it and which one will remain marginal and unable to support a coherent reading.[1]

> In fine, the relevance of biblical interpretation can be found only in a relevant interpretation.[2]

Which quote was written by a famous Italian novelist a few years ago as part of a talk on 'overinterpretation' and which opened the first issue of the Christian biblical journal *Interpretation* in 1947? (Answer in footnotes.) If the difference is mysterious, interpretation has indeed changed over the last fifty years, but there are still limits to what can and cannot be done and, most would argue, to what something can or cannot mean. The range of meanings is not limitless, and the limits are different depending on the text and its readership. How has interpretation of biblical texts developed in ways that may serve as a model for criticism of early Irish literature? This chapter charts some of the milestones in the recent history of literary studies of the Bible and asks whether they could have relevance for the way we read early Irish texts.

We read not just for historical information, as the unnamed historian in the last chapter suggested, but also for pleasure. Writing is more than recording and the text is more than a record. The early Irish were capable of using writing as more than a means of recording—and of recording in ways that are not obvious at first glance. The difference between the genaealogical tract 'Of the Race of Conaire Mór' and *Togail*

---

1. U. Eco, 'Reply', in U. Eco and R. Rorty (eds.), *Interpretation and Overinterpretation* (Cambridge: Cambridge University Press, 1992), p. 146.

2. H.H. Rowley, 'The Relevance of Biblical Interpretation', *Int* 1/1 (1947), pp. 3-19 (19).

Bruidne Da Derga (The Destruction of Da Derga's Hostel about Conaire Mór) illustrates this point.[3] In this case we have a version of the story with only the 'essential' information. But the tale as we have it (*BDD*) does not tell the information in the shortest number of words possible; in fact the telling is rather protracted and ornate. At each juncture in writing, choices are made and words are left unwritten. We may not see what is written in the (blank) margins, but we can acknowledge the choices that must have been made to get to the words we have. *BDD* uses language it need not if revealing history was all it set out to do. If it was merely out to provide proof of Conaire's greatness, it could have been much shorter and simpler. What are the rest of the words for?

The Hebrew Bible has also long been read for its historical information. As a sacred text for at least two world religions it has an enormous social and cultural role to play. Yet it has also been read for other than patently spiritual 'information'. As literary studies has permeated the consciousness of theologians and of members of various religious institutions, interpretations of the Bible have changed. As these developments in larger literary circles and not biblical criticism's alone have set the tone for interpretation in the twentieth century, I will also refer to criticism of texts more generally here.

There are few scholars who write about reading the Bible who have not begun by defining themselves as Jews or Christians. Mieke Bal, whose work is discussed below, is one of a few significant exceptions who have come to the Bible as scholars of literature in general. In another sense, the interplay of secularized literary studies and literary studies of the Bible has always existed: the history of biblical interpretation has framed concepts of literary analysis in Western Europe. One religion's interpretative methodology has proved more recalcitrant to newer critical techniques and the other has anticipated them, but they do not exist independent of secular literary theory.

No matter what their background, most readers are in pursuit of understanding and perhaps of enjoying a text. For some, enjoying is equivalent to understanding. To use a metaphor reminiscent of deism, a sacred text is like a precious watch: some will want to keep it in a china cabinet behind glass, intact. Others will feel its perfection is best used everyday to see and refer to, as a way to tell the time—at the risk of

---

3. L. Gwynn, 'De Síl Chonairi Mór', *Ériu* 6 (1912), pp 138-41; W. Stokes, 'The Destruction of Da Derga's Hostel', *RC* 22 (1902), pp. 9-61, 165-215, 282-329, 390-437.

scratching its casing. Some will love a watch so much they must know how it functions, examine its parts one by one, marvelling at its works, trusting that its perfection is such that it will always fit back together again.

For each lover of the watch(words of his faith), the other views seem ridiculous or worse, heretic. It is not obvious for some that the Bible can be taken apart like any other text, that its other roles as a symbol of faith and a stronghold of spirituality will not evaporate once the words are looked at. What concerns us here, as we look to the last part of the history of biblical criticism as a guide to how early Irish texts may be read, is that the Bible shows no signs of having been dismembered or polluted by this process. One can read an article on why the story of Sarah and Abraham is about someone's divorce and still read about Sarah and Abraham in the Bible with the fullness of one's previous faith. Furthermore, such an article may shed light on the way one reads the story in future, without necessarily leading one to the same conclusion.

In one sense, the study of early Irish texts as literature has come further than biblical literary studies. The work of editing texts—a staple of early Irish studies—involves constant (if usually unacknowledged) interpreting. In that sense, early Irish studies is flexible indeed. However, while the number of translations of the Bible is constantly increasing, there are never enough translations of early Irish texts. (This is mainly because the number of available translators of the Bible is exponentially more than the number of translators of early Irish texts!)

In fact, early Irish texts contain information which serves the disciplines of critical theory as well as anthropology and philology. Such has been part of the progress in biblical studies—interdisciplinary concerns have made for a major advance in perspective. Biblical studies have got there slowly too, however. It would take a longer, philosophical/theological essay to chart its progress; this is not the place for a survey of the use of 'literature' relative to 'the Bible' nor of the development of literary and proto-literary approaches to the Bible. There are books devoted to such information, as well as numerous articles.[4]

That progress involves a reappraisal of texts and a development of their use from being sources to being sources as well as literature.

4.   For example, R. Detweiler and V.K. Robbins, 'From New Criticism to Post-structuralism: Twentieth-Century Hermeneutics', in S. Prickett (ed.), *Reading the Text: Biblical Criticism and Literary Theory* (Oxford: Basil Blackwell, 1991), pp. 225-80.

Much of this chiefly involves an acknowledgment of critical pursuits already in place under less 'offensive' labels. When Jonas represents Columbanus's exploits in a way that conceals something embarrassing about the saint's career, then already it is clear that history/hagiography does not deal with 'the Truth' alone. When Clare Stancliffe produces a paper on this topic, she is not just addressing the *Life of Columbanus* as a historical source, but she is trying to read it as literature, to explore the distance between events and their telling.[5] In some fundamental way, she gives a voice to something unheard but present in Jonas's work. It is a small step from there to believing that the non-Truth bits could also be of interest other than as murky or crystalline reflections of the Truth.

It is difficult to make this move to documents as literature, though, when there are so few documents, and so few scholars to read them. These are virtually the only sources for the period—how else but by reading them for this legal and sociological information can historiography progress? The answer is that literary readings do not detract from historiographic ones, but rather complement them. Theodore Dreiser's *Sister Carrie* provides great insights into turn-of-the-century Chicago, but there are enough other documents from nineteenth-century Chicago that Dreiser's work is more usually explored for literary details. Moving forward in time again, it is absurd to suggest that Raymond Chandler's novels be used *primarily* as sources of insight into Los Angeles history in the 1930s and 1940s—although they are indeed sources for the same.

Conversely, any theory of literature that demands a completely ahistorical approach is flawed. What is needed is equal time for both, so that the result is neither 'naive historicism' nor 'blind modernism', terms which Paul Zumthor used [in 1979] to refer to ways of 'reading' the Middle Ages.[6] At that point, studies of other mediaeval literatures were so advanced that its scholars could parley literature in terms of the Other while still being aware of the particular challenges ancient texts posed to their own literary appraisal. These issues are far removed from the rudimentary but evolving concerns of reading early Irish literature

5. C. Stancliffe, 'Jonas' *Life of Columbanus* and his Disciples', in J. Carey, M. Herbert and P. Ó Riain (eds.), *Studies in Irish Hagiography* (Dublin: Four Courts Press, 2001), pp. 189-200.

6. P. Zumthor, 'Comments on H.R. Jauss' Article', *New Literary History* 10/2 (Winter 1979), pp. 367-76 (370).

today. Zumthor is addressing not whether it is acceptable to treat historical documents as literature, but how historical distance affects the reading of (inherently literary) texts.

Zumthor was aware of the dangerous assumptions involved in the teaching of mediaeval studies (some of which were addressed in the last chapter), factors which slow down the process of interpretation. He writes,

> The fathers of mediaeval studies... never questioned the ideological and philosophical implications of their manner of working, of collecting information, and of transmitting it to their students and readers. Hence the unreflecting tenacity with which they held to contingent criteria that they put forth as absolute: organicism, authenticity, and others. These criteria led to an analogical type of argumentation that was never declared as such: thus the risk of misinterpretation.[7]

It is true that the literature he has in mind is centuries older than the ones under discussion here, but the juxtaposition of ancient texts, the legacy of nineteenth-century criticism and the late arrival of twenty-first-century critical tools is the same. The use of these tools produces new issues for the reader of ancient texts, be they early Irish or biblical. The concern for detail that the 'fathers of mediaeval studies' felt is not replaced but supplemented:

> At each moment in reading the mediaeval text, there is a double necessity: to determine its 'historicity' (I mean the formal aspects of the manner in which this text entered the culture of its own time) and, simultaneously, to redefine, adapt, and sometimes reject modern critical concepts, so as to render them appropriate in seizing this historicity.[8]

Zumthor's article (and others in this volume of *New Literary History*) anticipate later reflections on the methodologies of studying the past and its alterity. As a historiographer, Brian Stock is one of very few others to address the past with a knowledge of both critical theory and a wide range of mediaeval material. He seems uniquely qualified to grasp the conflicts involved in interpreting these documents as literature:

> The passing of a century has brought neither marriage nor divorce [between empirical historians and students of literature] but rather, after the fashion of mediaeval romance, endless extensions of an increasingly frustrating courtship. To some historians, all literary statements, including literature in the normal sense as well as laws, contracts, and other

7. Zumthor, 'Comments', p. 371.
8. Zumthor, 'Comments', p. 372.

records, contain varying degrees of subjectivity... Other writers have rediscovered narrative discourse, and look upon this primary shaping as an advantage. But ... [m]ost social historians still use literary sources for providing illustrations of what is more precisely demonstrable from evidence uncontaminated by human reflection, or so they think.[9]

Stock captures the irony of the situation neatly, expounding on the same point of naive historicism and blind modernism that Zumthor located. The reading of ancient texts as literature is not straightforward either:

Literary critics propose that texts must be analysed within a system of purely semantic relations, rather than with reference to events in the outside world. Somewhat ironically, historians would agree, not because they wish to restore the integrity of the text but in order to exclude the problematical literary element from their field of endeavour. The science of one group thereby becomes the superstition of another.[10]

As developments in literary approaches are of greatest concern here, it is appropriate to focus on some of Stock's arguments against 'blind historicism'. In early Irish texts, information is never straightforward by the terms of twentieth-century discourse. There are seemingly endless mysteries and anomalies from the level of grammar on. History and philology cannot answer them, and it becomes important to ask, for example, how much energy should be expended on trying to locate Hinba?[11] The alternative to a preoccupation with 'scientism' is not in ignoring these phenomena either. Stock writes muscularly:

Take the miracle. Counting the number can be instructive, especially if sex and generational differences, geographical distribution, and the frequency of psychological irregularities are also recorded. But ... in all probability, it did not take place.

This sort of reasoning, however, only confuses the understanding of a many-sided phenomenon by imposing a bogus scientism on it. The point is not whether a miracle 'took place', but that people whose social affiliations can be the object of empirical study have explained an aspect of their behaviour in terms of it... The miracle is a catalyst that focuses

9.   B. Stock, *Listening for the Text: On the Uses of the Past* (Baltimore: The Johns Hopkins University Press, 1990), p. 78.

10.   Stock, *Listening*, p. 78.

11.   Hinba, according to *Ad VC*, was an island residence of Columba's. No one knows which Hebridean island the name refers to, but there has been much speculation.

> the attention of the original actors or the later observers on the stresses
> and accommodations within the social system as a whole.[12]

This argument does not point ipso facto to the necessity of assessing documents as literature, but it does reshape the relevance of that assessment in a way that leaves room for more disciplines. Stock, of course, is writing for a world that has already acknowledged the literary value of their documents and thus he can argue in favour of it or against it without affecting the existence of that branch: there will be hundreds of undergraduates writing literary essays on *Beowulf* and the *Chanson de Roland* this year. For early Irish studies there is always more in the balance.

What developments have there been in interpretation as a way of assessing and enjoying the Hebrew Bible, whose commentary is the critical model here? The formation of the journal *Interpretation* is a place to start. Today its methods would not seem avant-garde (nor would they at the time to anyone who had read Freud, Propp, Bakhtin, or any of the other important thinkers of the early twentieth century). In 1947 in American Christian religious circles, however, it seems fair to assume that *Interpretation* smacked of heresy, or was at least shocking. Perhaps to counteract this impression, H.H. Rowley states the case clearly in the introductory article that the journal is representing not just any interpretation, but interpretation with a view to understanding the Christian scriptures in a Christian way. *Interpretation* putatively set out to keep up with other disciplines in some sense, but it was still committed to dealing with the sacred texts in as 'sacred' a way as before. As such, it was in keeping with certain age-old traditions of interpretation.

Frank Kermode has written a useful summary of Christianity's methodological history of interpretation in 'The Plain Sense of Things'.[13] He highlights its developments and radical difference from rabbinical traditions; it would seem as strange to the rabbis as they to it. It is obvious, however, that one of them has become dominant while the other has been made to keep to itself for nearly two thousand years. The limits of Christian interpretative methodology inform the whole history of interpretation in Europe.[14] Kermode writes this about the Bible:

12. Stock, *Listening*, p. 85.
13. F. Kermode, 'The Plain Sense of Things', in Hartman and Budick (eds.), *Midrash and Literature*, pp. 179-94.
14. This view is expanded on in S. Handelman, *The Slayers of Moses: The*

That which is edifying is so only because it already conforms with the New Testament, and the unedifying has to be made edifying by figurative reading in New Testament terms.... There was a Jewish or carnal sense, to which one might attribute more or less importance; but the true sense was Christian and spiritual, and that sense could be interpreted as the plain sense. The figurative becomes the literal.[15]

As the Church evolved it was a surprisingly small step from looking for the 'plain sense' of the Hebrew Bible and the Christian scriptures to subjecting other written words to the same treatment. Kermode writes (in the present tense), 'The literal sense of the New Testament confers on the Church the right to declare the true meaning of any text.'[16] Thus, a major foundation is laid for traditions of thinking in the West and we see a possible origin for the pervasive hermeneutic notion of a 'plain sense', a 'bottom line'. (It is interesting to note that it is the contemporary institution and not the ancient sacred texts themselves which calls the shots.) What is significant here is that this sense-seeking is a choice, one possible method. All too often this way of reading is considered simply 'normal', the only way to read. In fact, other cultures have other traditions of reading—and even within a culture, people read in different ways.

The idea of reading a text for many senses is not singularly Jewish, but it is indeed Jewish. Joseph Dan argues that seeing vast possibilities of interpretation demands an original document (and will not work with a translation the same way). In this case he has in mind the Hebrew of the Hebrew Bible, the endlessly rich and endlessly obscure text of the rabbis. Christianity, by contrast, has always worked from translations when it refers to the Bible, and cannot look at the letters' manifold possibilities with the same authority. For the rabbis it was strange and unnecessary to look for a bottom line in one of the Bible's verses. 'Dogmatic thinking must rely on an unambiguous text. The Hebrew Bible does not lend itself easily to the formulation of dogma, because of the obscurities which haunt almost every biblical verse.'[17]

Emergence of Rabbinic Interpretation in Modern Literary Theory (Albany, NY: State University of New York Press, 1982), and in Kermode, 'The Plain Sense'.

15. Kermode, 'The Plain Sense', p. 185.

16. Kermode, 'The Plain Sense', pp. 188-89.

17. J. Dan, 'Midrash and the Dawn of Kabbalah' in Hartman and Budick (eds.), *Midrash and Literature*, p. 129.

Thus at least two fundamentally different ideas of interpretation have always been in motion in biblical studies. At every stage, it would seem that the interpreter is the authority and not the interpreted, although some schools of thought are more open than others. The irony is in the very nature of the word 'interpretation':

> It is in the heritage of ... two etymological senses—translation *of* a text and translation *for* an audience—that we might try to capture a working definition: 'interpretation' is 'acceptable and approximating translation'. Each term here provokes additional questions: (1) Approximating *what*? (2) Translating *how*? and (3) Acceptable to *whom*?[18]

Significantly, there was a journal for biblical criticism called *Interpretation* in 1947; there is still none in Irish studies. This may be because the existing journals publish the full spectrum of thought already; it may also be that there is doubt at the end of the question 'acceptable to whom?'

One branch of interpretation is literary criticism. It is not the object here to summarize the history of that discipline, even insofar as it concerns the Bible, from its roots in the Higher Criticism of the nineteenth century to the present day. It is addressed at great length elsewhere in whole volumes, to the extent that there are volumes summarizing just one critical standpoint, as well as collections of readings in this or that vein. Instead, a few key examples will be cited.

Books of literary criticism of the Bible are usually addressed to the scholar who has never heard of literary criticism before. There are always long and semi-apologetic introductions and extensive summaries. These act to establish the flexibility of this 'new' language that permits the scholar to ask questions like '*Why* does Saul do that?' It is the rare article or book that is literarily and not just theologically sophisticated. Mieke Bal, Robert Alter, and Meir Sternberg are some exceptional scholars who write authoritatively about literature generally while being au fait with the Bible's language and milieus. More often, copies of parts of Bakhtin's oeuvre fall into the hands of restless theologians who then squeeze their ideas through his sieve.

18. S. Mailloux, 'Interpretation', in F. Lentricchia and T. McLaughlin (eds.), *Critical Terms for Literary Study* (Chicago: University of Chicago Press, 1995), pp. 121-34 (121-22).

Are there any ground rules to literary criticism, then? Most would answer with some reference to Northrop Frye and his *Anatomy of Criticism* (1957). Frye sometimes reacts specifically to the state of biblical criticism, but for the most part he is writing about the study of literature more generally. In this passage, he writes about a particular biblical book, but its relevance to scholars of early Irish is patent—indeed, it resonates in Ó Cathasaigh's and Dooley's own 'polemical introductions' (alluded to in the previous chapter): 'I am trying to make sense of the meaning of the Book of Job as we now have it, on the assumption that whoever was responsible for its present version had some reason for producing that version.'[19]

Thus Frye sets out to interpret not the history of the vellum or parchment, but the words on the page (later critics will go back to seek the palimpsest). This is an all-or-nothing approach. It is in the heyday of literary criticism that the strongest antipathy towards the then dominant historical criticism is expressed, as Frye and others propose a severing from concepts of 'original function'. Again, although the relationship of mediaeval texts to their original readership and to the present reader may be particularly complicated, Frye's words resonate today:

> Even the most fanatical historical critic is bound to see Shakespeare and Homer as writers whom we admire for reasons that would have been largely unintelligible to them, to say nothing of their societies. But we can hardly be satisfied with an approach to works of art which simply strips from them their original function. One of the tasks of criticism is...the recreation of function in a new context.[20]

Frye wants to 'interpret ... in terms of a conceptual framework that belongs to the critic alone'. As subsequent critics mentioned here have noted (Stock, Bal, Davies), historians use just such conceptual frameworks, too, and interpret with as bold strokes. The difference is that they do not state that those are conceptual frameworks so much as God's Truth.

Regina Schwartz cites Robert Alter as the one to bring literary critical principles into biblical studies in 1975 with his 'ground-breaking' essay 'A Literary Approach to the Bible'. Alter calls for 'serious analysis',

---

19. Frye, *Anatomy*, p. 189.
20. Frye, *Anatomy*, p. 345.

the manifold varieties of minutely discriminating attention to the artful
use of language, to the shifting play of ideas, conventions, tone, sound,
imagery, narrative viewpoint, compositional units, and much else; the
kind of disciplined attention, in other words, which through a whole
spectrum of critical approaches has illuminated, for example, the poetry
of Dante, the plays of Shakespeare, the novels of Tolstoy. [21]

Alter and Kermode's *Literary Guide to the Bible* gives just such
attention to the Bible, to name one very important book, and although
early Irish literature has no convenient canon, an equivalent publication
in this field would be invaluable. David Gunn and Dana Nolan Fewell's
guide, *Narrative in the Hebrew Bible* (1993) is another useful book
with one foot in theory. Its format is representative of books of literary
criticism of the Bible: one passage is looked at through the critical
lenses of assorted techniques over two thousand years of (Christian)
exegesis.

There have also been contributions to literary textual criticism which
focus more closely on those specific language traits of the Hebrew
Bible which make it, according to some, fundamentally unreadable by
any extrabiblical critical technique. Meir Sternberg lays down those
rules in *The Poetics of Biblical Narrative: Ideological Literature and
the Drama of Reading*. Sternberg explains how to read this singular
text, with respect to its own particular system of writing. In a related
vein is Adèle Berlin's *Poetics and Interpretation of Biblical Narrative*.
Here a word or arrangement of words is allotted a unit of strength of
literary impact: *hinneh* will have *this* force *here*, and so on.

One thing which the absence of this type of book from early Irish
studies implies is that early Irish literature has no such dimensions, that
is, its tales are not as rich, interesting or pleasurable as is the Bible or,
for that matter, *Pinocchio*.

The only way to prove this point is to try to illustrate it, not just by
assembling quotes from Ó Cathasaigh's or Nagy's work, but by using
new material. In *Critical Terms for Literary Study*, to name one good
college textbook of many, thirty thinkers analyse texts on different
bases, some working with Wordsworth, some with Dante, to demonstrate what approaches mean and that they are possible, plausible and

---

21. R. Alter, 'A Literary Approach to the Bible', *Commentary* 60 (December
1975), p. 70-71, cited in R. Schwartz, *The Book and the Text: the Bible and Literary Theory* (Oxford: Basil Blackwell, 1990), p. 2.

productive.[22] In the same format I will work from the Old Irish tale *Táin Bó Fraích.*

Táin Bó Fraích is a good place to start for several reasons. For one, it is fairly accessible to non-Celtic scholars (a point to consider when urging an interdisciplinary approach!): the DIAS edition by Meid has recently been reprinted, and Jeffrey Gantz includes an adequate translation of that edition in his small collection published by Penguin.[23] Gantz even furnishes us with a literary nod, contentiously informing us that the tale is 'neither mythic nor heroic so much as literary and psychological. More attention is paid to motivation here than in any other early Irish story... Even the dialogue is unusually subtle.'[24] Will a short passage reveal the layers Gantz locates?

Ailill and Medb are trying to embarrass or test Fróech who has been intimate with their daughter Findabair. In this scene, Fróech is in a pool and the others are watching from the shore. Lines 194-219 are as follows:[25]

> 'Don't come out', says Ailill, 'until you've brought me over a branch from the rowan tree on the other side of the river. I think its berries are beautiful.'
>
> He sets out, breaks a branch off the tree, and brings it back with him through the water. (Afterwards, whenever she saw something beautiful, Findabair would say that the sight of Fróech moving across the dark pool was more beautiful to her, the body so white and the hair so lovely, the fine face, the very blue eyes, and he this gentle young man, with a face narrow beneath and broad above, complete and flawless, and the branch with the red berries between his throat and his white face. This is what Findabair used to say: that she had never seen anything which possessed even half or a third of his beauty).
>
> After that he brings the berries out of the water to them.
>
> 'The berries are fine and lovely. Bring us some more of them!'
>
> He sets out again until he comes half way across the water. This beast in the water grabs him.

22. F. Lentricchia and T. McLaughlin (eds.), *Critical Terms for Literary Study* (Chicago: University of Chicago Press, 1995).

23. W. Meid, (ed. and trans.), *Táin Bó Fraích* (Dublin: DIAS, 1967); J. Gantz (trans.), *Early Irish Myths and Sagas* (London: Penguin Books, 1982), pp. 113-26. Carney has a translation too; I mention Gantz because someone unconnected to Celtic studies can easily buy it.

24. Gantz, *Early Irish Myths*, p. 114.

25. My translation. I am grateful to Colm Ó Baoill for his corrections. For Irish, see Appendix I.

'Get me a sword!' he says. And there is not a man on land who dares bring him one, for fear of Ailill and Medb.

After that Findabair removes her clothes and leaps in the water with the sword.

Her father sends a five-pointed spear after her from above—a throw's length—so that it goes through her two tresses, and Fróech catches the spear in his hand. He sends the spear up toward shore, the creature at his side. He releases the spear with a thrust and, by means of a kind of weapon play, it goes past the purple mantle and through the shirt that Ailill has on. At that, the youths rise up around Ailill.

Findabair comes out of the water, but leaves the spear in Fróech's hand. Thus he strikes the creature's head off (so it was by his side) and he brings the creature with him to land.

Some literary critical questions this passage poses are, What role do the berries play? (Out of reach, then carried by Fróech to adorn him in Findabair's eyes, inadequate for Ailill, an excuse for his violence.) Why does Ailill not have the monster attack Fróech on the first journey? (Just to give Findabair a chance to watch him?) Does the passage say more about father and daughter or about the lovers? Does Ailill arrange the whole show in order to try to hurt Findabair? (Does Medb approve of this tactic?) Would Fróech have survived without the sword; was it only a test for Findabair's love? (He does not use the sword to defend himself; the creature is *inna thaeb*, at his side.) Is it significant that Findabair should take off her clothes? What is the role of the creature in the events in this passage?

Literary criticism sees the exclusion of other disciplines, the bracketing of philosophy, history, and anthropology in favour of a 'pure' literary 'science'. It does not address the possibility that the words on the page (whatever varying qualities they may indeed possess) are read differently by different people. The questions of literary criticism proposed here still miss points about *Táin Bó Fraích* which would be crucial to another reader (and the picture of the narrative their answers may form is only one possible picture). There are many more issues involved in reading which operate at completely different levels of thought. Do people read a text in a vacuum, or is there always a group of texts that come into any reading process? Do *texts* really exist in a vacuum or do they subtly reflect the milieu that created them, politically or culturally?

Northrop Frye was not completely stuck in time—which goes part of the way to explaining why his books are still in demand. One important concept of his that existed before him and endured afterwards is that there are many ways to read, or many schools that prefer their own way of reading:

> The student must either admit the principle of polysemous meaning, or choose one of these groups and then try to prove that all the others are less legitimate. The former is the way of scholarship; the latter is the way of pedantry...[26]

This is a new flexibility in interpretation. One need not look for what a text is 'really' about, nor is a text *only* historically or literarily useful. The result of this freedom is not chaos but rather the establishment of new criteria for relevance, new languages and codes of expression, and new ways to make texts accessible to more people (often at the cost of 'deconstructing' previous authorities' methods).

We are still in the business of interpreting and understanding, however 'different' the way we go about it. Mieke Bal puts it dryly, writing about the Bible:

> One modest and legitimate goal has always been a fuller understanding of the text, one that is sophisticated, reproducible, and accessible to a larger audience.... [T]he criteria for the evaluation of interpretations are the traditional standards of plausibility, adequacy, and relevance.[27]

For many theories of narrative a structural awareness is a place to start. Structuralism is well established in early Irish studies, and thus it is unnecessary to summarize its history here. Melia and Ó Cathasaigh had produced in-depth studies involving structuralism by the early 1970s, as mentioned in the previous chapter. It is, thus, hardly the case that scholars of early Irish have their heads in the sand about trends in critical thought. Structuralism is discussed in Chapter 3. Here, however, we can return to the passage of *Táin Bó Fraích* to establish one way its structure could be assembled and listed. A preliminary list of actions might look like this:

> Ailill tells Fróech to stay in water, get berries (beauty the reason).
> Fróech brings berries.
> Findabair (in flash forward) watches (beauty the reason).
> Fróech brings berries.
> Ailill demands more (choice, delicious the reason).

26. Frye, *Anatomy*, p. 72.

27. M. Bal, *Lethal Love: Feminist Literary Readings of Biblical Love Stories* (Bloomington: Indiana University Press, 1987), pp. 12-13.

Beast grabs Fróech.
Fróech asks for a sword (no, for fear of Ailill and Medb).
Findabair jumps in water with sword.
Ailill throws a spear after her (pierces, not hurting).
Fróech catches spear.
Fróech throws the spear after Ailill (pierces, not hurting).
'Youths rise up around Ailill.'
Findabair leaves water, and sword.
Fróech kills (apparently pacific) creature.
Fróech brings its head to land.

Some questions of narrative revealed in *Táin Bó Fraích* might be, What patterns form on the basis of this sketch and what might they suggest? Other questions of narrative might include, Who speaks and when? (Ailill gives orders, Fróech gives one short demand/plea. The others are silent.) Whose point of view is revealed? Who acts? (Ailill stays still, talking. Fróech goes back and forth in the water.) What other actors are there and how do they affect the narrative? What force do the unnamed others have ('not a man on land dares bring him a sword' and 'the youths rise up')?

The kind of interpretation these questions (and their possible answers) shape might be seen as somewhat subversive, since it does not look for, let alone rely on, a 'plain sense'. New levels emerge that go beyond the putative intentions of the author (which are 'very difficult to find out and frequently irrelevant for the interpretation of a text').[28] Nor are the intentions of the reader straightforward—and there is also the factor of the intentions of the text that Eco refers to (in a way which may take theory back to where early Christian exegesis started). Theorists navigate by these obstacles.

Theories thus extend in various directions, parsing and rearranging the shape and stresses of texts, probing various aspects of structure, or demanding they be read in the light of an ideology. The advocates of each new intense approach do not necessarily demand that all others read the same way, but rather seek to define their terms and explain why they find them useful.

Bal describes the theory of narrative she has in mind, the way she reads the systems of texts, and what her intentions are. She draws attention to the way information is told, not just the information. Literary

---

28. Eco, 'Interpretation and History', in Eco and Rorty (eds.), *Interpretation*, p. 25.

theoretician J. Hillis Miller's comment makes a good preface to her work: 'Narratives are a relatively safe ... place in which the reigning assumptions of a given culture can be criticised.'[29] Bal wants to hear the 'voices' in a text that only careful listening will reveal. That way she feels she will understand something about the narrative that it may have sought to disguise, but which is part of the culture that created it.

By this careful examination, either the expected or the unexpected turns up, and light is shed on the culture in a new way:

> The simple questions Who speaks? Who 'sees'? Who acts? when applied to a specific text may either provide direct answers, and thus show the structure of meaning in its pragmatic dimension, or else prove to be problematic ... its ideological impact ... blurred ... Through their problematic structure, [texts] demonstrate the way in which the subject and its assumed unity were problematized.[30]

The next step is deducing information from the problems. If Findabair is watching Fróech and painting a mental portrait of him and not the other way round, as we might expect, then it might be argued that the narrative is 'problematized'. Fróech's passivity and not his might is being highlighted in a passage where, at first glance, he seems to be active, slaying a monster and defending Findabair from Ailill.

Some readings can be intensely personal, not designed to analyse some 'objectively' visible structure, but to grapple with the fact that even that is up to the reader. Even without getting into the thick of reader-response criticism there are many kinds of biblical literary criticism that include personal views. Richard Howard writes, 'I knew that Esther was about my mother, and that Mordecai was about the world—about my stepfather and the struggle for survival.'[31] Is the book of Esther really about Richard Howard's mother? No. The book of Esther is not even about *your* mother. He is writing a parallel text which can be read with the Book of Esther without replacing it. We can gain insight from his reading about what may be part of the 'intentions of the text' or not.

29. J.H. Miller, 'Narrative', in Lentricchia and McLaughlin (eds.), *Critical Terms*, pp. 66-79 (69).

30. Bal, *Lethal Love*, p. 21.

31. R. Howard, 'Esther Apart: Hearing Secret Harmonies', in D. Rosenberg (ed.), *Congregation: Contemporary Writers Read the Jewish Bible* (New York: Harcourt Brace Jovanovich, 1987), p. 407.

We may compare this approach with the following comment by Proinsias Mac Cana about the early Irish tale *Longes Mac n-Uislenn*: 'Above all it might be thought that Deirdre ... was a woman of flesh and blood, and certainly few writers, if any, whether in Irish or in any other literature, have succeeded in creating such a concise yet utterly convincing image of the feminine psyche.'[32] Mac Cana is not stating an opinion: we are made to know that just as sure as any of his other points are true, objectively and categorically—like that the Book of Invasions is a twelfth-century text—women are basically all like Deirdre. (In our propensity for ear-boxing? In our persistence in trying to dash our brains out?) This statement is unlikely to find favour with even the most conservative of feminist critics.

Biblical studies has vehicles not just for structuralist articles but for new developments in theory. The 'in' for these essays has often been the periodical *Semeia*, which served as 'the centre of an emerging biblical structuralism'[33] beginning in 1974 with its issue 'A Structural Approach to the Parables'. Unlike *Interpretation*, in *Semeia* the aim is to 'involv[e] non-biblical colleagues and specialists, and [to keep] in touch with parallel initiatives in the American Academy of Religion'.[34] Instead of an apology to God in the introductory essay, *Semeia* offers an invitation to the world's thinkers. It called and calls itself:

> an experimental journal of biblical criticism ... devoted to the exploration of new and emergent areas and methods of biblical criticism. Studies employing the methods, models, and findings of linguistics, folklore studies, contemporary literary criticism, structuralism, social anthropology, and other such disciplines and approaches are invited. Although experimental in both form and content, *Semeia* proposes to publish work that reflects a well-defined methodology that is appropriate to the material being interpreted.[35]

Its limits, then, are few, theoretically. But it still does not say where it draws the line on a 'well-defined methodology' or what is meant by 'appropriate'. The questions are ones that exist outwith biblical studies; they weave in and out of developments in critical thought. Does the author or the text determine meaning? Are there limits to interpretation?

32. P. Mac Cana, 'Women in Irish Mythology', *The Crane Bag* 4 (1980), pp. 7-11 (9).
33. Detweiler and Robbins, 'Hermeneutics', p. 258.
34. Wilder, 'An Experimental Journal', *Semeia* 1/1 (1974), pp. 1-16 (3).
35. This appears on the inside cover of every issue of *Semeia*.

Theory does not propose to solve these questions but it is not afraid to ask them. No mapping of actions of characters or speech acts proposes to eliminate the need for interpretation. The relevance and plausibility of interpretation cited by Bal and others is always open to debate.

Is it fair to dismiss completely a text's posited original function? Umberto Eco looks at the question of interpreting, using the unusual metaphor of a screwdriver to highlight the realness of a text's intended function (if only one will acknowledge it). Screwdrivers are for driving in screws, Eco cries:

> A screwdriver can be inserted into a cavity and be turned inside, and in this case could also be used to scratch one's ear. But it is also too sharp ... and for this reason I usually refrain from [this]... This means that, as well as *impossible pertinences*, there are *crazy pertinences*. I cannot use a screwdriver as an ashtray.[36]

That is, it is one thing to ignore a text's intended function (a penitential text, say—a guide to penance for a particular sin) and use it effectively for something else (an index to the author's penchant for necromancy), but there is a line where that interpretation seems crazy—contrary to the very essence of the text, insupportable except by the most arcane logic (a catalogue for fishing gear). To deconstruct a text, to see it as useful for something for which it was not manifestly intended may be acceptable, but not for anything: 'To decide how a text works means to decide which one of its various aspects is or can become relevant or pertinent for a coherent interpretation of it, and which ones remains marginal and unable to support a coherent reading.'[37]

Eco's words are partly intended as a response to Richard Rorty's article 'The Pragmatist's Progress' in the same volume.[38] For Rorty there is no overinterpreting, or at least no way of defining a 'plain sense' and pointing to it:

> The notion that there is something a given text is *really* about, something which rigorous application of a method will reveal, is as bad as the Aristotelian idea that there is something which a substance really, intrinsically *is* as opposed to what it only apparently or accidentally or relationally is.[39]

36. Eco, 'Reply', pp. 145-46.

37. Eco, 'Reply', p. 146.

38. R. Rorty, 'The Pragmatist's Progress', in Eco and Rorty (eds.), *Interpretation*, pp. 89-108.

39. Rorty, 'Progress', p. 102.

This flies not in Eco's face so much as in all the critics' who do not permit polysemous meaning, conservative as well as (politically) 'liberal'. As discussed above, I believe the rabbis would agree with Rorty (much as Davies claimed the glossators to his camp), and would see idolatry in their monomaniacal arguments where Rorty sees 'occultism'.[40] (The rabbinical tradition is discussed below.) The lines of acceptability are not drawn only according to individual taste (which is acceptable enough) but they are continually redrawn according to trends in thought over time. A strict Freudian reading of a text would seem 'crazy' in one decade of the twentieth century for being too radical. To others throughout that century it might seem merely 'impossible' and to a theorist in this decade it would be too conservative and limited to be written.

For my own part I agree with Rorty as I pursue a demonstration of schools of theory of narrative that have seemed outlandish at some point in their history. Rorty asks us to 'scrap the distinction between using and interpreting and just distinguish between uses by different people for different purposes'.[41]

Another important school of narratological analysis is psychoanalytic theory. The important idea here is the unconscious: there are things that go on in a dream, for example, of which the dreamer himself is not aware. In parallel, there are things that go on which are repressed from consciousness. The connection between this idea (so simplistically stated here) and its various guises in twentieth- and twenty-first-century thought is elaborate. This idea emerges in critical theory as texts other than the dream take the dream's place. Freud himself turned to literature and even to ancient literature to uncover things about the unconscious.

Indeed, Freud makes much not only of Sophocles's *Oedipus* plays as a subject for analysis, but refers to the long-standing traditions of dream-interpretation in many cultures, even in the Bible. Psychoanalysis is obviously connected, then, to trends in interpretation mentioned already: there are voices in texts which are not immediately apparent, which only close examination will reveal. Different levels of sophistication in a psychoanalytic approach to literature determine what the analysand is exactly: do we look through the text to the author's biases or to the culture's bias? Or is it worth psychoanalysing characters?

40. Rorty, 'Progress', p. 103.
41. Rorty, 'Progress', p. 106.

Joe More's article 'The Prophet Jonah: The Story of an Intrapsychic Process' is an example of a psychoanalytic reading of a biblical text.[42] In reading the book of Jonah, More is aware of the text's linguistic particulars and works with them, not towards establishing a poetics of Jonah, but as clues to the portrait of the prophet. I read his work as still being on the safe side of dogma, not insisting that he is writing what Jonah is 'really about'. Rather he suggests a parallel text that can be read with Jonah. For example, he draws on his experience as a psychiatrist to conclude that 'Jonah's hatred of his brothers, which stemmed from his id, was able to become fused with parental (God's) demands into a morality that found its targets in Nineveh's sins'.[43] If Jonah did not really have brothers, it is hardly the point. More's article is a gloss, one way of explaining a confusing bit of text to a subset of readers. As such it may seem laughable or unnecessary to others.

We return to our exemplar, *Táin Bó Fraích*: what do we know about the characters? Ailill is controlling, demanding, acting as father figure, but strangely passive as he waits on the shore. He is the rival for his daughter's attention (his own wife, Medb, is absent from this scene). The narrative description of Fróech's beauty in Findabair's eyes eclipses his own preoccupation with wanting to possess beauty (his concept of the berries). Fróech performs every physical task better than Ailill had anticipated, and even mocks his spear-casting (read: confronts him with his sexual impotency). The berries that Ailill had used in an attempt to show up his rival become, in Findabair's eyes, the symbol of her new sexuality (framed by Fróech's skin, commemorated by her dive). Fróech gets Ailill's daughter on his own terms in the water realm (female sexuality) where he is in fact master, attracting Findabair in after accelerating her desire from a distance. She severs the parental ties, pointedly replacing the sexual object of the father with Fróech by undressing in front of Ailill but then going to Fróech's side. The monster, Ailill's emissary, echoes Ailill's impotence, even in this other realm of water: it threatens, but goes limp, serves only to adorn Fróech ('at his side') after its initial impetus and is then, like Ailill, symbolically castrated ('he strikes the creature's head off').

Psychoanalysis has had a more general influence on thought and has influenced language in several schools of theory and narratology. For

42. J. More, 'The Prophet Jonah: The Story of an Intrapsychic Process', *American Imago* 27 (1970), pp. 3-11.

43. More, 'Jonah', p. 9.

this reason we see it in *Semeia*, for example, in an apparently unrelated article about intertextuality and the Bible, to be discussed below. Or again, in the context of a folkloric reading of the Bible.

Susan Niditch writes, 'The shearing of Samson's hair is a sexual stripping and subjugation.'[44] This is an (unacknowledged) Freudian reading of Judges and shows how far along acceptance of sexual psychoanalytic language is in biblical studies. The gap between hirsute Samson asleep on Delilah's lap and skinhead Samson with his eyes gouged out has been filled by Niditch's effortless psychoanalysis. What has happened is that Freud's view of human relations and the unconscious has affected language in Western Europe (whether or not the debt to Freud is acknowledged). Freud, too, was merely picking up on a process that seems to be a constant part of humankind's experience, and labelling it in a particular way—but that is, of course, open to debate.

The overlap of studies of mythology and psychoanalysis is another area of interest again, as in the work of Otto Rank.[45] While each of these areas has achieved some currency in biblical studies they have not been used together as they have in other disciplines. At the same time, folkloric readings are at least as sophisticated in early Irish studies as they are in biblical studies, and need not be summarized here.

One of the things that distinguish Freud as an important thinker is his devotion to interpretation, his insistence on this in all his work. This has had the effect that his own texts have been interpreted again and again, by Jacques Lacan and others. He has been the object of interpretation for analysts-to-be, and for Freud-haters, but also for philosophers. Susan Handelman locates in Freud's own experience an Oedipus complex that will have a particular connection to my reading of Samson (in Chapter 5): 'The dead father in *Totem and Taboo, Moses and Monotheism* ... or all the fathers of philosophy in Derrida: all enforce upon the living sons a certain contract to guilt and a desire to be free of that burden.'[46] (This, for its part, is directly relevant to the Bible because Handelman connects Freud to a tradition of thinking begun by the rabbis.)

Thus even if we do not 'buy' Freud's particular theories, which may indeed be structured round 1900s Vienna, and his own foibles, we can

---

44. S. Niditch, 'Samson as Culture Hero, Trickster and Bandit', *CBQ* 52/4 (October 1990), pp. 608-24 (616).

45. Cf. O. Rank, *The Myth of the Birth of the Hero and Other Writings* (New York: Vintage Books, 1959). This overlap is discussed in Chapter 4.

46. Handelman, *Moses*, p. 138.

appreciate the process: 'Freud's most enduring legacy is that his text, more than ever, calls for interpretation.'[47]

From the sexually audacious language of Freud's writing we can move to a discussion of 'gender studies', which broad label includes feminism, discussed above. Gender is not something to be 'applied', of course. Philosophy and politics enter into the reading and writing processes, some theoreticians argue, and new issues emerge when we study texts. We 'ignore' gender-relevant language at our peril. 'Acknowledgment' involves reaching back behind literary criticism to the time when we believed culture could be read through the text, but this time the culture's intentions, like the instincts of the unconscious, are sometimes hidden.

This interpretative (and political) stance involves a closer reading than the intentionalists practise. This means, for example, that the text to be read need not have main women characters for attitudes about women to be revealed. Everything is highly politicized; why should that stop in a culture's fictional texts? 'It turns out that all the time writers and critics thought they were just creating and explicating transcendingly in a separate artistic language, willy nilly they were speaking the contemporary cultural wisdom.'[48]

Such reading has much to do with feminism, but also with a new lens, generally. Although this kind of reading may go 'against the grain' of the text, it points to a level of interpretation which it seems foolish to ignore:

> It is as if the novel itself had found a female voice and the language to say things its male vocabulary could not articulate and therefore did not know, or did not know it knew. The term 'gender' can empower criticism in the same way, enabling it to pose new questions and thus discover new levels of interpretation.[49]

This is a major part of the rationale behind readings by Dooley and Findon, discussed above, as well as for a great deal of Mieke Bal's work. She is looking to articulate the feminine but she is trying to be aware of gender more generally. Bal's is a strong voice in biblical criticism in several ways at once; one of them is that she for difference.

47. J. Lechte, 'Freud', in *Fifty Key Contemporary Thinkers: From Structuralism to Postmodernity* (London: Routledge, 1994), p. 23.

48. M. Jehlen, 'Gender', in Lentricchia and McLaughlin (eds.), *Critical Terms*, p. 264.

49. Jehlen, 'Gender', p. 271.

'Bal…wishes to amplify the prophetic, celebratory, simultaneously nur-
turing and destroying female voice of the narrative that, if heard …
will change the nature of biblical scholarship.'[50]

This means not looking for strong female characters but reading
carefully. In her intense readings of Judges she customizes narratology,
theories of gender, and readings for a political or cultural Other. Her
work is important also for theorists of other ancient literatures because
she works from a strong knowledge of the culture from which the
biblical text emerges. The questions that Stock provokes about literary
theory and mediaeval texts are of relevance to Bal's work with biblical
texts. With Bal, however, a fine line is walked (as I suggested above
with reference to the work of other feminists):

> Insofar as Bal's reading continues to depend on a frame of reference in
> 'real' history for its validation, one must wonder whether her strategy of
> containment inadvertently allows for the theologically driven nation-
> alism so basic to the rise of biblical 'Higher Criticism' especially in
> nineteenth and early twentieth-century Germany.[51]

A somewhat old-fashioned reading for women's voices in *Táin Bó
Fraích* might turn out like this:

Ailill and Fróech may appear to control the situation for their loud
words and thrashing about, but the text clearly revolves around Findabair. It is her words above and beyond the details of the present scene
which are inscribed for eternity, to be cited as if part of an existing
myth in the narrator's time, framing the whole episode: 'Findabair said
afterwards… Findabair used to say…'[52] She casts Fróech as her sexual
object (distorting the usual sexual roles) not for his power or might, but
for looks. We note his passivity as she casts him as object. Indeed,
Fróech is passive throughout, merely confronting the various tasks
brought upon him by Ailill and Findabair, his one original task being to
kill an already unthreatening monster! Findabair further exerts her
strength as the focal point of this narrative by confronting Fróech and
her father with her nakedness (which is, again, acting against cultural

---

50. Detweiler and Robbins, 'Hermeneutics', p. 263.

51. T. Beal, 'Ideology and Intertextuality: Surplus of Meaning and Controlling
the Means of Production', in D.N. Fewell (ed.), *Reading between Texts: Intertextuality and the Hebrew Bible* (Louisville, KY: Westminster/John Knox Press, 1992),
pp. 27-39 (35).

52. Dooley has seriously and justifiably made a similar observation about Deirdre
in 'Heroic Word'.

norms), disobeying authority by seeking her own love object, and han-
dling weapons in a way more reminiscent of Scáthach than even the
strong-willed Deirdre. She saves her man because he cannot do it
himself (and because no *man* ['ní fer'] is brave enough to do it). Ailill's
entire ploy to embarrass her is thus thwarted and she emerges first from
the water, still naked, triumphant, her lover left speechless, as is her
father, pinned to a tree nearby.

The presence of such readings means that race and class can come
into discussions of the Bible, where perhaps the relevant dividing line is
between those who have a covenant with God and those who do not.
Can there be said to be such a division in early Irish texts? Can they be
read not just for gender but for 'race' (Connachtmen, Ulstermen, and so
on)? Such a discussion could connect back to O'Leary's work, where
codes are investigated, but this time in a way that works 'against' the
text. Such readings could be connected back to sociology to suggest
more about the functions of narrative in early Irish society. (But this
process is fraught by the fact that a certain narrative may be the only
text from that period.)

For Bal, such readings for the value-laden language of texts affects
more than the world of the past. Her hopeful words encapsulate this: 'It
is only when the disciplines that study ancient texts are open to interdisciplinary collaboration ... that the social function of narrative and the
narrative function of social changes ... can be properly analysed and
understood.'[53]

With that, a sort of pinnacle is reached in biblical criticism, and we
can safely go back a millennium or more to the ever-existing rabbinical
traditions of interpretation. Their legacy is another source to draw on,
although their ideas cannot be 'applied' any more than gender can be—
theirs is a whole way of thinking. 'At bottom midrash is not a genre of
interpretation but an interpretative stance.'[54] They are both more and
less than a lens, however, and while it is unforgivable to discuss different approaches to the Hebrew Bible without mentioning these primary inheritors of Scripture, the connection to early Irish texts does not
lie merely in the example of the way they read the Bible.

53. M. Bal, 'Dealing/With/Women: Daughters in the Book of Judges', in
Schwartz (ed.), *The Book and the Text*, pp. 16-39 (37).

54. J.L. Kugel, 'Two Introductions to Midrash', in Hartman and Budick (eds.),
Midrash and Literature, p. 91.

There are several relevant points about midrash and the rabbinical traditions. This is Judaism finally making the front pages of European thought after a thousand years or more of exile. Here is a mediaeval tradition which can serve both as a model of critical thinking for modern times, and in itself as a text to be read today. (Contemporary theorists are also learning from the logic of other ancients, who seem to have anticipated very recent developments in thought.) On a third level, this tradition can be said to have 'resurfaced' in the thinking of Freud, Derrida, Harold Bloom and a few others. Stephen Prickett tries to capture this in a way that makes sense for his intended Christian readership:

> With Derrida, Hartman, Bloom and Alter and other twentieth-century critics ... we find almost for the first time in two thousand years a public contribution to that interaction [of analysis and 'twentieth-century philosophical problems of theology'] which is distinctively Jewish.... Not merely does this constitute the resurfacing of an older and different critical tradition from a different religious perspective, with a different arrangement even of the basic texts; it also means the presence of what amount to totally different ways of thinking about hermeneutics.[55]

What, then, is this methodology and how does it relate to biblical criticism and literary theory, and how can it be related to early Irish studies?

Handelman uses 'rabbinic' to refer to the literature and attitudes that began to be formed from the fourth century BCE onwards. It is obviously impossible to capture all their ways of thinking and analysing here, or even to try to explain the difference between theirs and the 'normal' structured thought of Graeco-Christian traditions. In summarizing, Handelman says that the rabbis prefer 'multivocal as opposed to univocal meanings, the play of *as if* over the assertions of *is*, juxtapositions over equivalencies ...'[56] An example of Rashi's logic ends the last chapter, where we see that kind of thinking in action. Conflicting views are presented one next to the other without an implied hierarchy.

There is certainly question as to whether the text (the Bible) can be wrested from a definition of 'rabbinic' without rendering the term meaningless, however. Is it midrash because of the thinking or because

55. S. Prickett, 'Introduction', in Prickett, *Reading the Text*, p. 9.
56. Handelman, *Moses*, p. 32.

of the fact that the thinking is directed toward the Bible?[57] This does not mean that a layman may not think midrashically, but should perhaps refrain from calling himself a rabbi (although Handelman takes on 'Reb Derrida' with glee).

In this spirit, Harold Fisch writes about Daniel Defoe's *Robinson Crusoe* where 'the story of Robinson's many trials on the island may be used as a kind of midrash on Jonah'.[58] He supports this with sketches on Jonah's and Robinson's adventures, but what he need not prove is its relevance or its 'truth'. The ultimate in his argument would not be 'And thus we know that Defoe used Jonah as his model'. It may be tempting to think of this historical connection, but his argument does not rely on it any more than if he had written 'The story of Jonah's many trials can be read as a kind of midrash on *Robinson Crusoe*.' The whole hunt for categories is not pertinent and yet the result is not chaos, either. He relies on midrash's breadth: 'Midrashic statements are... essentially independent of one another; they do not demand to be related to one another by some Aristotelian principle of form and order.'[59]

The rabbis demonstrate flexibility and the many-voiced nature of thought and writing. The example is beginning to serve biblical criticism now, much as it has begun to be appropriated by the latest thinkers in critical theory (or even less recent ones like Emmanuel Levinas). If this were imported into early Irish studies, it would mean that articles with conflicting opinions would deserve to be seen in print, side by side, without one threatening the validity of the other. Here we might conflate the logic of the rabbis and the glossators again, as at the end of the last chapter. What remains to be done is the exporting of some of the logic of the ancient glossators into the realms of reading, not just for their etymological prowess this time, or legal know-how, but for their methodologies.

Questions come to the surface such as, how do they treat words? What are their methods? As Susan Handelman (among others) has examined the *methodology* of the rabbis so could the methodology of the glossators be analysed not just with a view to literary analysis but

57. Handelman argues that they can indeed be discussed independently (*Moses*, pp. 41-42, 80, *passim*). Harold Fisch disputes this in 'The Hermeneutic Quest in *Robinson Crusoe*', in Hartman and Budick (eds.), *Midrash and Literature*, p. 231.
58. Fisch, 'Quest', p. 218.
59. Fisch, 'Quest', p. 231.

as concerns philosophical, historiographic, and religious thought (as Thomas O'Loughlin has implied about Hiberno-Latin sources).[60] Rolf Baumgarten has made a similar point.

Baumgarten examines mediaeval Irish etymology on its own terms and calls modestly for a 'systematic appreciation of these, admittedly marginal, features of Irish literary tradition according to their own purpose and environment'.[61] He also understands why they have been ignored for so long as a source of insight—for much the same reasons that the rabbis were ignored: the methodology is Other. 'Mediaeval philosophical etymology is *per definitionem* different from modern etymology in purpose and methodology, though constant modern abuse and ridicule directed towards its results have prevented epistemological appreciation.'[62]

In both cases it is this 'different' which has stigmatized the methodology—the culture chooses a point as 'normal', erases what came before and denies what comes afterwards.

Where other scholars asked, 'What are these gloss-ridden texts good for?', Liam Breatnach asks us to look at the texts. He cites the critics who ask the first question, the enemies of the intricate, marginal thinking typical of the glossators: '[M]ost of their work consists of elaborate variations on themes ... They weave a crazy pattern of rabbinical distinctions, schematic constructions, academic casuistry, and arithmetical calculations, none of which has any value ...'[63]

The scholar D.A. Binchy wrote these words. It is only the word 'rabbinical' in this text that gives away the object of its tirade; otherwise a reader would assume the rabbis themselves were being criticized by traditional Christian exegetes, perhaps for *gematria* or *notarikon* specifically.[64]

---

60. T. O'Loughlin, 'The Latin Sources of Medieval Irish Culture: A Partial Status Quaestionis', in McCone and Simms (eds.), *Progress*, pp. 91-106.

61. Rolf Baumgarten, 'A Hiberno-Isidorian Etymology', *Peritia* 2 (1983), pp. 225-28 (226).

62. Baumgarten, 'Etymology', p. 225.

63. D.A. Binchy, 'The Linguistic and Historical Value of the Irish Law Tracts', *Proceedings of the British Academy* 29 (1943), pp. 225-26, as cited in L. Breatnach, 'Law', in McCone and Simms (eds.), *Progress*, pp. 107-21 (114).

64. Where *gematria* is 'The method by which the values of letters in words are calculated and then interpreted, often by comparison with some other word with the same numerical value' and *notarikon* is that 'in which the letters of a word are

A midrash on *Táin Bó Fraích* is easily imagined, but could be performed only by a scholar with a knowledge of early Irish texts as encyclopaedic as the rabbis' was of the Bible. So would a canon help with such an exercise. A rabbi might turn to lines 214ff., which baffle editor Meid ('The exact meaning of the phrase is uncertain'): 'Léciud ón co forgabáil.' He might elaborate on its sense, 'went through' as in 'permeated' but did not 'pierce', as Reb Dillon wrote 'cast with check'. But is there not a *gabáil* into the cauldron in *Scéla Mucce Meic Dathó?*[65] And thus Ailill is pierced into, as Reb Carney says 'a cast with a thrust'. Or we might take *léicid* in the sense of 'let, allow' because the spear was destined for Ailill's heart, and Fróech merely *released* it, but controlled it, in so doing, from actually killing Ailill, because she is Findabair's father.[66]

Breatnach has called attention to the danger of ignoring the writings of the early Irish themselves in his characteristically polemicized way: 'Do those who indulge in such comments really mean to imply that they know more about early Irish society than the authors of the very texts which are probably our most important source of information for that society?'[67]

Furthermore, when scholars quote the rabbis, they are quoting from biblical exegesis, laws, biblical commentary, jokes and anecdotes— glosses almost all of them on some aspect or other of literature or culture. It remains to be asked why so many people have quoted Bergin's fake gloss (cited in the last chapter). Perhaps because despite its being a parody, it is not only educational, but amusing—it shows imagination (and not just Bergin's), and flexibility, wandering meaning, and the greatness and obscurity of language.

The words and letters of the Hebrew Bible can be expounded on and unfurled down to the letter, like the laws of the early Irish. There was no concept of a 'true sense' of some verse for the rabbis, but rather an incredible number of possibilities, none of them contradictory, all of

taken to be abbreviations of other words ... or in which words reveal new meanings by being divided into two or more parts ...' Definitions are from Hartman and Budick (eds.), *Midrash and Literature*, pp. 363-65.

65. 'a taibred din chétgabáil, iss ed no ithed.' R. Thurneysen (ed.), *Scéla Mucce Meic Dathó* ('The Story of Mac Dathó's Pig') (Dublin: DIAS, 1935), p. 2.

66. Cf. *léicid*. 'The principle meanings are (a) *lets go, releases*, (b) *lets, allows, permits*, (c) *leaves (behind), allows to remain*' (*DIL*, p. 424).

67. Breatnach, 'Law', p. 116.

them possible within the letters of the Hebrew texts, and all of them 'permissible' (there is no notion of 'excommunication', of a 'Church', of dogma). Could the early Irish have had trouble with all the dogma of Christianity at once, maybe particularly because they were so word- and letter-wise when Christianity came along?

Thus, through several channels we see that biblical criticism serves not only as an example of criticism, but as a model of constructive comparison. Harold Fisch's interpretation of Jonah and *Robinson Crusoe* is just one example of what comparative thinking might mean. Mieke Bal has also produced comparative readings in *Lethal Love: Feminist Literary Readings of Biblical Love Stories*. In one chapter, she compares the story of Samson and Delilah in the original with a contemporary 'adaptation' in a children's Bible.[68] In another chapter she compares Victor Hugo's 'Booz endormi' with the book of Ruth: Hugo is a gloss on Ruth.[69] Similarly she refers to several of Rembrandt's paintings with biblical themes as insights into the nuances of texts.[70]

In another kind of comparison, Susan Lochrie Graham explores the Bible in an intertextual reading of the television show *Star Trek: The Next Generation*. She persuasively paints producer Gene Roddenberry's psychoanalytic portrait, describing how the Bible is revealed in spite of his conscious efforts. Then she reads moments in the series for their biblical language and themes: 'Intertextual theory provides a critical means of exploring the ways in which ideas and images are incorporated into a narrative, even in contradiction to the stated intention of an author.'[71] Dismissing definitions of 'influence' in favour of the more intricate 'intertextuality' she successfully reads 'against the grain'.[72] The present book uses a related approach, reading sometimes against the grain for a particular voice (without the benefit of an interview with the authors to help form my interpretations).

68. M. Bal, 'Delilah Decomposed: Samson's Talking Cure and the Rhetoric of Subjectivity', in *Lethal Love*, pp. 37-67.

69. M. Bal, 'Heroism and Proper Names, or the Fruits of Analogy', in *Lethal Love*, pp. 68-88.

70. Cf. M. Bal, 'Lots of Writing', *Semeia* 54 (1991), pp. 77-102, and M. Bal, *Reading 'Rembrandt': Beyond the Word-Image Opposition* (Cambridge: Cambridge University Press, 1991).

71. Susan Lochrie Graham, 'Intertextual Trekking: Visiting the Iniquity of the Fathers upon "The Next Generation"', *Semeia* 64 (1995), pp. 195-217 (195).

72. For a discussion of intertextuality and the Bible see Fewell, *Reading between Texts, passim*.

If the early Irish text were read as the core text, an equivalent inter-text might be a Brian Moore novel, say, in which the author might have an unconscious awareness of some early Irish writing which would then resurface in his work.

More obviously, an intertextual analysis might look at the relation-ship between *Buile Shuibne* and the Sweeney legend in some contem-porary Irish texts. Such later texts—like Seamus Heaney's *Sweeney Astray*—may be dubious as adaptations but, like the Targums, are valid texts for comparison with original ancient texts, and do not threaten those texts' legitimacy.

The fact that there have been relatively few literary readings of early Irish texts gives the false impression that there can be no valid literary reactions to characters like Cúrói, or insights into gender to be revealed in *Fingal Rónáin*. But they are not so ill-wrought so as to be boring, so obfuscated by manuscript transmission so as to be invisible, or so part of a serious discipline so as to be no fun, as I hope the readings of *Táin Bó Fraích* have demonstrated. If anything, the many incarnations of a character (Ailill) or concept (the Otherworld) in different early Irish tales should be an occasion for more writing, not dismissal.

In fact, early Irish has several advantages as a burgeoning field for literary enquiries. As there has been no real establishment of 'appro-priate' literary criticism of early Irish texts, new articles should have leave to skip around in the history of theory, exploring the boundaries of thought. Furthermore, there is no canon of early Irish literature, which means a certain freedom and the possibility to include all kinds of texts in theoretical essays: laws with genealogical tracts with hagiog-raphy with tales. It can also be spared the compartmentalization to which other literatures have been subject ('Mael Fhothartaig: Tragic Hero?').

However, there is something ironic about this comparison of method-ologies. Surely, one would expect the secular discipline to be less reluc-tant to admit that its documents are not gospel than the ecclesiastical one. Deeply religious people have found that biblical texts can be appreciated from various angles, including referring to salvation pas-sages as 'narrative' and the foci of spirituality as 'texts'. If religious institutions can withstand examination of their texts, so can early Irish studies.

Scholars of early Irish literature and culture are no strangers to careful readings. History books have underplayed the Celtic contribu-

tion since the beginning of historiography. When Celtic scholars con-
struct a course on some aspect of Scottish history, for example, they
must rewrite what English scholars have left them, and enunciate a
voice that was there all along but not listened to. When they do that
they are already at the frontiers of theory.

In the next chapters, I will use some of the tools described above to
render visible voices or patterns within certain passages. This approach,
whereby the means is at least as important as the ends, has a precedent
in the work of Mieke Bal. In *Lethal Love*, as mentioned above, Bal
examines four biblical stories. In each of her readings she uses an
alternative version of a text, or a critique of it, as a comparative text to
the original (Masoretic) text, and in each one she is looking to articulate
women's voices. Moreover, with each story she looks at—drawn from
different parts of the Bible—she is using different critical tools. In
reading the story of Adam and Eve, for example, she refers not only to
Genesis but also to Christian mythology. Then she introduces the
hermeneutic framework within which she will read those texts. In a
similar way, the texts to be studied here fit into the general scheme
shown in the Plan of Comparison opposite (other texts will also be
mentioned in particular chapters). This collection features a range of
languages and kinds of story as well as approaches. In the body of the
book the critical material will be assessed at length.

Plan of Comparison

Bible text	Early Irish text	Biblical 'genre'	Early Irish 'genre'	Hermeneutic framework
The book of Jonah	*Ad VC*; *BCC*	minor prophet (Prophets)	hagiography	structuralism (Lévi-Strauss); (psychoanalytic theory)
The story of Samson (Judges 13.1-16.31)	*TEm*; *AOA*; *SC*	judge (Prophets)	'Ulster Cycle'	psychoanalytic theory (Freud); (post-structuralism; literary criticism; comparative mythology)
The book of Esther	*TBec*	(Writings)	'Cycle of the Kings'/ 'Historical Cycle'	reading for gender, 'class', the 'Other'; (reading alternate versions [Targums]; rabbinical commentary)

Chapter 3

WEAKNESS AND HUMAN FRAILTY: A READING OF THE BOOK
OF JONAH AND SOME EPISODES FROM LIVES OF COLUMBA

The book of Jonah features the famous reluctant 'minor' prophet whose
story has inspired works of art, plays and novels for centuries. Since its
composition around the fifth century BCE, the interpretation of its forty-
eight verses has filled volumes. The prophet's hesitancy alone has made
him a source for seemingly endless discussion, although it is arguably
the vehicle that the book provides for a display of God's lovingkindness
that has ensured it the important place it has in (Jewish) liturgical tradition.[1] A summary follows.

> 1. The word of the LORD comes to Jonah telling him to prophesy against
> Nineveh. Jonah, however, boards a ship bound for Tarshish (the opposite
> direction). At sea, the LORD causes a great storm and the sailors panic
> as Jonah sleeps in the hold until the ship's captain sends for him and asks
> him to pray. The sailors determine (through lot-casting) that the storm is
> Jonah's fault. They ask who he is and he tells them he is a Jew. He tells
> them to throw him into the sea to calm it, which they reluctantly do. The
> sea stops raging and the sailors offer a sacrifice to the LORD.
> 2. The LORD send a fish to swallow Jonah, where he stays for three
> days. From there he calls to God stating his present position (in the depths)
> and offering gratitude for his future position, promising a sacrifice. The
> LORD commands the fish to vomit Jonah up.
> 3. The word of the LORD commands Jonah to go to Nineveh again
> and Jonah goes. There he announces a brief dooming prophecy to which
> the Ninevites respond with all speed. The king reacts personally to the
> words, and orders all Nineveh to fast, down to the last cow. He orders
> them to desist from evil, hoping that God will see them and forgive
> them. He does.

---

1.   It is read on Yom Kippur. For a discussion of its place in Christian and
Islamic tradition, see J. Limburg, *Jonah* (Louisville, KY: Westminster/John Knox
Press, 1993), pp. 113-23.

4. Jonah is very upset about this and he prays to the LORD saying he had anticipated just such forgiveness, and that this is why he set out from Tarshish. He asks the LORD to take his life, but the LORD questions this anger. Jonah goes to the east of the city, makes a booth and sits there, watching Nineveh. The LORD makes a plant grow to give Jonah shade (Jonah is pleased), then causes it to wither, and sends a hot wind (Jonah is displeased). God asks whether Jonah is right to be angry 'about the plant', when it was not he who made it grow or perish. Similarly, God argues, should he (God) not spare Nineveh with all its many people and its great ignorance?

'And I said, "Oh, that I had the wings of a dove. I would fly away and find rest." '[2]

It is with this quote that Richard Sharpe begins his edition and translation of Adomnán's *Life of St Columba*, citing the Vulgate's translation: 'Quis dabit mihi pennas sicut Columbae...' and thereby implicitly attaching importance to the dove of the Bible and Columba's name. The original—*mî-yitten-lî 'ēber kayyônâ*—contains the element *yônâ*, which is transliterated elsewhere in the Bible as 'Jonah'.

Adomnán himself refers to the original, although such knowledge of Hebrew as he reveals is usually taken to be based on hearsay. He writes at the beginning of his second preface:

> There was a man of venerable life and blessed memory, the father and founder of monasteries, whose name was the same as the prophet Jonah's. For though the sound is different in three different languages, in Hebrew *Jona*, in Greek *Peristera*, in Latin *Columba*, the meaning is the same: 'dove'. So great a name cannot have been given to the man of God but by divine providence.[3]

What is significant here is not whether Adomnán's comment is grounded in an understanding of comparative philology, but what association he is deciding to make between the three languages.[4]

Adomnán seems intentionally to be suggesting some sort of semiotic relationship between saint and prophet.[5] Such midrashic linguistic cre-

2.   Ps. 55.7. All quotes from the Bible are from *TANAKH: The Holy Scriptures* (New York: Jewish Publication Society of America, 1988).

3.   R. Sharpe (ed. and trans.), *Adomnán of Iona's Life of St Columba* (London: Penguin Books, 1995), p. 104.

4.   Columbanus makes the same association with reference to his own identity in *Epistula* V, in G.S.M. Walker (ed.), *Sancti Columbani Opera* (Dublin: DIAS, 1970), pp 54-55.

5.   In his paper for the 1997 International Conference on Hagiography in Cork,

ativity is valuable in itself, and deserves to be taken seriously, as Morgan Davies has recently demonstrated with reference to other early Irish texts.[6] The fact that these words mark the beginning to the second preface of Adomnán's famous work makes them all the more significant for an understanding of Columba's portrait. What is the relationship between Jonah and Columba as characters?

It is not sufficient to provide a précis of Columba's adventures as parallel to the few words about Jonah's, above, and then imply that these are neatly reflected in the 'biographies' of Columba. The authorial intention as well as the stylistic and historical background to Adomnán's work are continually debated. Indeed, there is much more to his *Life of Columba* than a biography of the saint. It serves archaeologists, legal historians, philologists, and Iona-fanciers alike as a source of information about Columba, early Christianity, and more. Thus, to summarize Columba's career and then detail what aspects of it are 'picked up on' by his hagiographers is hardly appropriate.

Ad VC tells the story of a saint living (for the most part) on the island of Iona in the sixth century. He explains how the Irish saint got there, and what miracles he performed in his life. The three books contain many different kinds of adventure, but they add up to more than a list of the saint's 'accomplishments': Adammán's style is noteworthy in itself, the individual episodes intriguing. Columba heals people, he foretells the weather, he blesses cattle—but how he blesses cattle is for Adomnán to tell. In the particular episodes I will be looking at, Columba has the God-like role of predicting the appearance of sea disturbances. In these episodes, the way Adomnán depicts other characters is equally important.

The Bible may have been a major source of inspiration for Adomnán. Indeed, the intertextuality of both the Christian scriptures and the Hebrew Bible is a valid point from which to read all of Adomnán's work. Such readings take into account the historical and cultural possibility of influence but do not rely on that information. Rather, they can work from the information already available in the texts themselves, without having to resort to external material.

That is, it is hardly necessary to state that among the books Adomnán read was the Bible, including, of course, the book of Jonah. However,

---

'The Reproductions of Early Irish Saints', J.F. Nagy included this quotation as an example of the capacity of the early Irish for just such semiotic thinking.

6.   Davies, 'Protocols'.

as the citations from Harold Fisch and his arguments about *Robinson Crusoe* reveal (above), this does not mean that Adomnán modelled his seaside narratives on that book—nor need that be true for a comparison to be meaningful. Instead, the comparison I offer can be read as a midrash on *Ad VC*: a close look at some words from Columba's career as depicted by Adomnán, with a view to seeing what they may have in common with the prophet's career.

Much valuable work has been done about the political agendas behind hagiographies, and on their particular linguistic content, and historical contexts. There is still much, however, that can be explored about hagiographies as literature.

To acknowledge hagiographies as literary works involves discussing aspects of them previously ignored. The reason behind Columba's name cannot be answered conclusively by history, although historical documents help answer many other crucial questions. Hagiographies are imaginative discourse as well as historical documents, and as such, part of Ireland's remarkable body of mediaeval literature, and as deserving of attention as the rest of it. Máire Herbert has reminded us that 'literary works represent, rather than simply reflect, reality. Thus, no *a priori* assumptions should be made about the verisimilitude of what is portrayed by the hagiographer.'[7]

It is true that the study of hagiography would be greatly limited if a literary approach was the only one available. However, when attention is paid to the event of telling as much as to the event that has been told, there are things for which history alone cannot account. A knowledge of history cannot account for whales in the Hebrides which are the size of mountains and ready to swallow disobedient disciples—no more than can a knowledge of zoology, such as John Marsden demonstrates in his recent *Illustrated Life of Columba*: 'We can only speculate on the precise nature of this creature, as several species of greater marine mammal have been recorded in the Hebrides, and were certainly both more numerous and more evident in Columba's time than today.'[8]

It is therefore appropriate to look outside those disciplines and ask if there is a reading of the book of Jonah that is parallel to an aspect of Columba's legend in some way, as it is known through the Lives.

This paper will address the structural relationship between literary

7. M. Herbert, 'Hagiography', in McCone and Simms (eds.), *Progress*, p. 86.
8. J. Marsden, *The Illustrated Life of Columba* (Edinburgh: Floris Books, 1991), p. 60.

depictions of Columba in certain hagiographic episodes and the book of Jonah. I will look at §1.19 from *Ad VC*; from 'The Irish Life of Colum Cille' §55; and §105 and §233 from *Betha Colaim Chille*, compiled by Manus O'Donnell.[9]

First, there are associations between Columba and Jonah which exist as a background to these texts. The range of these associations would seem to include the terms *columba, yônâ*, Jonah, Iona, and the dove. Some of this multifaceted meaning is captured by another figure from early Christianity, in Columbanus's bilingual equation: 'Ego, bar-Iona (vilis Columba), in christo mitto salutem' (I, bar-Jonah [a poor dove] send greeting in Christ').[10] Columbanus went so far as to (invent and) identify with an adventure of Jonah's, 'whose shipwreck I have almost undergone'.[11]

Jennifer O'Reilly has also seized on another of the indications of this relationship in her article in *Scriptural Interpretations in the Fathers*.[12] Specifically examining iconography in part of the Book of Kells, she draws attention to the name 'Iona' in the Lukan genealogy and the 'fish-man' next to it, citing several scholars who believed the name—as 'Iona' and as Jonah's name—plainly 'called to mind' Columba.[13] In particular, she pursues the 'dove' connection, and its symbolic role in early Christianity.

O'Reilly's work calls attention to the changing nature of such symbols, against a temptation to imagine that the dove always symbolized 'peace', for example. The 'Iona' illustration in the Book of Kells func-

---

9. In this chapter, English translations from Adomnán's *Life of St Columba* are taken from Sharpe's translation. Editions of the original Latin can be found in A.O.A. Anderson and M.O. Anderson (eds.), *Adomnán's Life of Columba* (London: T. Nelson, 1961). The 'Irish Life' has been edited and translated by M. Herbert in *Iona, Kells, and Derry: The History and Hagiography of the Monastic Familia of Columba* (Oxford: Oxford University Press, 1988). The 1532 *Betha Colaim Chille* is edited by A. O'Kelleher and G. Schoepperle (Urbana: University of Illinois, under the auspices of the graduate school, 1918); English translations of that work given here are my own. I am grateful to Colm Ó Baoill for checking this translation.

10. Walker, *Sancti Columbani Opera*, pp. 2-3. I am grateful to Gilbert Márkus for the reference.

11. Cited in Sharpe, *St Columba*, p. 243.

12. J. O'Reilly, 'Exegesis and the Book of Kells: The Lucan Genealogy', in T. Finan and V. Twomey (eds.), *Scriptural Interpretation in the Fathers: Letter and Spirit* (Dublin: Four Courts, 1995), pp. 315-55.

13. O'Reilly, 'Kells', p. 318.

tions on that page of the Lukan genealogy as one of a number of 'meta-
physical conceits ... incorporat[ing] pictorial adaptations of rhetorical
techniques'.[14]

The present work is as concerned with literary detail, instead of
pictorial detail, in view of the many possibilities of literary meaning
and the structural study of myth. It is therefore appropriate to look here
at interpretations of the entire book of Jonah inasmuch as they connect
to particular episodes concerning Columba.

If Columba has many dimensions, Jonah has even more. It is not
enough to prompt a notional Jonah and assume that all readers conceive
of him in the same terms. As shown above with reference to McCone's
work, such asides can be misleading. It is worth clarifying my understanding of the book of Jonah before moving on to the possible common points of that book and the episodes mentioned above.

Elias Bickerman has charted the interpretation of Jonah through the
centuries, and Jack Sasson has included commentary and fiction pertinent to the story of Jonah from all over the world and from a remarkable range of time.[15] James Limburg has collected evidence of Jonah's
place in Islam, and has written about some of the pictorial representations of Jonah in every medium from stained glass to steel.[16]

'Jonah' can mean a 'jinx'—an identity that, in Britain, may have been
popularized by the *Beano*[17]—but he has also been seen as a prefigu-
ration of Jesus, as in O'Reilly's sources. In each case, one aspect of
Jonah has been seized on: the Jonah of ch. 1 who brings a storm to the
innocent pagan mariners, or the Jonah of ch. 4 who declares his reluctance to prophesy out of something which might be called pride.

Similarly, individual aspects of Jonah's career have been interpreted
in very different ways. His big fish, for example, has alternatively been
seen as a symbol of the grave and as a wonderful, underwater *bateau
mouche*: 'That fish was specially appointed from the six days of Cre-

14. O'Reilly, 'Kells', pp. 351-53.
15. E. Bickerman, 'Jonah, *or* the Unfulfilled Prophecy', in *Four Strange Books
of the Bible: Jonah, Daniel, Koholeth, Esther* (New York: Schocken Books, 1967),
pp. 1-50; J. Sasson, *Jonah* (Garden City, NY: Doubleday, 1990).
16. For Jonah's place in Islam see Limburg, *Jonah*, pp. 113-18. For a survey of
a few of the many representations of Jonah in art, see Limburg, 'Jonah and the
Whale through the Eyes of Artists', *Bible Review* 6/4 (August 1990), pp. 18-25.
17. I am grateful to Derrick McClure for drawing my attention to the *Beano*
reference, and to the origin of 'Jonah' in contemporary British English generally.

ation ... He entered its mouth just as a man enters the great synagogue, and he stood (therein). The two eyes of the fish were like windows of glass giving light to Jonah.'[18]

Jonah is an idea in flux and, like all ideas, determined by context, the reader, and time. Any aspect of his short narrated career could be the 'whole picture' and eclipse the rest of his career in the way he is remembered. For this reason I offer an interpretation of the book of Jonah in the following sections, before progressing with a structural comparison with episodes from Lives of Columba.

I am convinced by Paul Auster's commentary on Jonah in 'The Book of Memory'[19] that essentially Jonah is a figure whose solitude is central to the book. His weakness does not stem from cowardice, but rather from his being trapped in a paradox, as Auster writes:

> If the Ninevites were spared, would this not make Jonah's prophecy false? Would he not, then, be a false prophet? Hence the paradox at the heart of the book: the prophecy would remain true only if he did not speak it. But then, of course, there would be no prophecy, and Jonah would no longer be a prophet. But better to be no prophet at all than to be a false prophet.[20]

Thus the book is about the difficulties of Jonah's silence, the contradictions set up between his calling and his position, and his weakness/ hesitation towards his responsibilities. Carl Keller makes much of the fact that God is fairly silent in the book of Jonah as well as Jonah himself, which does not make Jonah's task any easier.[21] Yet finally that task is done. Indeed, it seems noteworthy that few have seized on Jonah's final success (within the terms of the book), a result of his close interaction with God. As Jonah chooses each milieu, ostensibly to escape from it, God agrees to base his next conversion there, first converting sailors, and then Ninevites, demonstrating along the way his dominance over flora, fauna and fish.

Thus, Jonah's recalcitrance itself is within God's plan, which, as Auster would point out, must depress Jonah even further. Kenneth

---

18. From *Pirke deRabbi Eliezer* (first century CE), cited in Limburg, *Jonah*, p. 106.

19. In P. Auster, *The Invention of Solitude* (London: Faber & Faber, 1978), pp. 71-172.

20. Auster, *Solitude*, p. 126.

21. Carl Keller, 'Jonas. Le portrait d'un prophète', *TZ* 21 (1965), pp. 329-40 (329-30).

Craig's statement that the art of Jonah serves its ideology comes into play here, but can be taken further.[22] The book's very occasions for humour are part of its message: whatever mood Jonah casts, God will be there (whether he likes it or not).

Most readers refer to Jonah's silence as stubbornness.[23] Jonah, they say, is guilty of a chauvinistic desire to have the monopoly on mercy. Many Semitic and anti-Semitic writers have urged this, alternatively seeing Jonah and the Jews in general as selfish.[24] As even the genre-seekers of Jonah would admit, however, if he is compared to other 'chosen' characters in the Bible, his hesitancy is hardly unusual in the Bible, especially given the difficulty of his task.[25]

Keller takes this idea even further, reading the story of Jonah right off the edge of the page: 'Jonah spoke the truth. By the time the author has told his story the city no longer exists.'[26] That is, by the time the story of Jonah was written down, Jonah's prophecy had come true, and Nineveh was no longer. (This account is similar to Nagy's readings for metafiction in early Irish literature, discussed above.)

One of the points that Bickerman cites as being at the core of anti-Semitic readings of Jonah through the Enlightenment is Jonah's reluctance to deliver his prophecy. Sandor Goodhart reacts to the same point in different terms: Jonah acts incorrectly because he wants to judge the Ninevites when, as God says, it is God's job to judge.[27] Keller defends Jonah vigilantly stating that the reason he is hesitant is not that he does not think the Ninevites deserved mercy. Rather, Jonah was reluctant to announce destruction because he knows that God is kind, and that it was contradictory to God's kind nature to destroy.

Thus, the prophet's reluctance and its basis are the paradox of Jonah. How can he serve God and be true to himself? The preacher in Melville's *Moby Dick* wonders the same thing in his sermon about

22. Cf. K. Craig, *A Poetics of Jonah: Art in the Service of Ideology* (Columbia: University of South Carolina Press, 1993), *passim*.

23. Cf. N. Rosen, 'Jonah: Justice for Jonah, Or a Bible Bartleby', in Rosenberg (ed.), *Congregation*, pp. 222-31.

24. See Bickerman, 'Jonah', pp. 1-50, *passim*, for a survey of some of these.

25. Compare, for example, even Moses' hesitancy.

26. 'Jonas a dit vrai. Au moment où le poète rédige son conte, la grande ville n'existe plus' (Keller, 'Jonas', p. 340). My translation.

27. S. Goodhart, 'Prophecy, Sacrifice and Repentance in the Story of Jonah', *Semeia* 33 (1985), pp. 43-63.

Jonah: 'If we obey God we must disobey ourselves.'[28] The text investigates the question of disobeying oneself in the context of an ever-
present, omniscient God. This paradox is also relevant to the episodes
from Columba's Lives discussed below.

Structuralism suggests that there are common patterns in myth and in
language, as well as differences. These patterns need to be rendered
visible to get at the essence of the myth. The work of Claude Lévi-
Strauss is most often cited in connection with structuralist approaches
to myth.

His work is often used to illustrate not the kind of anthropological
insights that he was working towards, but rather to understand myths or
literary structures and patterns in themselves, with a view to showing a
systematic logic or the presence of a natural phenomenon behind them.

To that end I have attempted a structural sketch of the book of Jonah
along the lines of Lévi-Strauss's 'The Story of Asdiwal'.[29] Lévi-Strauss
would divide a myth according to sequences and 'schemata'. The sequences are

> organised at planes at different levels of abstraction in accordance with
> *schemata*, which exist simultaneously, superimposed one upon the other;
> just as a melody composed for several voices is held within bounds by
> two-dimensional constraints: first by its own melodic line ... and second
> by the contrapuntal schemata.[30]

This is the sequence of events in Jonah according to location:

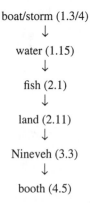

boat/storm (1.3/4)
↓
water (1.15)
↓
fish (2.1)
↓
land (2.11)
↓
Nineveh (3.3)
↓
booth (4.5)

28. H. Melville, *Moby Dick* (London: Penguin Books, 1994), p. 41.
29. Claude Lévi-Strauss, 'The Story of Asdiwal', in *idem, Structural Anthropology*, II (Chicago: University of Chicago Press, 1983), pp. 146-97.
30. Lévi-Strauss, 'The Story of Asdiwal', p. 161.

The delineation of schemata in the book of Jonah is more complicated. Lévi-Strauss uses four levels of schemata in 'Asdiwal'—cosmological, geographical, techno-economical, and sociological. Each of these exists more on a logical plane or more on a spatial plane than the next with reference to the sequence of events in the story. In the context of the book of Jonah, however, these categories are confusing. Weather, for example is both divinely relevant ('cosmological') but also functional ('techno-economical'). The weight of prayer and dialogue with God are also significant levels within the biblical idiom. Thus, a looser reading of Lévi-Strauss is perhaps more appropriate, if still experimental.

The chart on p. 84 gives some of the schemata happening in the book of Jonah at the same time as the sequence above (the arrows do not indicate equivalent elapses in narrated time).

An attempt at Lévi-Strauss's 'global integration' leads to the following axes, a result of distilling the information in the chart of schemata on p. 84:

obeying God	(Jonah) obeying his own will
toward Nineveh	away from Nineveh
eastwards	westwards
spiritual ascent (praying, obeying God)	descent (marked by use of *yarad* 'going down')
exposure	enclosure
advance	retreat

This sketch underlines the consequences of disobeying God and its opposition to Jonah's wellbeing, showing the way physical levels mirror Jonah's spiritual direction: as he disobeys God he fails in every possible way. As axes these points may be useful to associate with the Jonah narrative. That is, as much as offering a conclusion about the nature of the book of Jonah as myth, they call attention to various levels at which it can be said to operate.

There are many ways a comparison with Columba could be broached. One could interpret any one part of Jonah as being its central motif, look it up in Dorothy Bray's helpful guide, and see if there was a match in the Columba section.[31] Such an approach would ignore many more much closer parallels, however, in myth and literature internationally. Indeed, Stith Thompson has more than a dozen entries under the motif F9114:

---

31. D.A. Bray, *A List of Motifs in the Lives of the Early Irish Saints* (Helsinki: Suomalainen Tiedeakatemia, 1992).

Schemata in the Book of Jonah

Geographical: down to Joppa → (not east to Nineveh but) west to Tarshish → down into ship → down into water →
down into fish → out onto land → east toward Nineveh → east into Nineveh → east out of Nineveh to sukkah

Meteorological: damp → (extreme) wet → dry → warm → shaded → (extreme) hot

Expositional: indoors (hold of the ship) → out in the sea→ inside fish → out on (dry) land → indoors (sukkah) → exposed to sun

Cosmological: Word to Jonah → Jonah flees from the Word → lot is cast on Jonah → Jonah says he is a Jew → sailors pray →
Jonah prays → word comes to Jonah → Jonah prays (for death) → God talks to Jonah

'Jonah. Fish (or water monster) swallows a man'. If a longer sequence of events is looked at, however, the number of overlapping accounts in other literatures becomes fewer, until a match seems remarkable, and the idea of comparison attractive.

'Comparisons imply affinity *and* divergence', wrote Raymond Cormier in a critique involving early Irish and Old French literature.[32] The first anecdote for such comparison here is §1.19 from *Ad VC*, 'How the saint spoke with foreknowledge about a great whale':[33]

> One day, while the blessed man was living in Iona a brother called Berach, who was on the point of sailing for Tiree, came to St Columba in the morning for a blessing. The saint looked at him closely and said:
>
> 'My son, you must be very careful today. Do not try to go directly across the open sea to Tiree, but instead take the roundabout route by the Treshnish Islands. Otherwise you may be terrified by a monster of the deep and find yourself scarcely able to escape.'
>
> With the saint's blessing he set off and boarded his boat, but he went against the saint's advice as though he thought little of it. While crossing the open sea between Iona and Tiree, he and those with him in the boat saw—look!—a whale of extraordinary size, which rose up like a mountain above the water, its jaws open to show an array of teeth. At once the men dropped the sail and took to the oars, turning back in terror, but they only just managed to avoid the wash caused by the whale's motion. Remembering what the saint had foretold, they were filled with awe.
>
> That same morning Baithéne was also going to sail in Tiree. The saint said to him:
>
> 'In the middle of last night, a great whale rose up from the depths of the sea, and today it will heave itself up on the surface of the sea between Iona and Tiree.'
>
> Baithéne answered him: 'That beast and I are both in God's power.'
>
> 'Go in peace', said the saint. 'Your faith in Christ will shield you from this danger.'
>
> Baithéne was blessed by the saint and set sail from the harbour. They had already crossed a considerable stretch of sea when Baithéne and those with him saw the whale. While all his companions were terrified, Baithéne without a tremor of fear raised his hands and blessed the sea and the whale. Immediately the great creature plunged under the waves and was not seen again.

32. R. Cormier, 'Cú Chulainn and Yvain: The Love Hero in Early Irish and Old French Literature', *Studies in Philology* 72/2 (April 1975), pp. 115-39 (115) (his italics).

33. Sharpe, *St Columba*, pp. 125-26.

In the Andersons' edition, there is a footnote to this episode: 'This "whale" is here assimilated to the traditional idea of Jonah's sea-monster.'[34] That is, they are suggesting that the episode uses the same kind of 'sea-monster' at this point—*cetus*, 'whale'—which the Vulgate uses for Jonah's *dag gadôl*, 'big fish'.[35]

How should the Andersons' words and inverted commas be understood? They imply that there is something Jonah-esque about Adomnán's intentions in this anecdote. The Andersons must be positing an original sea-monster, one perhaps more like other Columban serpents, which has here been 'corrupted' to 'whale', with the intention of making the passage seem more like the book of Jonah. This, then, is a backhanded corroboration of the present thesis.

Jacqueline Borsje refers to the *cetus* of this episode as being an arbitrary name for 'a huge water monster': 'One can only speculate on Adomnán's reasons for using this vague terminology.'[36] This is the very terminology that had received only one comment related to style previously, namely Andersons', that the terminology is *not* vague. The logic I have pursued is different from both of theirs. Not 'He's calling it a whale for no good reason', but 'Could there be a reason he calls it a whale?'

Paragraph 1.19 is reminiscent of the two trips in the book of Jonah, one of them sanctioned by the word of God and one of them not, one of them a confronting of terror and one of them an avoidance of terror. One character dispatches the other, and the other meets the terrible thing against which he had been warned. He prays to God and sets off a second time, this time making it past the terror. The fact that there are two monks in §1.19 can be used constructively if Norma Rosen is right to locate two Jonahs: a 'before-the-fish Jonah and an after-the-fish Jonah'.[37]

A structural sketch of the two episodes may be helpful here. In the following comparison, Berach and Baithéne are analogues to Jonah. Is it fair to conflate them? Sharpe notes that the monk Berach is not known outwith this anecdote, although a monk Baithéne is historically

34. Anderson and Anderson, *Columba*, p. 246.

35. *Monstruoso*, *beluino*, and *bilua* are also used.

36. J. Borsje, 'The Monster in the River Ness in *Vita Sancti Columbae*: A Study of a Miracle', *Peritia* 8 (1994), pp. 27-34 (33).

37. Rosen, 'Justice for Jonah', p. 227.

known as Columba's cousin and coeval.[38] Baithéne is, however, sufficiently indistinct in this story to be erased entirely from Manus O'Donnell's retelling of it (to be discussed below).

Thus it is proposed that the two monks be labelled B1 and B2. It is not impossible that Adomnán named them alliteratively to emphasize the repetition of the tasks they perform and the simple but all-important difference in the way they go about them. Instead of one man being presented at first as a sullen, disobedient wretch, then as one who knows God's might, here a separate party takes each of these roles. Berach is like the Jonah of the first half, and Baithéne something like the Jonah of the second half of the book of Jonah.

Previous structural studies of hagiographies have focused on a different level of detail. Jean-Michel Picard has examined 'Structural Patterns in Early Hiberno-Latin Hagiography'[39] and Dorothy Bray's *List of Motifs in the Lives of the Early Irish Saints* has already been mentioned. But while the overall structure of several hagiographies or the sequence of events in a particular hagiography has been analysed, relatively little work has been done on the content of individual episodes in the hagiographies. That is, the how of what is being told, more than the why or the what.

Although structuralism is limited in ways, it has some capacity for flexibility, as shown by the fact that the structures of two different stories can be compared successfully although their mythical outcomes may be different.[40] One story can be said to have an identical structure to a story with a completely different order of events.[41] In the chart *Jonah and* Ad VC (below) those smallest units of action in Jonah are compared with a similar list of actions in §1.19. Marked with a recycling symbol are those mythemes which were rearranged.

38. Sharpe, *St Columba*, p. 279.

39. J.-M. Picard, 'Structural Patterns in Early Hiberno-Latin Hagiography', *Peritia* 4 (1985), pp. 67-82.

40. As an interpretation of the work of Claude Lévi-Strauss, this appropriation robs his work of its anthropological weight, and focuses on the literary aspects of a posited myth. Similarly, his own work does not include everything it could, perhaps, for the literary theorist, historian or folklorist, such as the relevance of the *telling* of the myth (cf. A. Dundes, 'Structuralism and Folklore', *Studia Fennica* 20 [1977], pp. 75-93).

41. Cf. C. Lévi-Strauss, 'The Structural Study of Myth', in *idem, Structural Anthropology*, I (New York: Basic Books, 1972), pp. 206-31.

Jonah and Ad VC (§1.19)

1. Jonah is called to travel in one direction.

   Jonah disobeys: he goes on a ship, with other sailors in the other direction.

   There is a huge storm.

   The rest of the sailors are scared;

   Jonah is not scared, nor of being thrown into the sea.

   When the sailors finally give up fighting the storm,

   (Jonah is thrown overboard and) saves the whole ship.

   The sea is calm.

   The sailors fear God exceedingly, and pray.

   —

   B asks C's blessing to sail to Tiree. C says to take another route, or he might meet a monster.

   B disobeys: goes on a ship, and 'the sailors that were with him', in the 'other' direction.

   There is a huge whale.

   The rest of the sailors are scared ⇕, but

   B is not scared of the whale. ⇕

   The rowers give up and turn back. ⇕

   He saves the whole ship. ⇕

   The beast disappears. ⇕

   They all remember C's words, and marvel.

2. God commands a fish ('whale')

   to swallow Jonah (as a reminder of God's omnipotence[?])

   Praying, Jonah finally mentions God (where he was silent before).

   He puts faith in God and thanks him for deliverance (most interpretations would add: in advance, for rescue from the whale).

   The fish spits him up to safety.

   —

   (The whale appears according to C's words) ⇕

   to threaten all (a reminder of C's omniscience?)

   B finally mentions God (where his predecessor was silent):

   'I and that beast are in God's power'. ⇕

   C: 'Your faith in Christ will protect you.' B thanks C and Jesus in advance for safe passage past the whale.

   B makes it safely across. ⇕

3. God tells Jonah a second time to go to the place he suggests.

   He goes to Nineveh, according to God's directions.

   He confronts the horrible Ninevites with (God's) prophecy.

   They repent (and recede from the narrative).

   God reverses his anger toward the Ninevites.

   They are all spared.

   —

   C tells the second B to travel in the way he suggests.

   B sails, according to C's directions.

   He confronts the horrible whale with a blessing. ⇕

   The whale goes away. ⇕

   (The whale, now 'in God's power', reverses his anger.) ⇕

   They are all spared. ⇕

From this comparison it seems that Columba is only like Jonah inasmuch as he is a prophet in the sense of seer. (In fact, by some interpretations Jonah's foresight is weaker than Columba's.) It is Columba's
friends in this posited analogy who play the more didactically ambiguous role of Jonah. Columba himself is like God, and it is Columba's
omniscience that is at the core of the story. God and Christ may be
mentioned in §1.19, but it is Columba who provides the occasion to
notice them.

The two missions of §1.19 happen simultaneously: 'Also on the same
day, in the morning, the saint gave news of the same whale to Baithéne.'
Columba's warning to B2 is similar, but his response is different. The
qualitative difference in their responses is that B2 does not act arro-
gantly. B1, by contrast, had acted 'as though making light of the saint's
command'.

The first time that Jonah is asked to go to Nineveh, he sets off in the
other direction, 180 degrees the other way, as fast as he can. The second time, Jonah is pushed off towards Nineveh, confronts his task of
prophecy, and respects God's command. Most critics see the two halves
of Jonah as reflections of each other, two tries at the same thing, with
the fish a horror as great as Nineveh.[42]

Despite Jonah's reluctance, he is close to God, as evidenced by many
things, not least of which is the two characters' verbal rapport, as
Luther commented: 'He chats so uninhibitedly with God as though he
were not in the least afraid of Him ...'[43] It is significant in §1.19 that B1
is not some fool who acts disrespectfully, but one close to Columba,
who calls him 'my son'. The one who questions God/Columba in both
stories is, at the same time, close to him.

It is also significant that the whale is not something to be killed in the
Columba story but, quite the opposite, something to be blessed. It is
thus unlike many a Columban sea-monster. The divine pedigree of the
whale in §1.19 is the same as Jonah's fish. The second obstacle to
Jonah, Nineveh, although a horror, is *'îr g^edôlah le'lohîm*, literally 'a
great city of God'; and God indeed comes to its rescue. The idiom
really means 'an enormously large city', however, and Nineveh is in no

42. Cf. A. Lacocque and P.-E. Lacocque, *Jonah: A Psycho-Religious Approach
to the Prophet* (Columbia: University of South Carolina Press, 1990).
43. Martin Luther, *Jonah, Habakkuk*, in H.C. Oswald (ed.), *Luther's Works*, XIX
(St Louis: Concordia Publishing House, 1974), p. 92, cited in Limburg, *Jonah*,
p. 119.

sense divine. Its not knowing good from evil, however, highlights the same point that is articulated elsewhere in the book of Jonah: good or evil, God is looking after it.

The diagram below shows the movements of Jonah 1 of the first half and Jonah 2 of the second half as compared with those of B1 and B2. In the book of Jonah the tasks are performed one after the other, by one character. In §1.19 the tasks are performed simultaneously but by two characters. In O'Donnell's retelling—which O'Kelleher says is 'literally' based on this episode—it is again one character on two trips.

Jonah 1 → wrong way (disobeys God, avoids calling) → whale
Jonah 2 → right way (obeys God) → Nineveh (confronts calling)

B1 → wrong way (disobeys CC) → whale
B2 → right way (obeys CC) → whale (confronts calling)

B1 and B2 also react like two Jonahs to the question of the horror that can conquer or be conquered. B2 sees the whale and brings the word to it ('he ... blessed the sea and the whale') and it goes away 'in the same instant'. Jonah 1 sees the horrible fish and it takes him over, literally swallows him, then spits him up. Jonah 2 sees Nineveh and brings the word of God to it and, with a speed that has amused critics for centuries, Nineveh is tamed. The whale appears as a servant of God, whose example of obedience may have been sent simply to shame Jonah into reverence.

Significantly, the whole of Jonah 4, where Jonah sits and whines as God teases him, has no analogue in this Columba anecdote. This last scene puts the lesson of fish and Ninevites in a different context as if they had been only images swimming in a crystal ball, with God the fortune teller and Jonah learning warily about himself through what he sees. As a posited hagiographic analogy, this would be an unfortunate element to include in a story about a whale and the all-importance of prayer.

Ad VC was one of the sources we know Manus O'Donnell worked from in compiling *Betha Colaim Chille*. Around 1532, Donegal chieftain O'Donnell commissioned the writing of a Life of Columba to be based partly on the oral tradition surrounding the saint. O'Donnell, like Adomnán, was a kinsman of the saint, although a few more generations removed. Some of the material he assembled is based closely on episodes from *Ad VC* (where there is usually some shift in style, emphasis or detail), and some material is from legends and songs about the saint which had persisted since (and possibly before) his death. Also collected were poems about and 'by' the saint. O'Donnell is especially pertinent to this study, despite being outside the early Irish period, as a source of alternate versions of *Ad VC* episodes.

Of course, O'Donnell lived in Ireland in the 1500s, so in many senses the Columba that emerges from his work will be a totally different one from Adomnán's. For this reason, the flavour of this collection is different, and in some sense the two works would be completely incomparable, were it not for the name of the hero in both. Sharpe calls O'Donnell's *BCC* 'a good read',[44] provided one does not want the 'real' truth about Columba (which is available elsewhere?) It could be argued that O'Donnell may be read as a gloss on the saint's life (which we do indeed know mainly through Adomnán) or as a later interpretation comparable to Victor Hugo's 'Booz endormi' relative to the book of Ruth (as Bal suggests, mentioned above). This seems an especially accurate description considering that nearly a thousand years separate Columba and *BCC*. *BCC* is thus an intertext that can be read to illustrate *Ad VC* or the legend of Columba more generally.

Paragraph 233 features the same story as §1.19 from *Ad VC*, above:

> One day Colum Cille was in Iona and a certain monk by the name of Bera came to him, who was going to another island by the name of [Tiree] on monasterial business. And he asked Colum Cille to give him his blessing. And Colum Cille answered him, saying:
>
> 'I will give you a blessing', he said, 'but all the same, avoid the usual route people take to that island, and go around the other small islands in front of you, lest you see something which would terrify you.'
>
> Then the monk went into his ship and took the route that Colum Cille had warned him against, because he was not afraid, since he had Colum Cille's blessing. And he was not long out when he saw a terrible beast raising her head out of the sea—and a mountain top was no bigger than she. And she opened her mouth and she would have liked to swallow the ship and its crew down her throat. And when they saw that, they lowered their sails and rowed the ship back around. And the beast had put so much turbulence and turmoil into the water that if God had not been watching over them and if they had not had Colum Cille's blessing they would not have reached land without drowning. And they realised that it was for fear of that beast that Colum Cille had told them not to take that route.
>
> And then they took the route that Colum Cille had told them, and they arrived in one piece, free from harm. And it is clear from that story that it

44. Sharpe, *St Columba*, p. 92.

is not only [concerning] land[45] that God gives insight into his very own
secrets to Colum Cille, but he also gave him insight and knowledge
about the beasts of the sea, and the ocean.

In this version, instead of two characters, one character, Bera, makes
two trips. Once he ignores Colum Cille's advice, once he follows it.
However, there are no two dangers in *BCC* as there are in Jonah and
Ad VC. Here Bera gets it right the second time and avoids facing any
danger at all.

Another difference is that the word by far most frequently used in
Ad VC to refer to the sea creature—*cetus*—has become *péisd* in *BCC*,
'beast'. If the use of *cetus* is an intentional likening to Jonah's fish, as
the Andersons imply, then this change is a conscious departure from
that similarity. Furthermore, when the sailors in O'Donnell see the
péisd, they do not marvel at divine power the way Jonah's sailors do at
the sea, and the way Adomnán's do at Columba's foresight. Instead, the
focus is on the logic behind Columba's warning: 'They realized that it
was for fear of that beast that Colum Cille had told them not to take that
route.'

Indeed, the place of religion is generally different in the two versions.
In *Ad VC*, Bera delivers a prayer/enunciation of God's power, which is
linked to Columba, to faith itself, and to 'Christ'; Bera has the right to
evoke God's name. There is no such moment in *BCC*. Similarly, in *Ad
VC*, Bera is blessed only once he has proclaimed his faith. Only then
does he face the danger and overcome it, proving not just Columba's
accurate prophecy, but the strength of faith (a message which, it has
often been argued, is part of the book of Jonah).

O'Donnell's agenda here is thus different, and the narrator states it:
'And it is clear from that story that ... God gives insight into his own
secrets to Colum Cille.' The emphasis is placed firmly on Colum Cille's
omniscience (and not the power of prayer or the importance of obeying
divine advice). Furthermore, it all goes to show that he is a good prophet, which information Adomnán covers in the title.

Does this proposed semiotic relationship continue on any level as the
legend of Columba continues? Can it be said to have some bearing on

45. 'nach ar tír amain tuc Dia radarc a sheicréde fen'. O'Kelleher and Schoepperle read 'not on land alone that God did manifest his secret things'. My translation agrees with Brian Lacey's: 'God not only gave an insight to His own secrets
about the land' (B. Lacey, ed. Manus O'Donnell, *The Life of Colum Cille* [Dublin:
Four Courts, 1998], p. 124, my italics).

the 'Irish Life of Colum Cille'? The jump of half a millennium from *Ad VC* is justifiable not merely by the terms of literary endeavour but also by the fact that the 'Irish Life' is the first Life of Columba since Adomnán's that 'may be classed as a new creation, and which is not merely derivative'.[46]

Paragraph 55 from Herbert's edition of the original follows with her translation:

> *Dia mboi tra Colum Cille i n-aroli lathi ic procept dona slogaib, luid aroli duine uadib darsin abaind bói i comfocus doib, na beth oc estecht fri brethir nDé. Not-mbenand in nathir he isin usce co rus-marb fo-cétoir. Tuccad a chorp i fhiadnaise Coluim Cille 7 dos-beirside croiss dia bachaill dar a bruinde cond-eracht fo cétoir.*

> On another day when Colum Cille was preaching to the crowds, a certain person went away across the nearby river to avoid listening to the word of God. The serpent struck him in the water and killed him instantly. His body was brought before Colum Cille, who made the sign of the cross with his staff over the man's chest, and he immediately arose.

This story can be summarized in a way that draws attention to its similarity to a reading of the book of Jonah:

1. Man hears word of the Lord.
2. Man enters body of water to get away from it.
3. Man encounters dangerous sea creature.
4. Man is not only forgiven by the Powers that Be, but resurrected.

This episode seems particularly noteworthy because of Colum Cille's uncharacteristic forgiveness (i.e. the 'resurrection'), which is usually reserved for the obedient. An example of this is the preceding anecdote, §54, where the saint revives a dead boy who had been struck down by the devil for his *belief* in the saint's word. As Gertrud Brüning noted of another Columba: 'Woe is him who despises him or his friends: the punishment is eternal misfortune and sudden death.'[47] Picard comments also that the nature of [Adomnán's] Columba 'manifests itself sometimes by extreme kindness, sometimes by irrational violence ...'[48]

46. Herbert, *Iona ,Kells, and Derry*, p. 181.

47. 'Wehe dem, der ihn oder die Seinen verachtet; ewiger Unsegen und plötzlicher Tod ist die Strafe' (G. Brüning, 'Adamnans *Vita Columbae* und ihre Ableitungen', *ZCP* 2 (1917), pp. 213-304 (235).

48. Picard, 'Patterns', p. 79.

The episode can be read as proof of Colum Cille's enduring, if sporadic, mercy, no matter what the situation. It is also possible to read it, with Brüning and others, as an unlikely version of Adomnán's §11.27. Read as a version of a Jonah myth, however, the issue of Colum Cille's reviving the dissenting man makes sense: he is somehow divinely approved in a way which makes him worth saving.

A comparison of points in both stories, with a focus on the opening of Jonah looks like this:

The Book of Jonah	'Irish Life of Colaim Chille' (§55)
Jonah is called by God and tries to escape it (?)	A person hears the word of God and tries to escape it,
by fleeing away onto a ship.	by fleeing away across a river.
Jonah is swallowed by a fish	A serpent strikes him and kills him.
and prays to God	
promising to do better,	
and thanking him for his deliverance.	
By divine command, the fish spits him up	Colum Cille makes the sign of the cross and revives him
from the depths up onto dry land.	'and he immediately arose'.

The first chapter of Jonah can be said to be about three things: Jonah's flight from the word of the Lord onto a ship, the storm at sea that ensues because of his presence there, and the other sailors' spontaneous conversion when—after they have thrown him in—the sea goes calm. The chart shows a similarity to the first point and to part of ch. 3.

By the rationale of this comparison, Jonah's big fish is analogous to the sea snake, *nathir*. Both beasts defy the bounds of conventional zoology in their capacity for damage and both the fish and the sea serpent attack or devour the person as a direct result of his reaction away from the word of God. Both beasts are God's workers in an implicit or explicit way. In Jonah, the fish is doing just what he is told: 'The Lord commanded the fish and it spewed Jonah out onto dry land.'

In §55 the sentence about the sea serpent follows directly the sentence about the man's fleeing from the word:

> On another day when Colum Cille was preaching to the crowds, a certain person went away across the nearby river to avoid listening to the word of God. The serpent struck him in the water and killed him instantly.

Both narratives can be read to suggest that the sea creature is reacting to blasphemy.

Of course, the intent of Jonah's fish is by no means clear. Was it intended as punishment or rescue? Did Jonah recognize it as one or the other? The serpent here does not give the dissenter time to be ambiguous, let alone deliver a psalm while still in the water. So whereas it is possible to view the fish as the source of Jonah's relief—by way of explaining the thanks he gives while still inside it ('From the belly of Sheol I cried out, and you heard my voice')—this serpent is only a dead end.

Jacqueline Borsje has examined this very episode from the Irish Life with a view to comparing it to two other ecclesiastical texts that feature saints and snakes.[49] She offers a close reading inasmuch as she acknowledges some of the elements of the individual actions in each episode, and does not stop with an allusion to the paragraph number. However, neither in this article nor in her Celtic Congress paper on a related aquatic topic (in which she discussed Greek, Roman and ecclesiastical water disturbances and beasts) does she mention biblical concepts of the sea and sea creatures, let alone Jonah's fish.[50] If her approach is flawed it is because it insists that her view is the only possible one, that the original 'source' must be one she has discovered.

In 'A Study of a Miracle' Borsje focuses on the pattern of §55 from the Irish Life, suggesting that this episode is 'modelled on' a segment of *Ad VC* which in turn is 'modelled on' a segment of the *Dialogi* of Sulpicius Severus. The latter episode, from the fifth century, is as terse as our episode and has only two sentences.

Borsje is working in an interesting direction by urging a more inclusive view of the text than what the historical/zoological approach had thus far offered. In comparing the different 'versions', however, she cuts off one of §55's 'toes' in order to fit it into the 'glass slipper' of the *Dialogi*: she leaves out of her summary the first of §55's three sentences. Even before a reading for a similarity to Jonah or the *Dialogi*, this sentence is central to the outcome, as well as being structurally significant within this short story. That first sentence determines that there is a saint preaching to people, one of whom refuses to listen and swims away; it does not begin with the serpent arbitrarily biting

49. Borsje, 'The Monster'.

50. J. Borsje, 'The Movement of Water as Symbolised by Monsters in Early Irish Texts', in R. Black, W. Gillies and R. Ó Maolalaigh, *Celtic Connections: Proceedings of the 10th International Conference of Celtic Studies* (East Linton: Tuckwell, 1999). Borsje has recently published a full-length study in this area: *From Chaos to Enemy: Encounters with Moses in Early Irish Texts* (Turnhout: Brepols, 1996).

someone. Borsje refers §55 back to a paragraph in *Ad VC* which features swimming monks, and no heretics (2.27). Brüning had made the same observation, and it remained unchallenged as one of a list of 'obvious' derivatives.

In an article mentioned in the introduction, James Carney referred to the very same paragraph as being the source for the moment in the tale *Táin Bó Fraích* when Findabair dives to Fróech's rescue, with as much intentionalism.[51] (By intentionalism I mean that Carney assumes that Froech's author's intentions are patent. In this case they are ostensibly to cover up for the fact that he is copying from *Ad VC*.)

Carney sets up an equation featuring the parts of the tale he wants to see—the sending of someone by someone else to jump into the water—and constructs a parallel. Borsje sets one up on the basis of the part she sees, which is finally no more specific than an interaction of a saint and a sea creature.

Rather than aspiring to infallibility, it is more constructive to be flexible when dealing with so many unknowns. It must be admitted, therefore, that the structural comparisons here have involved parts of the first three chapters of the book of Jonah, without ever touching on the end of that book.

In ch. 4, Jonah cajoles God for leaving him high and dry and God asks him to consider his actions. The 'props' for this scene include a *kikayon* plant—which has never been adequately translated—a *sukkah*, or booth, a stiff wind, and a worm. Terry Eagleton called this part a 'small Dadaist drama',[52] and indeed it has caused critics much irritation in determining whether Jonah is tragedy, farce, parody, melodrama, or situation comedy.

Jonah is angry and sitting in a booth east of Nineveh after having watched the Ninevites repent and be spared:

> Now Jonah had left the city and found a place east of the city. He made a booth there and sat under it in the shade, until he should see what happened to the city. The LORD God provided a [*kikayon*], which grew up over Jonah, to provide shade for his head and save him from discomfort. Jonah was very happy about the plant. But the next day at dawn God provided a worm, which attacked the plant so that it withered. And when the sun rose, God provided a sultry east wind; the sun beat down

51. Carney, 'Background', p. 223.
52. T. Eagleton, 'J.L. Austin and the Book of Jonah', in Schwartz (ed.), *The Book and the Text*, pp. 231-36 (231).

on Jonah's head, and he became faint. He begged for death, saying, 'I would rather die than live.' Then God said to Jonah, 'Are you so deeply grieved about the plant?' 'Yes,' he replied, 'so deeply that I want to die.'

Then the LORD said: 'You cared about the plant, which you did not work for and which you did not grow, which appeared overnight and perished overnight. And should not I care about Nineveh, that great city, in which there are more than a hundred and twenty thousand persons who do not yet know their right hand from their left, and many beasts as well!'

The following paragraph (§105) comes from the 1532 *Betha Colaim Chille*:

Another time Colum Cille and another holy man by the name of Baithín were walking by the sea at a certain place and they saw a ship that was sinking. And Baithín asked Colum Cille why God saw fit to let the ship sink.

'[For the sake of] one sinner who was on board', said Colum Cille, 'God has seen fit to let all the people on the ship drown.'

'It seems to me', said Baithín, 'that God has done wrong by the people on the ship.'

And Colum Cille let that pass, and he did not give Baithín an answer at that point.

And he filled his glove with bees and he gave it to Baithín to watch.[53] And a bee came out of the glove and stung Baithín intensely, so that it hurt him badly. And on account of the wound that the bee had given him, he killed all the bees that there were in the glove.

'Why did you kill the bees?' asked Colum Cille.

'One of the bees hurt me intensely', said Baithín.

'Listen, Baithín',[54] said Colum Cille, 'as the bee stung you, so does man sting God by sin. And as you killed a glove full of bees for being hurt by one bee, so does God allow a lot of people to die for the sin of one person, which is clear since he allowed the people on the ship to drown just now for the one sinner who was on board.'

'I understand, holy father', said Baithín, 'that it is right that this example was given to me, and I will never marvel again at the works of God, nor will I challenge them any more as long as I live.'

The similarity to Jonah would seem to be more than structural, but as it is inadequate to suggest an 'obvious' likening, it is worth sketching the story in structural terms.

---

53. 'tuc da coimed'. O'Kelleher and Schoepperle: 'gave it to Baithin to keep'.

54. 'Bidh a fis agad, a Baithín'. O'Kelleher and Schoepperle: 'Wit thou well'. I have translated this into English although a literal translation might read something like, 'May knowledge of it be at you'.

The Book of Jonah	Betha Colaim Chille
... Because of God's lovingkindness	... Because of God's anger
all the Ninevites are spared.	all the sinner's fellows are killed.
Jonah thinks this is unjust.	Baithín thinks this is unjust.
...God sends Jonah a *kikayon* plant for a while.	Colum Cille gives Baithín a glove of bees to hold for a while.
God makes the plant wither, leaving Jonah exposed to the hot sun, which hurts him.	A bee comes out of the glove, stings Baithín and hurts him.
He begs for death (which God calls feeling sorry for the plant).	He kills the bees (in anger).
God: Sad? (Feeling compassionate?)	CC: Feeling murderous?
Jonah: Yes.	Baithín: Yes.
God: See? Am I not obliged to feel great compassion for my personal creations?	CC: See? God is obliged to feel just such rage for personal attacks on him.
≠	Baithín: Yes! I will never question God's judgment again.

Here there is no sea creature, or an exploration of prophecy, although there is a declaration of faith. The closeness of the two episodes comes at the end.

Conversely, the sense of the two episodes is reversed throughout. Although in the book of Jonah the whole ship would sink because of one man (Jonah), the ship does not sink. In fact, Jonah never brings bad luck to anyone but himself. Rather than drowning the sailors, in the book of Jonah God makes the sea go calm for them.

In §105 God is a malicious, rigid character who might kill a city for one sinful man. In the book of Jonah, God is a forgiving, playful character who would spare a city if there was one good man in it. The characters in §105 are witness to a God whose judgment is full of wrath and should not be questioned. The characters in the book of Jonah are witness to a God whose judgment is insurmountably merciful and who invites questions (although he does have all the answers).

What is yet more singular-seeming about the texts is the relationship of Baithín and Colum Cille as parallel to God and Jonah's. If Nineveh is equivalent to the ship that Baithín and Colum Cille see, this is even more strongly expressed. In both cases, the focus of the passage is on the relationship between the two main characters, and not on what disaster or inconvenience they witness. Nineveh's repentance may be seen to serve only as background for the conversation and lesson between the two main characters. The drowned shipwreck victims or sackcloth-wearing cattle are forgotten.

Baithín is not as uninhibited with God as Jonah is, but he does chat uninhibitedly with Colum Cille. Also, Baithín is close enough to the saint that he can question him. Where before there were only proclamations on one end and silence on the other, here there is exchange. Although Colum Cille refuses to answer the first time Baithín protests ('Ni tuc se frecra an uair-sin ar Baithín' 'And he gave no answer at that time to Baithín'), this time he is open to dialogue: 'Cred far marbais na beich?' 'Why did you kill the bees?'

Not only is Baithín close to Columba, but he is credited with intelligence. Columba expects Baithín to understand the metaphor of the bees (although he tells him its significance), much as Jonah is asked to interpret the withering of the gourd, as Harold Fisch has noted.[55] So Baithín is indulged as much as Jonah is, is as worthy of instruction, with as unorthodox learning aids. (The fact that early Irish society did have legislation concerning bee stings makes the episode no less remarkable in this respect.)

Thus, both stories feature the reaction to presumed injustice, and the opening of dialogue between the omniscient one and the one who can only observe omniscience. The figure of omniscience is the saint, and the parallel of the book of Jonah's God to Columba is never more intriguing than here. Certainly the points in §105 when Colum Cille speaks are the same as the points in the book of Jonah when God speaks. Daithí Ó hÓgáin comments with reference to this episode that 'Colmcille's quick anger is ... comparable to that sometimes attributed to God, and [this] story shows him pointing out the paradoxical nature of God's justice.'[56] Of course, as in Genesis 18, alluded to above, God does not act angrily all the time—and God's paradoxical nature in the book of Jonah is entirely more obscure, leading Luther to write at another point, 'If it were not in the Bible, I'd consider it a silly lie'.[57]

To the extent that his is a didactic tale then, Jonah is being taught compassion through a personal example of self-love. Baithín is being taught the benefits of violence through the example of self-defence.

55. Fisch, 'Quest', p. 221.

56. D. Ó hÓgáin, *The Hero in Irish Folk History* (Dublin: Gill & Macmillan, 1985), p. 33.

57. *D. Martin Luthers Werke. Tischreden*, III (Weimar, 1914), p. 551, trans. by and cited in Limburg, *Jonah*, p. 120.

Inevitably, they are both being taught that it is inappropriate for them to comment on what God has decided must be, and that they will get hurt if they do so. Paragraph 105, seen as a version of Jonah, does away with the idea of mercy.

Before Jonah is accepted as a 'source' for this episode, it is worth comparing at least one narrative outside the sphere of Irish or biblical literature, by way of example. The following text, attributed to Aesop, might be compared with the above §105:

> A man who saw a ship sink with all hands, protested against the injustice of the gods. Because there was one impious person on board, he said, they had destroyed the innocent as well. As he spoke he was bitten by one of a swarm of ants which happened to be there. And though only one attacked him, he trampled on them all. At this, Hermes appeared and smote him with his staff, saying: 'Will you not allow the gods to judge men as you judge ants?'
>
> Moral: Let not a man blaspheme against God in the day of calamity, but let him rather examine his own faults.[58]

Jack Sasson cites this passage and comments:

> The fable's affinity to the sequence of events is ... arresting. Moreover, its moral is two-stranded: one is delivered by a deity and is uncannily reminiscent of God's apothem in 4.10-11; the other is appended to the fable's end, and its message cannot be totally alien to the many pregnant lessons that Jonah seeks to teach.[59]

Was Aesop or the Bible O'Donnell's source? The closeness serves to underscore the point that it is always difficult to prove one source over another.

Lévi-Strauss felt that a paradoxical question was often at the core of a myth, like 'How can there be a first man and a first woman if they were not brother and sister?'[60] Such a question about the book of Jonah might be 'How do you combine total obedience with self-respect?' Common to Jonah and these Columba episodes is the related question: 'How can you teach someone to respect divine power without killing him?'

---

58. Cited in Sasson, *Jonah*, p. 316.

59. Sasson, *Jonah*, p. 316.

60. This and some other paradoxes of Lévi-Strauss are summarized helpfully in E. Leach, 'The Legitimacy of Solomon: Some Structural Aspects of the Old Testament History', in E. Leach, *Genesis as Myth* (London: Cape, 1969), pp. 25-84.

Also common to these passages are demonstrations of that divine power. As the book of Jonah is organized to demonstrate God's omnipotence and omniscience, so do these episodes work to prove Columba's.

Some of the concepts of the two texts would not seem to point in the same direction, however. None of the episodes shares a definition of prophecy, for example. Sharpe notes that Columba's prophecies are 'not like those of the Old Testament prophets'—but there are many kinds of prophet in the Bible.[61] (Jonah, for example, is probably not a prophet in the 'Old Testament' sense: he is very good at foreseeing, and balks at the declaring. Part of O'Reilly's contribution to the study of the Jonah/Columba relationship is that she brings recognition to the fact that behind a comparison may be a different system of thought and interpretation than what is 'obvious' about prophecy or images.)

Another major aspect of Jonah which has no place in the hagiographic excerpts examined here is repentance. There is something that may be called forgiveness, but no repentance to precede it. Berach in Adomnán's §1.19, for example, just vanishes from the narrative when Columba begins patiently to instruct Baithéne. Similarly, in §55 from the 'Irish Life', Colum Cille revives the bitten 'certain person', but he does not appear to have deserved it.

Viewed as a whole, the episodes collected here suggest that none of the men who challenges the saint in one way or another deserves to be forgiven. Rather, forgiveness, like condemnation, need not make sense, and should just be marvelled at. Perhaps it would weaken the didactic impact of Columba's power, in rhetorical terms, if a disciple actually earned his forgiveness, and did not have it magnanimously bestowed upon him.

It must be acknowledged, however, that the book of Jonah is much longer than any one Columba story. Partly for this reason it is arguably under less duress, if any, to get a lesson across, and can explore more rhetorical avenues. Jonah is good and bad, God loves him and punishes him, he is a man of vision and a (reluctant) man of action, he is sometimes too exposed or too enclosed. Jonah's weakness and indecision, if those characteristics are indeed part of his portrait, do not detract from the impact of the narrative. That weakness can be located in the figures

61. Sharpe, *St Columba*, p. 57.

of Columba's helpers, but with the narrative spotlight shining in the other direction.

Whether or not it should be classed as satire, parody, parable, or 'straight' prophecy—all of which have been asserted by different critics with equal vigour—the book of Jonah is ambiguous, and this ambiguity is a condition for humour, and for intellectual play.

Structurally speaking, some of that complexity is to be found in Columba episodes, but distributed differently. As part of a posited analogue, no one character in these hagiographic episodes is saddled with Jonah's burden of ambiguity. Columba's place in the narrative, for one, is certainly not as flexible as Jonah's. This has to do with the tradition of hagiography into which Adomnán and others were consciously writing, as has been shown by Picard, as much as with the historical developments of Christianity, and the political agendas of the hagiographer.[62]

It may just be that these more intricate philosophical conflicts—how can he be a spokesman for God and still be true to himself? How can someone be ordained yet unworthy?—are too complex to emerge in a relatively short hagiographic anecdote. At four chapters, Jonah still comes across as packed with ambiguity and 'many pregnant lessons'.

Furthermore, the biblical narrator is capable of manipulating that ambiguity so that the 'delivery' of the 'lesson' between God and Jonah is part of the lesson. In a sense, the Columba stories involve the same blend of art and ideology but a different art and a different ideology.[63] The message here is 'Fear God. Be amazed by Columba.' The art is as direct and brief.

There are also significant differences in each hagiographer's depiction of Columba. For example, Adomnán's Columba is often humble, and always humbly described. The narrator of the 'Irish Life' praises the saint as 'meeker' 'more obedient' and 'more humble' than any man in Ireland. The narrator of the 1532 *BCC*, however, is anything but humble. In *Ad VC*, it is an honour for Columba to have something in common with even one biblical character, and certainly with Jonah.

---

62. For more on the politics of hagiography, see Picard, 'Patterns', and Herbert, *Iona, Kells, and Derry*.

63. The concept of art in the service of ideology is borrowed by Kenneth Craig (*A Poetics of Jonah*) from Meir Sternberg (Cf. *The Poetics of Biblical Narrative: Ideological Literature and the Drama of Reading* [Bloomington: Indiana University Press, 1985], p. 44, *passim*) to refer to the book of Jonah. Craig does not, however, locate the same art and ideology that I do.

The narrator of the 'Irish Life' devotes a significant amount of time to establishing the majesty of Abraham and his descendants, before even mentioning the saint.[64] By contrast, the narrator of the 1532 *BCC* has it that Colum Cille is better than the whole lot of them, as when he says

> *As eidir lind a radha go ndechaidh se a céim foirbfechta os cind hIsahias*
> *an med co midh a lan d'faidetoracht Isahias dorcha dothuicsena...*[65]

> We may say that he went a step of perfection above Isaiah inasmuch as Isaiah's prophecies were difficult and hard to understand.

A literary reading reveals new aspects of the texts, and a close historical reading of various versions of the same story reveal different political agendas behind the texts. Such investigation as Herbert has done on *Fled Dúin na nGéd* and its relationship to 'The Battle of Allen' and 'The Battle of Mag Rath' could be imitated on versions of the 'same' story which appear first in *Ad VC*, then elsewhere in Columban legend. [66]

---

64. Paragraphs 1-10 (about one sixth of the whole work) do not mention Colum Cille.

65. O'Kelleher, p. 429.

66. M. Herbert, 'Fled Dúin na nGéd: A Reappraisal', *CMCS* 18 (1989), pp. 75-87.

Chapter 4

WEAKNESS AND MASOCHISM: A READING OF THE SAMSON
STORY AND SOME TALES ABOUT CÚ CHULAINN

1. *Introduction*

Part of the dynamic of reading the story of Samson involves knowing
(or thinking you know) who the 'bad guy' is, and why. Mieke Bal has
written much exploring the similarities of female characters' actions
throughout the book of Judges, similarities that have been obscured by
the fact that tradition teaches us which side is good. In other words,
'a human community is defining a certain "us" over against a certain
"them". Israelites and Philistines laugh at different places when they
hear this story.'[1]

> 13. An angel warns Manoah's wife (who is barren) that she will bear a
> Nazirite. She tells Manoah and he panics, asks for verification and guid-
> ance. The angel reassures him, the woman bears a son, and names him
> Samson.
>   14. Samson (now a young man—at least) goes down to Timnah and
> sees a Philistine woman there whom he wants. His parents object (but
> they do not know this is the LORD's doing). As they all go down to
> Timnah, a lion comes at Samson; he (secretly) tears it apart. Then he
> arranges to marry the woman the next year.
>   At that point he finds the lion's skeleton full of (bees and) honey, which
> he eats and has his parents eat. At the wedding feast, Samson propounds
> a riddle to the party which confounds them. Seven days later, the wed-
> ding party tells Samson's wife that they will burn her alive if she does
> not find out the answer to the riddle. She nags him until he tells her (the
> answer has something to do with honey, a lion, and sources of strength).
> Samson is enraged when the Philistines produce the right answer. The
> LORD is in him: he kills thirty men and goes home. His wife leaves him.

    1.   J. Wharton, 'The Secret of [the LORD]: Story and Affirmation in Judges
13–16', *Int* 27/1 (1973), pp. 48-65 (53).

15. Later, Samson comes back and finds the woman married to another. In anger, he sets fire to Philistine crops using incendiary foxes. The Philistines burn Samson's estranged wife and her father. In retaliation, Samson attacks the Philistines, and then goes down to Etam. The Philistines have the Judahites bring Samson up from there, but as they are about to deliver him into the hands of the Philistines, the LORD is in him and he kills a thousand with the jawbone of an ass.

16. Another time, Samson goes to Gaza and sleeps with a whore there. The Gazites try to ambush him there but he steals out in the middle of the night and tears down the town gates.

Then, in the Wadi Sorek he falls in love with a woman called Delilah. The Philistines pay her to find out why Samson is so strong. She asks him, and he makes up a story about how he might be subdued. She sets up an ambush according to that information, warns him of it and watches it fail. Three times they do this and then she starts nagging him for the truth. He says he might be subdued if his hair is cut—because he is a Nazirite.

Again she sets up the ambush and this time it works: the Philistines seize him, gouge out his eyes, and make him a slave. Later, they bring him out to dance for them in a celebration in honour of their god. Samson calls to the LORD for help in revenge, asking to die with the Philistines. He pulls down the temple and kills everyone in it, including himself. He is buried with his father.

Samson, like Jonah, has always been a popular source for exegesis, partly for his ambiguous 'goodness' by any biblical terms. Like Jonah, he does not pray to God except to ask for help, and he seems to work for God only against his own instincts. His strength and sexuality are arguably the most memorable aspects of his portrait, perhaps more than his role as a judge for Israel, or a paradigm of a good leader. We are told that he ruled for twenty years, but Samson is more commonly associated with specific brief adventures in his career, and his antics with one woman in particular. His short story is about the same length as Jonah's, and as packed with enigmatic moments which probe the question of what weakness is.

Samson seems by turns weak and proud. Broadly speaking, he resembles the heroes of other early literatures for his brawn. Closer readings reveal, however, that his interpersonal relationships and peace-time actions tell just as much as does his warrior's prowess about his character and perhaps about the culture that produced him. He is not just a strong man with bad taste in women.

As much as his interactions with women, his character is framed by the fact that he is a Nazirite, that his contract with God determines everything he does. Samson may not be the total folk hero that David is, for example, but he does embody many features of a condensed heroic biography, from his type-scene birth, to the amount of hope invested in him, to his apartness, his wild strength, his path of initiation, and his eventual downfall.

In some ways a comparison between Samson and Cú Chulainn seems obvious. Something about Samson's brief and violent career invites comparison with that of an Old Irish hero—his bluntness, perhaps, his masculinity, and his memorable adventures with women. At the same time he exists ostensibly just to serve a contract between him and his people/God, the Nazirate. Some other things Samson and Cú Chulainn seem to share are riddles and courtship, sexual, martial and tribal initiation stories, the isolation brought on by heroic status as well as warp-spasms and strongman feats. Most of these points are about masculinity and sexual relationships, but are reactions to the contract the hero has with his people.

Because there is no early Irish canon, Cú Chulainn can be understood only as his character is refracted through so many narratives and episodes. Throughout this essay I will examine several examples from different tales involving Cú Chulainn which I think have parallels in aspects of Samson's career. My approach will involve a close reading of all the stories involved, with a view to learning about them as much as to 'proving' ultimately what they are 'really' about. Implicitly, however, the choice of what is compared shows that I think that they do indeed have something in common. That common factor is their particular brand of masculinity which involves weakness.

Previous critics have compared the mythological motifs in Samson's career with those of masculine heroes from other cultures' literature, from African myths to Greek. As with Cú Chulainn's, however, there is more to this 'strongman profile' than meets the eye. Critics may be naive to suggest that Samson is secretly reluctant to be male, or that Cú Chulainn has an endearing femininity underneath everything. But equally, it is a mistake to take the tale of their masculinity entirely at face value like Tarzans ourselves: Cú Chulainn—strong; strong—good! Reading 'against' or 'with' the text should reveal more than a single group's 'voices', male or female. Furthermore, I will not be asserting texts' wilful misogyny, female authorship or subversive femininity. In the final analysis, although a man's actions and the code he must follow form the core of the narratives here, the stories reveal information about interaction between men and women alike.

A number of critics have already commented on Samson's 'unbiblical' nature. His story 'poses a number of questions because of its inconsistency with the biblical world'.[2] Robert Alter called Samson 'the only strongman-hero in the Bible'.[3] Samson is soon labelled a folk hero because of this and, despite the shortness of his story, several scholars have looked for connections between Samson and figures in international mythology. While I will refer to the work of some of these scholars, I offer a more literary study, re-examining exactly what is being compared.

Since Samson's tale is relatively short, it is important to enunciate even small episodes within it. In this chapter I evoke some of Samson's most remarkable features and compare them with the portrait of Cú Chulainn I reveal. (Any such choice is of course subjective—the critic chooses which aspect of the hero is to be called his essence.)

Of the many analyses of Samson, there may be said to be two groups: those that focus on women and those that do not. Some studies try to highlight Samson's military prowess, his strength and significance as a 'judge'. In these portraits, the women in Samson's story are a distraction from his mission, whether that mission is seen as theological or strategic. More recent scholarship has returned to the Samson story to look at its 'gender'-related messages. However, all too often, this means woman-hunting, in one of several ways, as Simon Gaunt summarizes (with relevance to another but comparable discipline involving ancient literature):

> One strand seeks either to discern (and condemn) misogyny and patriarchal structures within mediaeval texts or to detect (and congratulate) writers who were critical of the oppression of women. Secondly, various critics have written what they themselves call 'images of women' criticism, which describes how women are portrayed (usually by men) in mediaeval texts, and seeks to explain the different images and to evaluate the disparity between such images and what we know of the experience of mediaeval women. Thirdly, mediaeval women writers have

2. O. Margalith, 'Samson's Riddle and Samson's Magic Locks', *VT* 36 (1986), pp. 225-34 (225).

3. R. Alter, 'Samson without Folklore', in Susan Niditch (ed.), *Text and Tradition: The Hebrew Bible and Folklore* (Atlanta: Scholars Press, 1990), pp. 47-56 (47).

attracted a good deal of attention. Finally, and perhaps most excitingly, counter-readings of texts have been offered by positing the response of women readers—mediaeval and modern—to male-authored texts.[4]

The existence of a gender category has given scholars leave to discuss the sexual ramifications of Samson's career, but mainly as it pertains to the 'victim' women he encounters. Similarly, some scholars have read not only 'against' Cú Chulainn texts but past them in looking for women. Instead of the feminine, in these readings I would like to articulate the masculine.

I would look at Cú Chulainn first, then Samson, describing then comparing aspects of their characters according to several critical approaches outlined above, but mainly relying on psychoanalytic theory. In the end I hope to show that both stories reflect the conflicting loyalties of a hero's life, the choice between personal and public responsibility, which is in turn a reflection of masculine identity. In other words, I claim that the Samson and Cú Chulainn stories have similar narratological themes as the action progresses, generally.

More specifically, I hope to show that the hero faces a partly psychological struggle between responsibility to himself and to the 'Law', or society. It is true of Cú Chulainn as has been observed about other masculine heroes that he is 'defined in relation...to the law of patriarchy which specifies the culturally acceptable positions (and the delimitation of) masculine identity and desire'.[5] I find this relationship manifest particularly in the hero's dealings with women.

This essay, like the last one, is concerned with an examination of the theme of weakness. I will be looking here at a different breed of weakness from Jonah's: the weakness of the masculine hero and two literatures' interpretations of that theme.

We may refer to the book of Judges' own comments on the Samson story's place in this biblical time when 'everyone did what he pleased'.[6] It was a time of good guys and bad guys when 'major judges...fought on behalf of a beleaguered tribe to throw off the yoke of foreign

---

    4. S. Gaunt, *Gender and Genre in Medieval French Literature* (Cambridge: Cambridge University Press, 1995), p. 2.

    5. Frank Krutnik, *In a Lonely Street: Film Noir, Genre, Masculinity* (London: Routledge, 1991), p. 86 (summarizing Freud).

    6. Judg. 17.6; 21.25.

oppression'.[7] If Joan Radner is right, this is similar to the time when 'the *Táin* is said to have taken place': 'a metaphorical time-out-of-time, a liminal period of chaos'.[8]

Each hero has a place in the narrative of his people as an important champion in that liminal time. His weakness, however, serves a purpose too, and not just in literary terms. Both bodies of literature here set out to explain a Golden Age in the life of a people, and in this time part of what sustains that age is the 'contract' between a hero and his people. 'Loyalty to kindred is an absolute value, and it is love of kindred which saves Ulster...'[9] The narrators, however, must also explain why that golden age is over, and that people no longer in power when they are writing, hundreds of years later.

What is revealed about the hero within his tradition? Is such socio-logical speculation profitable, or indeed possible? Partly, we cannot know the exact relationship of reality to the events in the Ulster Cycle or the book of Judges. There is, of course, archaeological evidence from earliest Ireland (from which murky past we may guess these stories emerged), and there is political information about early Christian Ireland (when we may guess the stories were given literary body and a written record), but where protohistory ends and imagination begins remains open to debate.

Cultures seeking heroes are nothing new, even when biblical heroes alone are the 'model', or old: 'Biblical epics tended to be made mostly after both world wars, when America, as "leader of the free world" had a need to wrap itself in the sanctimonious mantle of previous Chosen Peoples.'[10] The need to be a chosen people is evident in the *Lebor Gabála* (The Book of Invasions) (discussed in Chapter 5) but that alone does not establish a particular biblical model for any part of early Irish literature. Such parallels are only too easy to find.

Equally broadly speaking, there are fundamental differences in the narrative contexts of the two literatures that are under discussion here. In the Bible, Palestine is promised land, due to a particular people, but

7. J. Crenshaw, *Samson: A Vow Ignored, A Secret Betrayed* (Atlanta: Scholars Press, 1978), p. 59.

8. J. Radner, '"Fury Destroys the World": Historical Strategy in Ireland's Ulster Epic', *Mankind Quarterly* 23/1 (1982), pp. 41-60 (53).

9. Ó Cathasaigh, 'Mythology', p. 131.

10. P. Lopate, 'Judges. Samson and Delilah: Tests of Weakness', in Rosenberg (ed.), *Congregation*, pp. 72-73.

not always in their possession. This is vaguely comparable to Ulster and its possession by Ulstermen (as opposed to Connachtmen). The concept of a family or line of kings (like the House of David) as being due power is something like the political lineages that make up part of the background to the Ulster Cycle and the historical reality of early Christian Ireland. But the contract between the people Israel—their cause and destiny to be monotheists—and God remains constant and emerges as the thread that connects good adventures and bad in the Hebrew Bible, pre- and post-exilic. So when the narrators of the Bible deconstruct the glory of a fabulous king, there will always be another leader and another unexpected hero, ignored prophet or loyal disciple to take his place on the scene.

Ulster's glory, by contrast, is fixed in time: the end is the end. There is no contract or cause other than the honour code itself, which, by the narrator's time, is inadequate and the supporting structure for a people who are gone. It froze them (sometimes literally, as in their 'pangs', *cess noínden*) when they most needed fluidity and adaptability, and thereby ensured their extinction.

The narrators of the Ulster Cycle know that their stories will live on and are legends already by their time; their intended audience implicitly knows it too. But the eternal contract with the future is different; the underlying metaphor is different. Few are the Irishmen who read the Ulster Cycle today as a manual for their faith in a continuing Irishness. Many more are the readers of the Bible who understand Abraham as their father, or exile as a simile for their exile, even in a post-biblical zone such as America.

Thus the comparison of peoples can go only as far as the immediate extent of story time, as if at the end of each early Irish tale there is a full stop and at the end of each Bible story ellipses. Narratologically and morphologically similar though the heroes' roles in the tales may be, the framing and conclusion of the tales are essentially different.

The early mediaeval Irish storyteller had motivations that are still being discussed by historians and anthropologists. He had political allegories to create about his current province, and patron saints' hometowns to glorify. In the case of Ulster he was creating or telling the story of a people who had a special contract with each other and revolving around a main hero (Cú Chulainn) or group of heroes (the Ulstermen). The narrator is not, however, an inheritor of the heroic code, does not participate in an Ulster contract.

By contrast, God's contract with Israel and the lineage of Israel is not just history or mythology for the narrator of the Bible. So even if there are similar political allegories to be made or figures from contemporary history to glorify, his agenda is fundamentally different. When he writes 'God of Abraham' he means 'my God', and he suspects that it will mean 'my God' for whoever reads it after him. The mythological function of Israel's past is continuous, a limb of an existing body of Jews.

This 'frame' affects the details of the Samson and Cú Chulainn stories in ways that will be evident. There are fundamental differences in the margins. The reactions of characters to God, and God's responsibility to them far exceeds the importance of Ulster's conduct as a tribe/ cause. For example, God may take strength away from Samson but it is not an accident, done from passivity or inflexibility, but with his people's longer term needs in mind (and if we doubt it, the narrator reminds us). When the Ulstermen are paralysed and cannot help Cú Chulainn it is because they are simply too weak to do so. This paralysis continually marks a difference between the narrative world of early Irish literature and the Bible's.

I have already discussed the pitfalls of motif-hunting with regard to Jonah and Columba, but a study of Samson and Cú Chulainn would be incomplete without some reference to mythology. Part of its relevance comes in connection to psychoanalytic theory, to be discussed below. Also, in the case of these two heroes, more than with any of the others in this thesis there is a body of critical work about them. Daniel Melia, Nagy and Ó Cathasaigh are among the scholars to have devoted attention to the Ulster Cycle's place in international mythology. There will be reference to their work here, as there will be to that of the critics who have looked at Samson through this lens.

For each student of myth, the significance of a particular narrative is redrawn. Lord Raglan sketched Cú Chulainn in a way that showed Cú Chulainn's commonalities with Moses, among others.[11] David Kenneth Jaeger counts Samson's adventures in a structure that has him a reflex of a type that includes David and Jonathan.[12] Jaeger never mentions the

11. Lord Raglan, *The Hero: A Study in Tradition, Myth, and Drama* (London: Cape, 1936), pp. 89-97.
12. D.K. Jaeger, 'The Initiatory Trial Theme of the Hero in Hebrew Bible Narrative' (Unpublished PhD thesis, University of Denver, 1992).

women in Samson's story because they do not sufficiently 'interfere' with the overall pattern he has located to alter its comparability to other, less sexual heroes' patterns. The fact that Jaeger's pursuit of this mythological agenda causes him to leave out of his summary major sections of the Samson story does not make his survey worthless, but it does reflect the choices that even such seemingly clinical studies involve. For that reason, a mythological assessment seems best used as one of many approaches.

For this reason, I will not be pursuing the following Birth of the Hero motifs as the main similarity between Samson and Cú Chulainn. (Authoritative scholars like Rank and Raglan could be referred to for a serious rendering of this theme, as well as Ó Cathasaigh for the place of early Irish heroic biography in world mythology.)[13] A mythological look at Samson and Cú Chulainn's birth stories that sought primarily to conflate them might lead to this list of 'identical' features:

1. The mother has been initially disappointed about the prospect of bearing children (Samson's mother is barren; Dechtire has had a child die in her care).[14]

2. The mother has been singled out by supernatural means in a dream or vision and told that she will bear a boy child (although the newsbearer does not have sex with her).

3. She is told that this is part of a plan belonging to someone divine or semi-divine (God; Lugh).

4. There is a special condition to his upbringing (that he not cut his hair; that he be named Sétantae, that colts be raised with him).

Perhaps this arrangement makes the comparison more attractive. But the collocation seems to set out to limit the stories as much as to make them accessible. Poor Elijah does not do well in Raglan's twenty-two-point pattern, for instance, and we may imagine a compère adding, 'Although he *does* disappear in a chariot of fire and has a holy sepulchre, I'm afraid we can give him only nine points. But he won't go away empty-handed ...' A less exclusive method should bring more points to light. The whole fly-swallowing episode with Dechtire, for one, has no place in the above plan, but is surely significant.

13. Cf. Ó Cathasaigh, *Biography*.
14. Cf. 'Compert Con Culainn'(The Birth of Cú Chulainn) which can be found in A.G. van Hamel, *Compert Con Culainn and Other Stories* (Dublin: DIAS, 1933), and in translation in Gantz, *Early Irish Myths*, pp. 131-33.

The main critical tool employed in my readings of *Tochmarc Emire*, *Aided Óenfir Aífe*, *Serglige Con Culainn* and the Samson story is psychoanalytic theory. This is not unconnected to mythology, which Freud called 'psychology projected onto the outside world'. In previous chapters I have addressed the prospect of the psychological interest of early Irish literature and the implicit acknowledgment of this in Philip O'Leary's work, and elsewhere. Where do psychoanalysis and mythology overlap?

In one sense the overlap is obvious: the story of Oedipus is a myth about a question of culture and life. So is it for Freud:

> Freud's interpretation of the drama is not so removed from the Greek one as might appear at first glance. For the Greeks, as for Freud, the problem of Oedipus is one of knowledge of the most vital kind: knowledge of the self... But for Freud, the story of Oedipus traces the unconscious wish of every (male) child.[15]

In *Totem and Taboo*,[16] Freud investigates certain mythic structures of 'primitive' peoples as they connect back to psychoanalytic patterns. For all their flaws, Freud's ideas here suggest a provocative connection between a culture's myths and its psyche.

Otto Rank, a disciple of Freud, also did much on psychoanalysis and myth. In his *The Myth of the Birth of the Hero*[17] he analyses a collection of 'international' birth tales and suggests that they can be interpreted as the product of an imagination, as Freud interprets dreams. The tenacity with which he clings to his universalist conclusion (that all are about youths breaking away from their parents, where the child becomes the hero of myth) matches Freud's insistence on a not unrelated father–son conflict. Freud, however, is more interested in the particulars of the culture producing each individual myth.

C.G. Jung is even better known for his psychological approach to myth, but he is also even more devoted to the 'allegedly pan-human archetypes' that mythologists are wary of.[18] Dundes sees the Jungian

15. F. Meltzer, 'Unconscious' in Lentricchia and McLaughlin (eds.), *Critical Terms*, pp. 152-53.

16. London: Routledge & Kegan Paul, 1950.

17. *The Myth of the Birth of the Hero and Other Writings* (New York: Vintage Books, 1959).

18. C.G. Jung, 'The Psychology of the Child Archetype', with introduction by Alan Dundes, in A. Dundes (ed.), *Sacred Narrative: Readings in the Theory of Myth* (Berkeley: University of California Press, 1984), pp. 244-55 (244).

and Freudian approaches as fundamentally different and seems to side with Freud, whose observations can be empirically tested at least. What is more significant, perhaps, is that Freudian theory is not so universalizing: it is concerned with myths as projections of childhood which vary, as childhoods vary between cultures.

I will not be positing the psyche of an ancient Irishman here, let alone a universal trait. I do, however, accept the premise that what may be interpreted about the tales of a culture may have some relation to the psychological needs of that culture. In this case I am interpreting a particular masculine hero pattern found in two narratives (which may be called myths as easily as tales or texts). The conclusions I draw about the culture that created them are tentative, but comparable to those that others have reached by other methods: that there is a conflict between personal and public obligation being explored, one presumably germane to the lives of the people who told it and/or wrote it.

2. *Tochmarc Emire*

There are dozens of sources for tales that chronicle Cú Chulainn's many and varied adventures. For each of those tales, different versions reveal different aspects of Cú Chulainn's character, according to the literary and even political agendas of the author(s).

Táin Bó Cuailnge is not about Cú Chulainn alone, but it is concerned with his career, as well as currently being the most famous work of early Irish literature. (Critical literature about the *Táin* has already been alluded to; two important collections are *Ulidia: Proceedings of the First International Conference on the Ulster Cycle of Tales* and *Aspects of the Táin*).[19] Any narrowing down to a particular aspect of his career, or a particular recension is just that: an inevitable result of selection. In this case I have chosen to focus on a few stories central to his career, ones which contain reference to his dealings with women as well as to other parts of his heroic biography. By reading these closely, it is hoped that a certain kind of weakness will be revealed alongside depictions of his indisputable strength.

These particular stories also seem to have the most in common with Samson's portrait of all of Cú Chulainn's adventures. They draw attention to his apartness, his initiation, and the supernatural abilities he has which make him both an ideal saviour for his people and also a

---

19. Mallory and Stockman (eds.), *Ulidia*; Mallory (ed.), *Aspects of the Táin*.

hopelessly flawed leader who will die without leaving his people an heir. The progression detailed in these tales is not 'really about' women, but stories about Cú Chulainn that feature female characters are often those which reveal the most new information about conflicts in his character and the heroic codes to which he is bound.

By the 'time' of *Tochmarc Emire* in the implied chronology, Cú Chulainn is a young man with many admirers. His birth and boyhood deeds are behind him; he lives among the Ulstermen. Mythological motifs to do with initiation run throughout his adventures in this tale.[20]

Conchobor is king over the Ulstermen (Ulaid); they are prospering. His palace is gorgeous and the heroes of Ulster like to gather there in luxury, performing feats. Cú Chulainn is the best hero of all and the women love him for his greatness and beauty. The Ulaid want him to have a wife in order to keep their own wives and daughters safe from him, and to provide them with an heir. Conchobor sends men throughout Ireland to find a wife for Cú Chulainn but he fancies none of them. He goes after Forgall Manach's daughter, Emer.

He sets out with his charioteer Lóeg and finds Emer with her foster sisters. (She alone is worthy of him.) They meet and talk in riddles which seem to revolve around the process that led him to her, as well as around who they are. They boast to each other about their statistics and those of the ones who raised them. He is satisfied with her and finds her a good match; they discuss their union and he flirts with her. She flirts back, naming feats for him to perform. He agrees and goes away.

[A long *dindshenchas*[21] passage follows, some explaining the name Emain Macha, each an elaborate self-contained passage. Some refer to some of the more enigmatic remarks Cú Chulainn and Emer have said to each other.]

Cú Chulainn reaches Emain Macha. Meanwhile, Forgall Manach has found out what is under way between Cú Chulainn and his daughter, and determines to thwart Cú Chulainn. He goes to Conchobor in disguise and recommends that Cú Chulainn go away to Scáthach in Scotland for his training-in-arms. Cú Chulainn agrees, but goes to visit Emer first at which point she tells him of Forgall's intentions to destroy him.

Along the way Cú Chulainn meets many people, some who thwart him, some who help him. Among them is a frightening monster which turns

20. I will be working from A.G. van Hamel's edition of the tale featured in *Compert Con Culainn and Other Stories* (Dublin: DIAS, 1933, repr. 1978), pp. 20-68. The most readily available translation into English is to be found in T. Kinsella (trans.), *The Táin* (Oxford: Oxford University Press, 1969), pp. 25-39. This, however, excludes much that Kinsella finds irrelevant to the 'plot' of *The Táin*.

21. Folklore and pseudo-history built around place-names.

out to be quite helpful. Before reaching Scáthach he meets some of her disciples and then her daughter Úathach, who desires him. She gets hurt by him, and after the fight that ensues, Cú Chulainn offers his services to Scáthach. Using information Úathach gives him, he tricks Scáthach into agreeing to train him. He sleeps with Úathach. (Meanwhile suitors come to Emer but she scares them off.)

Scáthach is at war with another chieftain, Aífe, and she tries to prevent Cú Chulainn from helping her fight, but he goes anyway and defeats Aífe's sons. Then, using information Scáthach gives him, he tricks Aífe until she is at his mercy and must meet three demands, one of which is to bear him a son. She agrees, conceives, and says the son will come to Ireland at the age of seven. Connla is to be his name, but he must not reveal it. Cú Chulainn leaves a gold thumb ring for him and he is to wear it when it fits him.

A trained warrior now, Cú Chulainn says goodbye. Scáthach delivers a glorious but rather lonesome prophecy for him, and he goes homeward. Again he meets people on the way who delay him through good or ill will, among whom is a girl he rescues and narrowly avoids marrying.

Cú Chulainn makes it to Forgall's fort but has a hard time reaching Emer. Cú Chulainn kills people left and right in accordance with the feats Emer had asked of him, in places whose names were reflected in the *dindshenchas* passages. Just as Cú Chulainn and Emer are finally about to go to bed together, Bricriu points out that Conchobor, as king, must be the first to sleep with the virgin Emer, about which no one is happy, especially Cú Chulainn. They get past this by sleeping three to a bed, Cú Chulainn, Emer, and Conchobor. Then Cú Chulainn and Emer live as man and wife.

Tochmarc Emire begins with a description of Conchobor's happy reign and the elaborate finery of his court, much in the way that *Serglige Con Culainn* begins with a description of the gorgeous assembly there. In *Tochmarc Emire*, however, the emphasis is on the unity among the Ulstermen rather than their internal competitions. Still, Cú Chulainn emerges as the best champion, unequivocally.

In describing Cú Chulainn the narrator of *Tochmarc Emire* lists his faults: 'Trí lochta Con Culainn: a bith ro-ócc … a bith rodánae; a bith ro-álainn'[22] ('Cú Chulainn had three faults: being too young, too bold, too lovely'). This raises three questions immediately: (1) Why would the narrator be listing the faults of the hero? (2) Why would *they* be

22. A.G. van Hamel, 'Tochmarc Emire', in *idem* (ed.), *Compert*, p. 22. Translations are mine unless otherwise stated. I am grateful to Dáibhí Ó Cróinín for checking these.

considered faults (i.e. how can a hero be too bold)? (3) Why/How are these faults Cú Chulainn's?

Whether the narrator intends to mock Cú Chulainn or to hint at his eventual downfall, it is significant that Cú Chulainn has faults built into his heroic character. It comes across in the narrative as a conscious forewarning of defeat, or at least of problems in his character. Perhaps this serves as a reminder to the audience that it is the ex-hero Cú Chulainn who is being discussed. That is, as suggested above, the heroic age of the Ulster Saga is a closed time, one from which the narrator is removed. The narrator's task is always twofold: to glorify a time and people of great sentimental, or perhaps political value, while explaining its subsequent extinction. On a more self-conscious level, we may say that Cú Chulainn has flaws because it makes his character richer and more dimensional.

B.K. Martin notes the irony in early Irish tales generally about faults which seem not to be faults at all: '[T]o be heroic is to be strong and clever and bold and virile...yet the more energetically they display these qualities the more offence they give.'[23] The three faults of Cú Chulainn are based on this rationale. Is this logical? Perhaps we can say that Cú Chulainn's faults are 'faults' like Naoise's in *Longes Mac n-Uislenn*. His charisma, the *andord* (which emission, sometimes translated by 'crooning', has the effect of making cows produce two-thirds more milk in the best of times), is a kind of force that hums, having great positive effect when all is well, and wreaking havoc when all is not well.

Why is it a fault to be young? The narrator offers an explanation: 'Ar ni rofhasatar a renga rodaim, ar ba móide conceistis óicc anaichnid fai'[24] ('Because the reins of a team ox would not grow, and they would mock him all the more for being an unknown young warrior'). That is, he could not grow a beard, which meant that he could not convince warriors to fight him. This, of course, would indeed compromise his glory and dignity. (In other tales, Cú Chulainn will wear a false beard to show opponents that he is worth fighting.) Inasmuch as this, then, the 'too young' comment seems rational.

'Too bold' implies that his boldness brings too much conflict. This is a surprising comment on Cú Chulainn because it seems to be the

23. B.K. Martin, 'Medieval Irish *aitheda* and Todorov's "Narratologie" ', *Studia Celtica* 10/11 (1975–76), pp. 138-51 (149-50).
24. *TEm*, p. 22.

opposite of 'too young', which refers to his being withheld from battle. If we take 'too young' to mean 'too inexperienced', however, or 'naive', it complements 'too bold'. Both point to the wilful and unnecessary endangering of his own life.

That he should also be called 'too lovely' is interesting. The comment is conspicuous for its un-Irish aesthetic—usually beauty in men is a mark of strength, virility, noble birth, a blessing of body and soul, and one can hardly have too much of it. There are a few exceptions to this in early Irish literature, of course, when beauty bodes ill. (It is more likely, however, to mean bad luck in the case of a woman. In *Longes Mac n-Uislenn*, for example, Deirdre's loveliness and no other obvious fault ensures doom for one and all.)

Perhaps 'too lovely' refers to the distractions from women that will come into Cú Chulainn's life as a result of this. In this case, it follows that he would act badly because of his loveliness, allow himself to be distracted by women, act independently in moments which should be devoted to community (as in the episode with Fedelm in *The Táin*, discussed below). But even more generally, 'too lovely' suggests that his vanity will get in the way of his fulfilling his duty, drawing attention to his private nature, and encouraging his masculine desire, while detracting from his obligations to the tribe, to the heroic honour code and to the Ulstermen. (We may think of the episode in *The Táin* when Cú Chulainn arranges for a special session of exhibitionism: 'He came out to display himself by day because he felt the unearthly shape he had shown them the night before had not done him justice. And certainly the youth Cú Chulainn mac Sualdaim was handsome …'[25]) If this is what the narrator meant, then 'too lovely' does indeed make sense with 'too young' and 'too bold' because each involves a success for Cú Chulainn and a risk-taking not for him but for his people, the Ulaid, thus endangering not himself but the contract he has with society, with the patriarchy in which he lives as an (honoured) guest.

It is this meaning that makes the most sense in the terms of the next part of the exposition in *TEm*: the Ulstermen are keen to find Cú Chulainn a wife not because they want him to have a companion, but because his loveliness causes each man to worry about his own welfare, through the threat to his own wife's honour:

25. Kinsella, *The Táin*, p. 156. (Equivalent to *Táin* I, ll. 2336-42 [Cecile O'Rahilly, *Táin Bó Cuailnge, Recension 1* (Dublin: DIAS, 1976)]).

Baí comairle la hUlltu fo dáig Con Culainn. Ar ro carsat a mná & a n-ingena co mmór é ... sétig bad toga la Coin Culainn do thocmarc dó, ar ba derb leo comba lugaide no saigfed milled a n-ingenraide & fóemad serce a mban fer dia mbeth sétig a chomfrestail oca.[26]

The Ulaid convened to discuss the question of Cú Chulainn. Because their wives and daughters loved him so much.[27] A man with a wife of his own would be less likely to ruin their daughters and steal their wives' love.[28]

This is the first indication of how the Ulaid feel about their hero. Their finding a wife for him is presented openly as self-interest. They are not giving him a wife because they want to see to his well-being. They want to keep their own wives and, significantly, they would not be willing, let alone proud, to marry off their daughters to him. And they want an heir. In the end, both of these wishes, as the Ulaid initially intend them, are thwarted by Cú Chulainn: he rejects the women they choose for him and when eventually he has a son, he kills him, and dies without an heir.

The nature of Cú Chulainn's relation to the Ulaid is thus quite passive within *TEm* so far: his identity is delimited in terms of what he must do by his contractual relationship with them, and what he must not do: be their champion, but not attract their wives, for example. This is the nature of Cú Chulainn's Nazirate-of-sorts, his identity crowded not with the expectations of God, but with the tribe's. The Ulaid are equivalent to God in their role in this dynamic and more generally, as I hope to show.

When the Ulaid go to find Cú Chulainn a wife, he wants none of the ones they select. Instead, he seeks out Emer in the Gardens of Lugh. Vincent Dunn has pointed out that Cú Chulainn seems to be travelling further and further into the Other in pursuit of her, and the Garden of Lugh where he finds her 'may be thought of as being set apart from the world of mortals'.[29] (Later, it is interesting to note how mortal she becomes once she is his wife. As in *Serglige Con Culainn* her status seems to be dictated by Cú Chulainn's masculine desire: once she

26. *TEm*, p. 22.
27. My translation.
28. Kinsella, *The Táin*, p. 26.
29. V. Dunn, *Cattle-Raids and Courtships* (New York: Garland Publications, 1989), p. 69.

belongs to him, her very cosmological status is transformed! This argument also points out the centrality of Cú Chulainn in these stories, and not the women whose lives he affects.)

The possibility of comparison with Samson becomes particularly tempting at this point: young hero seeks exogamous bride despite the objection of his elders. In both Samson's and Cú Chulainn's cases, the girl is not only exogamous—outside the tribe—but outside the known world: the Timnite woman and others are not just not Danites like Samson, they are not Jews. Emer is not just not an Ulsterwoman, but seems to be from beyond Ireland (or above or below it).

Cú Chulainn uses the self-interest of the Ulaid against them, threatening that if Emer is not given to him as a wife, he will leave no heir: a bargain his side of which he does not keep. Though we tend to imagine the relationship between Cú Chulainn and the Ulaid as kind and fostering (figuratively and literally), we cannot fail to notice several instances where the relationship is fraught, as here.

Emer and her maids appear and hear the clatter of hooves. The action as Cú Chulainn's party arrives is described elaborately: ' "Feiced óen úaib", ol Emer, "cid dotáet inar dochum." "Atchíusa ém ann ..." ' (' "One of you go look [and see]", said Emer, "what's coming this way." "Well, I see..." ')[30]

We have Emer's point of view as she watches this creature of fierce love arriving. It is interesting that he comes to the courtship in this passive position: he is most often looked at and not looking, although he will subsequently spend some time looking down Emer's shirt. Many theories of narrative make much of who looks and who is looked at. If nothing else, this passage establishes Emer's strength.

In fact Cú Chulainn's introduction is set up like Emer's: at different points of the story Cú Chulainn and Emer are described, following a description of their surroundings, and how they emerge from them. Unlike Cú Chulainn's presentation in *SC* or Emer's in *Fled Bricrend* ('Bricriu's Feast'), in *Tochmarc Emire* they are the best without having to compete, according to their merits alone. The fact that Cú Chulainn is attractive to women is an extra mark of excellence for him.

Emer is described as possessing the six virtues (*búada*) most desirable in early Irish literature:[31] '... búaid crotha ... ngotha ... mbindiusa

30. *TEm*, p. 22.

31. For discussion of the place of these in early Irish literature and elsewhere, see R. Smith, 'The Six Gifts', *JCS* 1.1 (1949), pp. 98-104.

... ndruine ... ngaíse ... ngensa'[32] ('... the gift of looks, voice, sweet speech, embroidery, wisdom, and chastity'). She emerges as the most beautiful girl in Forgall Manach's court. What sets her apart, however, especially to Cú Chulainn, is her verbal ability.[33] It is interesting that in these paired emergences from their respective milieus, what distinguishes Cú Chulainn is a seemingly feminine attribute. While early Irish saga women are often good talkers, 'sweet speech', *bindius*, is a more masculine trait—and the mainstay of Emer's excellence in *TEm*, according to the narrator (and the evidence). Her verbal prowess establishes her as a worthy competitor in Cú Chulainn's own realm.

Of the six virtues Emer possesses, only two (embroidery and chastity) 'were regarded as distinctively feminine; the other four were also attributable to men'.[34] This overlapping of masculine and feminine serves not only to underscore the perfection of their match, but also to foreshadow the arrival of other women who excel in even more masculine arts: Scáthach and Aífe, the warriors. The perfection of a match implies a psychological compatibility, where Emer's dominance and Cú Chulainn's 'femininity' (passivity) complement each other and make a mildly sadomasochistic relationship (to be discussed below).

The riddles that pass between Cú Chulainn and Emer when they meet seem to be about the inscrutable and/or impossible paths that led him to her. Perhaps he refers to the improbability of their meeting, the odds he challenged, the society he was willing to disrupt to come to meet her. He seems to be saying that he came impossibly, on impossible roads: '...etir in día & a fáith ...etir in tríath & a séitchi ...'[35] ('between God and his prophet ... between the king and his wife').

Emer boasts how pursued she is and how strong her father is. Cú Chulainn says he will surpass all that. Emer asks what is so good about him and he tells her. She doubts him, or pretends to. He cites the expectations placed on him in childhood. And finally he says, 'Ar ní

32. *TEm*, p. 23.

33. This may not be a constant throughout the Ulster Cycle, however. In *Fled Bricrend* Emer establishes sexual appeal as her superior point among all the Ulsterwomen, as Joanne Findon has pointed out ('Emer and the Roles of Female Characters in the Medieval Irish Ulster Cycle' [Unpublished PhD thesis, University of Toronto, 1994], p. 85). See also Findon, *A Woman's Words: Emer and Female Speech in the Ulster Cycle* (Toronto: University of Toronto Press, 1997).

34. Smith, 'Gifts', p. 49.

35. *TEm*, pp. 26-27.

fúarus sa cosse ben follongad ind airis dála imacallaim fon samail seo frim'[36] ('Until now I had not found a woman who could keep up the subject of conversation as well as me').

Many seize on the remarkable nature of their riddling, but no one seems to be able to explain the individual riddles. This, though frustrating, serves to underscore the exclusivity of their arrangement; perhaps these words are really meant for only them to understand! Dunn points out that even Emer's foster sisters are unable to understand them.[37]

They continue in the same vein for some time, boasting and retorting alternatively:

> *'Ma atchotat do gnímae fessin dano', ol in ingen, 'cid dom nachit áirmébainn etarru?' 'Forglim féin ém, a ingen', ol Cú Chulainn ...*[38]

> 'If you really have such deeds', said the girl, 'then why don't I judge among them for myself?' 'Judge away, girl', said Cú Chulainn ...

While I agree with Findon that verbal sparring in early Irish literature is a sign of intimacy (e.g. the verse-capping that implies sexuality by its nature as much as its content in *Fingal Rónáin*), it is possible to read even more subversive uses of speech into *TEm*. When Emer taunts 'At maithi na comrama móethmacaáim', ol in ingen, 'acht nád ránac co nert n-erred béos.' 'Maith ém rom ebladsa, a ingen', ol sé...'[39] ('The triumphs of a tender youth are fine', said the girl, 'but they're still not as strong as a champion.' 'Girl, my upbringing was good indeed', he said ... '), it may not be to lure Cú Chulainn into revealing his pedigree, as Findon suggests, so much as to flirt by his terms: to defy him and to insult him, and thus be more attractive to him. His enthusiastic response of romantic interest to verbal abuse is symptomatic of a more thorough masochism which I find in his character in *SC*; Emer is the willing sadist for this round.

It will also be observed that like Delilah's in Judges (below), Emer's questions in *TEm* are singular in aim: she wants to know the source of his strength. Cú Chulainn is evasive in his answers (he could hardly be less evasive than Samson!), and is not tempted to reveal information

---

36. *TEm*, p. 30.
37. Dunn, *Cattle-raids*, p. 72.
38. *TEm*, p. 28.
39. *TEm*, p. 28.

that can kill him. Furthermore, Emer seems immediately to be more loyal to Cú Chulainn than to whatever party she had previously belonged to. Thus, for both Cú Chulainn's vigilance and Emer's underlying loyalty, our final picture of Emer is not as a betrayer, whether or not we think of Delilah as one. That is, their means are the same but not their ends: Emer has no ulterior motives, and pursues the dynamic between them for her own reasons.

As will be discussed with reference to Delilah, 'betrayal' is a term the sense of which depends on its context. Because the reader knows that Emer is a 'good guy' (despite her arguably Otherworld origins and femme fatale tendencies—Emer demands that Cú Chulainn, among other things, go sleepless for the better part of a year before he can have her), and because the reader may not identify with the Ulaid implicitly (as a Hebrew Bible reader may with the Jews), he may not think of this as betrayal. And yet, the bottom line is the same between the two couples: the woman offers herself to him as long as he is willing to die for it (nearly).

Narratologically, Emer is consistently stronger than Cú Chulainn in this part of *TEm*: First, she does the looking while he is looked at. When he arrives, she asks the questions and he answers.[40] While they riddle on equal terms, she does the insulting and he draws closer. Raymond Cormier has also observed Cú Chulainn's passivity: 'We may find a hint of the ludicrous in a meeting where the aggressive beauty manages to outmanoeuvre the great hero.'[41] As Bal and Crenshaw have noted about Samson's wooing (below), so is it worth noting with reference to Cormier that Cú Chulainn is in a traditionally female position, attempting to ensnare by concealing information (including his very name, in their wooing conversation) and retaining mystery. Part of the significance of this sex reversal is its relation to masochism. Freud writes of masochist fantasies that they 'place the subject in a characteristically feminine position'.[42] I believe their relationship is charged this way at this point.

40. For another narratological analysis of this, see J. Findon, 'Negotiating Female Territory: Cú Chulainn's Journeys in Tochmarc Emire', in R. Black, W. Gillies and R. Ó Maolalaigh (eds.), *Celtic Connections: Proceedings of the 10th International Congress of Celtic Studies* (East Linton: Tuckwell Press, 1999).

41. Cormier, 'Cu Chulainn', p. 120.

42. S. Freud, 'The Economic Problem of Masochism', in S. Freud, *The Standard Edition of the Complete Works of Sigmund Freud. XIX. The Ego and the Id*

'Atchí Cú Chulainn bruinne na hingine dar sedlachaib a léned'[43] ('Cú Chulainn caught sight of the girl's breasts over the top of her dress').[44] Their flirtation revolves around the audacity and intimacy of his repeated remark. 'Caín in mag so mag alchuing' ('I see a sweet country. I could rest my weapon there').[45] This is a suspense formula. His waiting and constancy of stare switch him to the subject position in the narrative as his remarks go on, undeterred by the obstacles Emer sets before him. Like Samson, when Cú Chulainn's mind is set on a thing, there is no stopping him. Both heroes experience *amour fou*, an over-valuation of the sexual object, and reach a point where looking becomes an end in itself, seemingly.

The other girls with Emer speculate on the dialogue between the thus far nameless young warrior and Emer. Forgall Manach, the prospective father-in-law, appears and he sets out to thwart them.

If we decide to compare the trickster aspect of Samson's character (below) with Cú Chulainn, the episodes to focus on in *TEm* are those concerning Forgall Manach. It is between the two of them that we see the most trickery and countertrickery in *TEm*. First, Forgall Manach comes in disguise to Ulster and tricks Conchobor into believing he is someone else. Then he tricks Conchobor into sending Cú Chulainn away and, he hopes, to his death. Emer works to betray her father and help Cú Chulainn. Cú Chulainn's agreeing to go away turns out to be countertrickery: the episode is his training-in-arms, and Forgall Manach's malicious advice will have had a beneficent effect on Cú Chulainn.

Forgall Manach is not acting to protect his daughter, but out of fear for his own life. This self-interest echoes that of the Ulaid when they seem to be looking out for Cú Chulainn's loneliness at the beginning of this tale, but are in fact only concerned that he leave them an heir.

Cú Chulainn sets off to look for Scáthach, first with his comrades and then, as a result of Forgall Manach's trick, alone.[46] Lonely for a mo-

---

and Other Works (London: Hogarth Press and The Institute of Psycho-Analysis, 1961), p. 162.

43. *TEm*, p. 31.

44. Kinsella, *The Táin*, p. 27.

45. Kinsella, *The Táin*, p. 27, using *dindshenchas* paragraphs to adapt this.

46. This is a section which Kinsella does not translate, making constant a picture of Cú Chulainn as an invulnerable loner, which sits perhaps more easily with his legendary status.

ment, he reacts with disgust to see himself feeling: 'Anais íarom de suidiu ó ro airigestar a immarchor & a anéolus'[47] ('Then he got up since he noticed his straying and his ignorance'). (Later in the *Tain* when he delays his campaign by sleeping with Fedelm Noíchride he feels the same disgrace. In both cases he has let only a ray of the personal into his patriarchy-serving mode.)

Then Cú Chulainn meets and tames a lion—or almost a lion: 'While he was there he saw a terrible great beast like a lion coming towards him.'[48] His relationship with the beast is as close to love as anything that he experiences: according to the text, he feels an equal coexistence with, and affection for the 'lion'. The taming of the 'lion' may be said to echo his triumph of riddling and taming Emer. But, perhaps more strongly, the 'lion' seems to be made of the same stuff as Cú Chulainn. We see the echo of Cú Chulainn's strength in the harmony with which he moves on the beast, riding him effortlessly.

Although the episode seems to have no place in the narrative— Kinsella leaves it out entirely—it is fair to assume that it does have some significance. We will see that both Samson and Cú Chulainn relate well to animals in general (remembering not only Samson's lion, but his foxes, and the jawbone of an ass) to the exclusion or detriment of people. As the onlookers jeer at Cú Chulainn and the 'lion' ('ar ingnáthaigi leo in phéist erchóitech ucut do beith i ngíallnai do duine'[49] ['how unusual it was for them—that dangerous beast serving a man']), so is Samson laughed at in alternation with his feats of revenge with animals. The hero has the last laugh in both cases.

Cú Chulainn finally reaches Scáthach's fort, where he encounters more obstacles, despite some of her helpful disciples. As he approaches, Scáthach sends her daughter Úathach to meet him. Úathach is gripped with passion. Cú Chulainn continues passively as Scáthach calmly advises Úathach to sleep with him. (As with Emer, his reaction to her is not described, he is the looked-at, not the 'looker'.) Between them is another trick and countertrick. Úathach pretends to be a servant in order to be near him. Cú Chulainn then manipulates her and the situation until she volunteers the information he needs: she tells him

47. *TEm*, p. 47.
48. 'A mbaí and co n-accai bíastai úathmair máir amal leoman ina dochum' (*TEm*, p. 47).
49. *TEm*, p. 47.

how to trap her mother Scáthach. This scene is an echo of Emer's desire for Cú Chulainn which also conquers any family loyalty she might have had.

Another echo happens simultaneously: Cú Chulainn pinches Úathach and as the whole fort rises up in reaction, Cú Chulainn kills one of Scáthach's strongmen. He then offers to fill the strongman's position, as he once replaced Culann's hound after killing it, to become the Hound of Culann. These last few episodes are thus a reminder of his first initiation. This time he is not pledging Conchobor's fraternity, but Scáthach's. It may be that his childhood surrounded by other young warriors needs to come to an end for him to be an appropriate masculine heterosexual hero, and his domain is filled with women.[50] In any case, this is his 'training-in-arms', by definition an initiation. But perhaps the more significant initiation happening is his integration into society, a process being marked by the course of females in a faraway land.[51] From these adventures he can return a trained warrior but also a would-be Ulsterman, having gone abroad, faced Otherworld odds, and returned, learning that he must obey laws over his own desire. This is also arguably the 'moral' of the Samson story.

The meeting with Aífe is another episode where Cú Chulainn seems to be a trickster, using information and not just strength to conquer a warrior. He tricks her with a 'look behind you!' gag, taking her by the breasts and threatening her with his 'naked sword' (*claideb urnocht*). Then he sleeps with her, and demands a son. Whether or not humour is intended by the description of this little James Bond who pulls tricks on larger-than-life women, turning violence into sexuality, is difficult to know. Certainly the episode asks many questions: How are we to understand his sudden loyalty to Scáthach, or his desire to sleep with Aífe? Why should he choose *her* to bear him a son and not Scáthach?

When Cú Chulainn leaves, Scáthach delivers the promised prophecy which includes the lines

> alone no matter where you stand ...
> alone and ringed by envy...

50. This would seem to agree with a Freudian reading of sexual development. Cf. S. Freud, 'Three Essays on the Theory of Sexuality', in *idem*, *On Sexuality: Three Essays on the Theory of Sexuality and Other Works* (London: Penguin Books, 1991), pp. 88-126.

51. Findon also suggests this in 'Negotiating', *passim*.

your career full of triumph and women's love
what matter how short.[52]

Clearly, these are meant to be encouraging words, and, within the terms of the honour code, his future is a totally heroic one. And yet, it is a hero's bane to be alone always. It does not demand too radical a reading of this prophecy to understand it as a mixed blessing: to be envied and alone is much how Cú Chulainn *already* is among the Ulstermen. This prophecy may not be what Cú Chulainn wants. Although it is perhaps irrelevant to the nature of prophecy whether or not the subject wants his destiny, what is worth pointing out, however, is the distance between that projected glory and his own desire, which might otherwise be assumed to be identical. We do not hear a reaction to this prophecy but we know, even from this tale, that in fact Cú Chulainn seeks the company and audience of many people. And while he does indeed like to win battles, being the envy of people has caused stress for him already in this tale, as it does 'subsequently'.[53]

Thus, this prophecy, which marks the end of his initiation, serves to confirm Cú Chulainn's particular role in the society to which he is about to return. As much as any martial techniques, this lesson is what *TEm* will teach him: it is his job to be alone in his career full of triumph.

Next, he comes across a maiden in distress, Derbforgaill, kidnapped by the Fomorians. He rescues her, and later leaves without identifying himself, in a passage that seems to progress as if Emer did not exist, judging from the aplomb with which Derbforgaill is betrothed to him. Later, at the time he and the girl have arranged to meet, he sees two birds. He shoots at them with his sling and two beautiful women appear: Derbforgaill and her maid. She has been wounded by the slingshot and he sucks the stone out, informing her that now he cannot marry her since he has drunk her blood. It seems as if he has contrived the situation in order to reject her honourably (in a kind of *geis*-avoidance logic), although it is not clear whether he knows she is one of the birds.

Cú Chulainn finally makes it back to Emer, but is reminded tauntingly by Bricriu that Conchobor, as king, has the right and duty to sleep with each new bride before the groom does. Cú Chulainn is enraged.

52. Kinsella, *The Táin*, pp. 34-37 (cf. *TEm*, pp. 57-60 for Irish).

53. I use inverted commas here and elsewhere because I am referring not to the chronological sequence of manuscripts but events within the 'implied chronology' of the Ulster Cycle. I borrow this respectfully from Findon's writing.

Like Samson with the foxes, Cú Chulainn conquers his anger at this consummation-delay by gathering all the animals and birds in sight from Slíab Fúait. In this case he acts under very similar circumstances to Samson: both have been thwarted in having the woman who is rightfully theirs, and react in a warp-spasm of anger.

These last two episodes in *TEm* have a common thread. In reading *SC* I draw a distinction between Cú Chulainn's achievements depending on where (cosmologically) his success occurs. I find in that tale that success seems to be tied to his time in the Otherworld. So in *TEm* he meets with success against the Fomorians in defending Derbforgaill on a scale not matched by his experience in Ireland. We may compare the welcome and betrothal from Rúad, Derbforgaill's father, with Ulster's desire to protect and conceal *its* daughters. His masculine desire is met outside of society and thwarted within.

Findon is right to look for a progression of types of women that Cú Chulainn encounters in *TEm*,[54] but it may not be so easy to conclude anything consistent on that basis. Findon's approach is feminist and therefore, although we are looking at the same coin, each of us has called a different side. I think Cú Chulainn's character, and especially his weakness and masculinity, deserves more attention as the fulcrum of the Ulster Cycle. Thus, where Findon sees the women in *TEm* as the centre, I see them as litmus tests for Cú Chulainn's development.

Once Emer has been accepted by the Ulaid as the appropriate wife for Cú Chulainn, even within *TEm*, she has ceased to be the exogamous bride. Emer is the contrast to other women, the one he will earn only after a process of initiation with several other women in a pattern comparable to Samson's (below). Findon explains:

> The persistence of female images along the way [in *TEm*] signals the hero's need for a journey into the female in all its aspects before he can emerge as a complete hero, ready for marriage to an equal. He must first pass through a landscape ... of strong legendary women, and then learn to cope with a variety of strong women in real life, before he is finally ready to win the ideal wife.[55]

I would add that it is only during that interval that she has *become* the ideal wife, in a way she was not at the beginning (perhaps echoing the MS transmission!) Indeed, Emer is so much a part of Ulster society by

---

54. Findon, 'Negotiating', *passim*.
55. Findon, 'Negotiating', p. 14.

the end that, despite her usual outspokenness, she does not protest against having to have sex with Ulster's king. So, although she represents Cú Chulainn's masculine desire in the first part of *TEm*, by the end she signifies patriarchy, is an ambassador of the Ulaid, and the proof that his long journey ends with a return to the 'Law of the Father'.

3. *Aided Óenfir Aífe*

'The Death of Aífe's Only Son' is not about Aífe. Aífe belongs to *Tochmarc Emire*, and to Cú Chulainn's martial and sexual initiation that begins there with herself and Scáthach. In *TEm*, in a move more out of Laurel and Hardy than the honour code of Ulster, Cú Chulainn tricks Aífe and demands, among other things, that she bear him a son. Seven years later this son, Connla, appears to the Ulaid.

Aided Óenfir Aífe (*AOA*), also included in Kinsella's *Táin* (39-45), chronicles the return of Connla, the son Cú Chulainn had fathered with Aífe during his training-in-arms with Scáthach.[56]

Here we see the closest interaction between father, son, and the Ulster society by whose demands Cú Chulainn must abide. Here, too, Emer also has an important role. It is a brief tale but central to any understanding of Cú Chulainn's character as well as of the 'contract' with Ulster he is part of.

> [The conception of Connla is (re)stated.] Seven years later the boy comes looking for his father. He approaches the Ulaid in a bronze boat and performs feats from that distance. The Ulaid are concerned because he is so capable and yet so young. They despatch someone to talk to him—to invite him warmly to land—but Connla embarrasses him with his refusal. The boy humiliates the next Ulsterman sent to meet him as well. It is thus time for Cú Chulainn to defend Ulster's honour. Emer tries to restrain him because she knows that this is his son. Cú Chulainn ignores her advice but agrees that this is his son he is out to kill. He goes down to see Connla. They meet and exchange blows. They seem evenly matched until Cú Chulainn uses his *gae bolga* which only he possesses. He slices Connla up and carries the boy's nearly dead body to the Ulaid on shore announcing it as that of his son. The Ulaid mourn: they could have ruled Europe with that boy. The boy greets them all lovingly, and his father, and dies.

The boy is recognizable as Cú Chulainn's son, not only in his strength and dexterity but by his very youth, which has always been a marker of

---

56. Here also I rely on van Hamel's edition in *Compert Con Culainn*.

Cú Chulainn's identity. Connla's youth is immediately manifest by whimsy and impulsiveness, as was Cú Chulainn's; when we meet Connla he is knocking birds out of the sky and then bringing them back to life, all from his bronze boat (a marker of his Otherworld origin). He is already playing with life and death in a feat that is like his father's bird games in *Serglige Con Culainn*. In that story, as in this, the birds' lives are not unconnected to the lives of their hunters.

Many Ulster Cycle stories open with an enunciation of Cú Chulainn's superiority, and *AOA* begins by establishing Connla's. Like his father, Connla needs to show off, and, like his father, he makes the Ulaid uncomfortable sometimes even as they want to admire him. When Cú Chulainn is too beautiful the Ulaid try to marry him off to prevent him from devastating their own wives. He may be their foster son and defender, but their attitude to him might be described as wary. Here Connla threatens the Ulaid directly.

Although Connla is as unusual a boy as the Ulaid have ever seen, it does not occur to them that he is Cú Chulainn's son. He is just some unforgivably arrogant and gifted boy in a bronze boat. As the title is a trick (why not *Aided Óenfir Con Culainn*, 'The Death of Cú Chulainn's Only Son'?) so is Connla's very presence there a trick. He is sent to confront the Ulaid and to trigger one of their flaws. (Again, we see the pressure on characters in the Ulster Cycle and its narrators. The story of a seemingly endless and finally futile cattle-raid is one of their products—as are the 'pangs' of the Ulaid and their taboos [*gessa*] [which other, non-Ultonian early Irish characters also suffer from]. These bizarre narratological devices prevent characters from doing what they want and need to do to survive.)

This short story presents succinctly all the paradox of the inevitability of the end of Ulster as well as elaborating on the contrast between personal and public responsibility in Cú Chulainn's character. Each step in *AOA* leads inevitably to the next, until Ulster's destiny is exposed. It is to be found in this short story because this story alone is about an heir to the prosperity the Ulstermen have known with Cú Chulainn in their midst; without an heir that prosperity dies with Cú. What makes *AOA* tragedy is just this inevitability: the characters do what they must do along the way, although each move ensures their demise. The whole story has the tension of the unfolding of a single *geis*, as in Conaire's career in *Togail Bruidne Da Derga*.

The boy appears and insults Condere, then Conall Cernach. By the reckoning of the honour code, Ulster's honour must be avenged. Even according to early Irish law, an insult, be it by a boy or a bee, must be avenged. Thus the first obligation arises, put forth by the Ulaid:

1. Ulster suffers if honour is not avenged.

Cú Chulainn shows up to address this. He approaches the boy whimsically—*oca chluichiu*, performing feats as he came—which serves to confirm that Cú Chulainn and Connla are indeed father and son. Emer hangs on Cú Chulainn as women do whenever he is about to do something rash, that is, something which will do more long-term damage than the short-term damage his action will prevent (cf. *Brislech Mór Maige Muirtheimne (Aided Chon Chulainn)* 'The Death of Cú Chulainn'). Emer advises him not to kill his son: 'Ná téig sís!... Mac duit fil tís. Ná fer fingail immot óenmac.... Bad Cú Chulainn cloadar!'[57] ('Don't go down there! That's your son there. Don't commit kin-slaying against your own son.... Let Cú Chulainn listen!')

Emer has produced the second obligation:

2. A man must not kill his son.

As Joanne Findon makes clear in her article 'A Woman's Words: Emer versus Cú Chulainn in *Aided Óenfir Aífe*', early Irish law is behind Emer in this judgment.[58] *Fingal* (kin-slaying) was a crime so heinous that legislation could not be devised for it.[59] Or, it was so logically impossible to a society structured around kin-groups that it could not be dealt with: kin cannot take revenge on itself. *Fingal* itself is thus a paradox of revenge, its punishment built in, where the crime actually exceeds the potential for justice or retribution. This is also part of the paradox of *AOA*: the woe for the death of Connla exceeds the justice of his being punished for what amounts to hubris.

---

57. A.G. van Hamel, 'Aided Óenfir Aífe', in *Compert*, p. 14.
58. Findon, 'A Woman's Words', pp. 143-45, 146.
59. The laws, however, do not convict Cú Chulainn of *fingal*, basically because neither party was clear on who was what to whom—an ambiguity that the title reinforces. In the late text 'Cuchulinn and Conlaech' 'Cuchulinn was then sued by the men of Ulster' although he killed Connla 'in mistake'. ('For he had slain him in mistake and he was an innocent person in the guise of a guilty person, although it was combat'; J.G. O'Keeffe, 'Cuchulinn and Conlaech', *Ériu* 1/1 [1904], pp. 123-27 [127]). Findon ('A Woman's Words', p.144) points out that according to a tract from the *Corpus Iuris Hibernicae*, Cú Chulainn's action was not quite *fingal* because, among other things, the boy did not acknowledge tribe or family.

Findon's main point is that Emer is the voice of law in a fight between law and the heroic honour code. Emer is also presenting the case for the Ulaid's longer term need for an heir and this, I think, exceeds in importance her role as mother-figure and general lover of good causes. The narrator would seem to agree that Emer is right; her being ignored has tragic consequences.

Cú Chulainn does indeed ignore her, with his own obligation:

3.   (A man cannot listen to women when) his people must be defended.

Connla's obligation is next:

4.   Connla cannot identify himself.

This restriction is built into Connla at his conception. Presumably Cú Chulainn has it in mind that Connla should establish himself as a warrior on his own merit and be known only to Cú Chulainn through the ring he gives Aífe. But the ring is never mentioned again. His being unknown means he can be killed.

One reading is that Cú Chulainn is setting Connla up to be killed from birth, part of a long anger at the Ulaid which he celebrates when he presents them with Connla's body: 'Aso mo macsa dúib, a Ultu' ('Here's my son, Ulstermen'). This also would explain his gaiety at approaching the boy, and his lack of remorse at his death. This illustrates the theme of the hero I have located (and will expand on): the conflict in Cú Chulainn is between his masochistic instinct and serving the Law of the Father, his contract with the Ulstermen. Elizabeth Gray observes the same conflict in slightly different terms: 'Connla's death is tragedy arising from the equally legitimate claims of personal, familial, and tribal honour, which neither Cú Chulainn nor his son seeks to avoid'.[60] In fact, he acts to undermine the weight of expectation against him.

When each of the characters has produced his card the whole house collapses: Cú Chulainn kills Connla, and immediately the restrictions are reversed:

4a.   Connla is identified: 'Aso mo macsa dúib, a Ultu!'

---

60. E. Gray, 'Lug and CúChulainn: King and Warrior, God and Man', *Studia Celtica* 24 (1989), pp. 38-52 (48).

3a.   Cú's people would have been better defended if Cú Chulainn
       had not killed Connla (and if he had listened to a woman).

2a.   A man has killed his son.

1a.   Ulster suffers more, her honour avenged.

The chiasmus suggests the futility and the ultimate tragedy: suffering
has matched, then exceeded benefit. Emer's point alone remains—as
undone as the others in action, but still true.

Here, Findon should be mentioned again as she notices the women
behind the action.[61] Aífe takes the title and Scáthach has provided the
difference between Cú Chulainn and Connla's training that allows Cú
Chulainn to kill him. He cries, 'Is ed ón tra ... náro múin Scáthach
domsa!' ('This is something Scáthach didn't teach me!')

Findon finds that Emer is 'the voice for [*AOA*'s] powerful critique of
the warrior ethic'.[62] While I would agree that Emer's voice is loud, I
think the whole story is carefully constructed and does not depend on
her ignored advice alone. I would also argue that a woman plays this
role not to represent the eternal mother–child link of pathos, but because the voice of restraint must come from someone outside that warrior ethic. All the Ulaid are extinct, men and women alike. Therefore it
seems logically inconsistent to suggest that the Ulstermen are being
made to seem anachronistic and the Ulsterwomen everlasting. (If this
were so then the Ulsterwomen would not be so utterly petty in *Serglige
Con Culainn*, *Fled Bricrend* and elsewhere!) Rather, the warrior ethic
must be critiqued by someone out of its bounds: a woman, Emer.

Connla's death does not directly affect Cú Chulainn, the very person
Emer would seem to be protecting. Cú Chulainn is not weeping alongside the Ulstermen at the end; in fact, it is possible to interpret his last
words to his son as gloating about having slain him. This is a particularly noticeable absence in a literature prone to laments (when condi-
tions are favourable) and indeed (another incarnation of) Cú Chulainn
is capable of remorse when he mourns the death of Ferdia, after he
reluctantly kills him in the *Táin*.

So why is it called 'The Death of Aífe's Only Son'? In addition to the
other paradoxes, the title supplies an echo of the shock that the Ulaid
receive. Just as they do not know until he dies that he is Cú's son, so is
the reader in the dark until he reads it, confirmed by Cú's own ejacu-

61. Cf. Findon, 'A Woman's Words', *passim*.
62. Findon, 'A Woman's Words', p. 139.

latory 'Voiçi!' The title also commemorates the boy's small contribution to the plot: the concealment of his identity (which meant his death). The title preserves that secret.

Interlude I

At this point I would like to offer an interlude in the Samson/Cú Chulainn comparison. As it is as important to discuss the stories as to compare them, it is worth including another biblical parallel relevant to *AOA*, although it is not about Samson. The 'Binding of Isaac' (Gen. 22) is another story of filial sacrifice.

Out of loyalty to God, Abraham agrees to kill his own son. The story of Abraham and Isaac in Genesis differs significantly from any early Irish story, of course. The most obvious difference to *AOA* is that Isaac does not die; God stops Abraham before it is too late. The main reason for this may be summarized as that Isaac had a better father than Connla had, and Abraham an even better one. That is, Isaac does not have to be killed because his father is a good man, and because God looks after Abraham.

The test that God puts to Abraham is twofold: 'Is it to test Abraham's faith that God will not go back on His promise, that somehow His design can be trusted? Or is it to test Abraham's unquestioning obedience, his faithfulness rather than his faith ...?[63] (In other words, God asks, 'Does he have faith that I won't let the boy be killed?' and/or 'Will he do anything I say?') Abraham says yes to both, of course, and his faithfulness and faith are well placed.

If Cú Chulainn's defence of his people's honour is a kind of duty of faith, a part of a contract like the one between Abraham and God, then Cú Chulainn's faith in that contract is betrayed. That this faith can be betrayed at all is part of the fault of the whole warrior ethic whose self-destruct mechanism is being explored in *AOA*.

Less significant differences between this and the biblical story are that Isaac is clearly only a victim and not an *agent provocateur*. The relationships are also clearly defined: Isaac is Abraham's son. If nothing else he is that. Equally, Abraham is God's servant. He does not show off, he is not amused by his task. God appreciates his duty to him, but that devotion would be of little worth if it were not clear that

63. W. Gunther Plaut, B.J. Bamberger and W.W. Hallo (eds., trans., commentary), *The Torah: A Modern Commentary* (New York: Union of American Hebrew Congregations, 1981), p. 149.

Abraham loves Isaac. God finds that his 'honour' is best served by the willingness to kill more than the actual killing itself.

This cannot exist in Ulster: an occasion for slaying is rarely missed. Furthermore, the Ulaid are not in a position to show mercy: they do not know what will happen if they spare Connla; only Cú Chulainn does, or seems to. Ulster is not served until blood is actually spilt: until then they are weak, vulnerable, and stuck. Inflexibility is the key to most extinction, and this inflexibility ensures theirs. Indeed, the Isaac episode secures Abraham's place forever ('I will ... make your descendants as numerous as the stars of heaven and the sands of the seashore ... because you have obeyed my command'). By contrast, the death of Connla ensures that the Ulaid will be one generation long.

Isaac's mother, as Connla's, is absent from the whole episode, but in both stories a new voice speaks up to stop the killing: 'Abraham! Abraham!... Do not raise your hand against the boy, or do anything to him.' In Genesis, it is an angel of the LORD who speaks, whom Abraham heeds immediately. In *AOA* it is Emer, whom Cú Chulainn ignores at his peril.

Thus, if *AOA* is read as an analogue to Genesis 22 we see that the messages of mercy are contorted or absent from the narrative entirely (as they were in the Jonah/Columba comparison). Emer, who might seem at first reading the voice of 'typical womanish pacifism', incapable of grasping men's honour codes, is in fact the analogue of an angel by the terms of this comparison. The possibility alone of this reading adds further credibility to the theme of Emer's strength in the plot, and her growing connection to Ulster establishment, while being outside its warrior code.

4. *Serglige Con Culainn*

The composite picture of Cú Chulainn from the Ulster Cycle is one of a fierce strongman with a capricious bent. From a twenty-first-century aesthetic standpoint it might be said that he lacks humanity, signs of weakness, three dimensions, or even the literary colour of an ancient Greek hero. Some of those levels are indeed present, however, encoded in the layers that make Early Irish literature so unusual, sometimes so conservative, and even inscrutable.

Translated in popular tradition and songs as 'The Sickbed of Cuchulainn', or 'The Wasting Sickness', this story charts an adventure in the life of an older Cú Chulainn.[64] Emer is now a fixture in his life (and part of Ulster) and not a maiden to be wooed away from her father. Her story is now in a new context that involves emotional intrigue and a change of worlds. Gantz calls the story 'part myth, part history, part soap opera'.[65]

> Every year the Ulaid have an Óenach, a wonderful assembly where they can show off. One Óenach they are all gathered and a beautiful flock of birds flies overhead. All the Ulsterwomen want a pair of them, especially Cú Chulainn's own wife, Eithne Ingubai ('E'). Cú Chulainn reluctantly goes out to hunt them and gets them, but he fails to get a pair for his wife. Then two special birds fly by and Cú Chulainn goes after them, although E tries to discourage him from pursuing these. Cú Chulainn keeps missing until he pierces one of them.
>
> Then he falls asleep and two women come to him. They smile and beat him to the point of death, then go away. The Ulaid try to wake him (although E says not to disturb his vision). Cú Chulainn gets up then, but cannot speak and is taken away (in some sense) to An Téte Brecc for a year.
>
> One day, before the following year's assembly, as all the Ulaid are gathered round him, a visitor comes and promises that Cú Chulainn will be cured by the daughters of Áed Abrat, in his country. He says he will send Lí Ban to him. Before the man goes he says he is Óengus son of Áed Abrat.
>
> Cú Chulainn wakes up and goes to the pillarstone where he had fallen asleep the year before. Lí Ban comes on behalf of Labraid Lúathlám ar Claideb who offers Fann as a mate in exchange for Cú Chulainn's cooperation in fighting enemies; Lí Ban assures him he is up to it. He sends Lóeg on ahead, however, to check it out.

---

64. M. Dillon (ed.), *Serglige Con Culainn* (Dublin: DIAS, 1953). Gantz's translation (*Early Irish Myths*, pp. 153-78) is the most accessible, if far from perfect. Like Kinsella, Gantz does not bother translating sections that seem to him to be outwith the main scope of the story (mainly the section where Cú Chulainn gives instruction to Lugaid Reóderg).

65. Gantz, *Early Irish Myths*, p. 153. Dillon and others (including such varied scholars as Alfred Nutt and John Carey) have drawn attention to this tale, not for its information about how Cú Chulainn deals with women or how these dealings illustrate his character, but for its place in mythological tradition, and specifically as a vision of the Otherworld: 'It is not only an Ulster tale but also an Otherworld tale' (J. Carey, 'The Location of the Otherworld in Irish Tradition', *Éigse* 19 [1982], pp. 36-43). See also Proinsías Mac Cana, 'The Sinless Otherworld of Immram Brain', *Ériu* 27 (1976), pp. 95-115.

Lóeg goes with Lí Ban to the island and a house with 150 welcoming women. Lóeg is now willing to talk to Fann (who is very beautiful). Just then Labraid arrives and Lí Ban addresses him sweetly, although he is in a bad mood. He welcomes Lóeg when he hears who he is. Lóeg goes with Lí Ban back to Emain Macha and Cú Chulainn is strengthened to hear his story.

[At this point representatives from the four provinces of Ireland are gathered to dispute the high kingship. Cú Chulainn gets up from his sickbed and gives his foster son proverbial advice about good ruling and fairness.]

Cú Chulainn tells Lóeg to go to Emer (as his wife is now named) and tell her that the women of the *síd* have been visiting and that she should come. E chides Lóeg for not finding a cure for Cú Chulainn and delivers a lay to that end: that the Ulstermen let Cú Chulainn down generally, and she misses his being awake. Then she chides *him* for being in this state for love of a woman. She wakes him up by telling him how beautiful this world is.

Lí Ban is there to tell him how worthwhile a trip to the *síd* is. Again Lóeg is sent in his place because Cú Chulainn rejects going on a woman's invitation. This time Fann comes back quickly with Lóeg. Lóeg tells how spectacular it is there, at length. Cú Chulainn goes along and is welcomed. Cú Chulainn confronts the enemy as requested, slays many of them, and is needing the three-vat treatment[66] afterwards, so angry is he. Fann is very moved by Cú Chulainn's beauty. Cú Chulainn tells how he won the battle. Cú Chulainn spends a month and a night with Fann and at the end she says she will meet him anywhere; they arrange a tryst.

Emer finds out, however, and comes along with knives and a few friends. Fann sees her coming and is afraid. Cú Chulainn is nonplussed and tells her so. Emer says Cú Chulainn will not be rid of her so easily. He tells her Fann is perfect for him. Emer reminds him of her love and he grows sad. They all discuss who will leave whom. Fann finally goes back to Manannan (whom she had left). Cú Chulainn suffers in his way and Emer seeks Conchobor's help in getting Cú Chulainn back to Emain Macha. Eventually, with some magic, Emer forgets her jealousy and Cú Chulainn forgets Fann.

Each text about Cú Chulainn provides another glimpse at his character, another interpretation or reading of the culture's hero. In *Serglige Con Culainn*, Cú Chulainn is a prized warrior. The story begins with a display of martial prowess by the Ulaid, as they are gathered at an

---

66. When Cú Chulainn gets very angry, it becomes necessary to submerge him in vats of water until his temper is normalized. The first two vats usually boil or explode.

assembly designed to give each warrior of Ulster a chance to 'boast of his valour and exhibit his triumphs. [They] put the tongues of those they had killed in their pouches—some threw in cattle tongues to augment the count...'[67]

A display of boasting that supplements the number of dead men's tongues with cow tongues? (One is reminded of the part of the book of Jonah where the Ninevites so totally repent that even their cattle dress in sackcloth. Some scholars cry: that is an even more sincere statement of repentance! Others say: livestock in sackcloth? Humour!) In *SC* we may have reason to consider this display of tongues an exaggeration, one of several examples of the Ulstermen's petty competitions. Certainly the Ulsterwomen who come on the scene immediately afterwards are considered petty by Cú Chulainn for just such competing, and he is reluctant to serve them for this reason. In *Fled Bricrend*, their competition is even more likely to be intended as humorous as 150 Ulsterwomen gather up their skirts and race because they have been made to think that the winner will be queen. It is parody because it is funny, funny because it is exaggeration and because it is rough-and-tumble when we expect dignity.

It is not as easy to dismiss the opening scene of *SC* as parody. Indeed the narrator seems impressed by the bounty and excessive wealth of the assembly where 'there would be nothing but meetings and games and amusements and entertainments and eating and feasting'.[68] In the context of this tale, however, which focuses on relations between men and women and jealousy, we cannot fail to compare the boasting of the men with the boasting of the women. The likely laughability of the women squabbling for birds sets off the laughability of the other half's competition. Men and women and the games they play to impress each other and themselves is at least as much part of the story of *SC* as are the poignant love and sacrifice scenes at the end.

The exposition also describes the Ulsterwomen's love-disfigurements which are something of a match to the Ulstermen's 'pangs', both of which are not special to this tale of the Ulster Cycle. In both, a

---

67. Gantz, *Early Irish Myths*, p. 155. 'Ba bés léu dano di ág inna comraime ferthain ind óenaig .i. rind aulabra cec fhir no marbtais do thabairt inna mbossán. Ocus dobertis aurlabrai na cethrae do ilugud na comram hi sudi' (Dillon, p. 1).

68. Gantz, *Early Irish Myths*, p. 155. 'ní rabe isin bith ní dognethe in n-eret sin léu acht cluchi & chéti & ánius & aíbinnius & longad & tomail' (Dillon, *Serglige*, p. 1).

sympathetic but involuntary physical ailment matches a poor but irresistible emotional/mental state. Seen in the context of *SC* as a whole, this mention of the Ulsterwomen's disfigurement illustrates the match of the physical and the emotional, and, on the other plane, the parallel of women and men. More obviously, the 'blemishes' show the intensity of love and its connection to getting hurt: pain is connected to love.

It is significant that *SC* opens with this exposition. It does not begin simply with Cú Chulainn out shooting some birds. Rather he comes in as a peripheral member of a group of men and women showing off, preoccupied with competition and looking silly for taking themselves so seriously. He is not part of it ('Have the sluts of Ulaid nothing better for us than to hunt their birds?'), but he must meet the Ulaid's expectations and as always he must compromise his own instincts to serve them.

The exposition shows that Cú Chulainn loves Emer or, to read more cynically, is afraid of her: 'Then do not be angry. When birds come ... you will have the most beautiful pair.'[69] Emer begins (named Eithne) as a contrast to the women of Ulster, their superior. In the end, she is a representative of Ireland, a contrast to the women of the *síd*, and their inferior. She evokes in him something other than the contempt that the Ulsterwomen do. But it is in going off to deliver on the above promise that he runs into the arms of the other women. He says twice that Emer is angry, although she denies this, and denies jealousy on the grounds that her love is special and without comparison. Perhaps Cú Chulainn is right, that she is angry now and angry later, jealous and competing in love.

He sees the perfect birds to present to his wife and he tries to shoot them down for her. Yet, for the first time in his life he cannot shoot straight. The bird-hunting that he did for the Ulsterwomen was easy and unimportant to him. Now he is in a position where he needs to appease his wife. And now, his martial success fails him. The birds embarrass Cú Chulainn in front of his wife and cause tension in his marriage while leading him to doubt his prowess as a warrior. In so doing they create a space for themselves in his life: he now needs a woman to love him and be proud of him, and a battle to win. This is just what they suggest and provide. (Since the birds are either Lí Ban and Fand themselves or their agents, we can consider the *síd* women the source for their effect on the narrative.)

69. Gantz, *Early Irish Myths*, p. 156. 'Nábad olc do menma trá ... Día tísat éoin ... in dá én ba háildem díb duticfat' (Dillon, *Serglige*, p. 2).

He wounds one bird and then soon falls asleep. 'While sleeping he saw two women approach ...' These women meet the hero of the Ulaid, whip him to the point of death, and smile. Why do they smile? In taking some possible guesses at the answer we may illumine some of the more obscure aspects of this bizarre situation.

1. Maybe they are enjoying watching him suffer. (Is he suffering? It does not say he is suffering.)
2. Maybe they are doing what they know is good for him (leading him into a shamanistic trance, for example, as Carey suggests[70]) and smile benevolently, Cú Chulainn's welfare in mind.
3. Maybe hurting is a good thing in itself in their world (or less likely, smiling is a sad thing).
4. Maybe they are acting according to an understanding with Cú Chulainn whereby hurting him is what they all want.

Which (if any) of these answers agrees with their actions in the rest of the text? The first answer seems wrong on the basis of information revealed later in the story: they later say 'Not to harm you did we come, but to seek your friendship'. Indeed a reading of flat-out abuse where the smiles are a sign of sadism is wrong because Cú Chulainn is somehow complicit in this mugging. These are the women he does finally go home with.

Reading sadomasochism in their behaviour makes the episode another case of the *amour fou* fantasy. This is what Cormier is doing when he writes, 'There seem to be a certain amount of sexual wishful thinking in the dream.'[71] As I will illustrate in relation to Samson, this agreement to abuse in a sexual context is an appealing concept to an overworked hero-strongman. If abusive women are not implicitly attractive, they are from Cú Chulainn's experience, even with Emer. In *TEm* she asks him to earn her love by a year's sleep deprivation, among other things—a situation hardly less cruel, and hardly less irresistible to Cú Chulainn. (At that point he and Emer were courting, and now he is courting [and being courted by] Fand and Lí Ban, if on a more fantastic level.)

70. J. Carey, 'Cú Chulainn as Ailing Hero' (paper given at 10th ICCS, 1995; proceedings forthcoming).
71. Cormier, 'Cú Chulainn', p. 126.

The link of combat and flirtation fits well within the context of Early Irish literature where the metaphor of one for the other comes up again and again, as it has already several times in this tale. That the word *comrac* is sometimes used both for martial and sexual encounters (as in the *Táin*: Cú Chulainn and Findabair, Cú Chulainn killing Ferdia)[72] is a good indication of the value put on strife as part of attraction.[73] Call it abuse or sauciness, this dynamic is part of the interest value of the dialogues between most women and men in early Irish literature. They are not usually nice to each other.

Moreover, Cú Chulainn does not or cannot ask them to stop. What is he doing as they smile and 'beat him for such a long time that there was scarcely any life left in him'?[74] As with Samson, we must ask whether something can be called betrayal or abuse if there is no indication that the one abused is not complicit in the act. (Early Irish law had this stipulation in cases where abuse was far more likely the case. If a woman screams for help while being raped it makes her case stronger, as in the Bible. Both societies would seem to agree that the victim must establish him- or herself as such vociferously.)[75] Whether he is partly complying with or enjoying the attack, it is clear later that he does at least briefly mistrust them, suggesting he was not totally pleased with his abuse, if only in retrospect.

We have seen that Cú Chulainn's responsibility as strongman of Ulster is great. The Ulstermen have him so much under their power that when their women want birds to adorn them, he must be the bowman. Even then, he cannot please everyone; first of all his own interests (here, his rapport with his wife) must fall by the wayside. His whimsical nature as it appears in earlier stages of his career is not part of his characterization in *SC*. His life is wholly a service to the Ulaid and a meeting of their expectations. This is the Law of the Father for Cú Chulainn.

---

72. I owe the insight of vocabulary to Patricia Kelly.

73. *DIL* defines *comrac* as an '(act of) meeting; encounter…"to unite"… single combat …"to rape"…' (p. 142). The word *dingbáil* also has a range of meanings which implies a link between worthiness as a mate and hostility or opposition (although these are not its only meanings). According to *DIL*, it can mean 'keeping aloof' and 'used of an enemy, passes into sense of *holding one's own against*, and hence by degrees to that of being a match for, an equal to' (p. 216).

74. Gantz, *Early Irish Myths*, p. 157.

75. This point is discussed in D. Ó Corráin, 'An dlí agus an sean-tiomna', *Léachtaí Cholm Cille* 20 (1990), pp. 32-48.

Fand and Lí Ban offer him a chance to rebel from those expectations
and that Law: a chance to be weak, to fail and achieve some degree of
normalcy as a man, and not only as a hero. Perhaps this is what the
mysterious Óengus mac Áed Abrat means when he promises 'they
would heal you, the daughters of Áed Abrat', when it would appear that
they are in fact the cause of Cú Chulainn's wasting-sickness.

Not too much later, these women come back and ask him for his
friendship, and at this point he seems hurt: 'Not good for me your
journey here last year.' (This is like the Samson who complains too
late, after the damage of his rebelling from the Law of the Father is
manifest.) She still expects him to come along, however, and is apparently disappointed to hear that Cú Chulainn is only willing to send his
charioteer, Lóeg, on to investigate, at first.

The Otherworld that Lóeg sees is comparable to other Otherworlds
depicted in early Irish literature in its bounty and beauty. Even without
the intertextual knowledge we have of those descriptions, we know that
this is some other place where, unlike in Ulster, women do not need
men to shoot down birds for them. They will not place Cú Chulainn in
the role of protector, and he will be the considerably freer character of a
mercenary warrior. This makes it all the more inviting to him.

Back in Ireland, Emer condemns the Ulaid for their passivity, for
letting Cú Chulainn remain in his wasting-sickness. Her talk illustrates
a few things.

1. When the Ulaid most need strength they are weak. They are
dependent on Cú Chulainn to lead them in heroism; they can do nothing
without him. (He is under that much more pressure.)

2. The Emer of *SC* is outspoken and sure of herself, as she is in other
Ulster Cycle tales. This talk in particular is reminiscent of *AOA* where
Emer is the voice of personal obligation,[76] the one free of the trance or
trance-like honour that affects all the men around her. She is active, but
acts best through words. When later in *SC* her strength is dimmed, her
desperation leads her to try using action instead of words: she wields a
knife at her female enemy, and this proves useless. Her manipulative
dialogue a few moments later is much more effective. Her words get
through to Cú Chulainn, at least prompting him to think about if not act
on what he thinks. Her words always wake Cú Chulainn up in some
sense, in *SC* as in *AOA*, as in *Aided Chon Culainn* ('The Death of Cú

---

76. As discussed above, and in Findon, 'A Woman's Words', *passim*.

Chulainn'). As I argue in my reading of *AOA*, Emer is perhaps not the dinosaur that her contemporary Ulaid are. As a woman she is outside the heroic code, and therefore more flexible. In *SC* she is so flexible that she can pass between worlds without an invitation (rare among women to make an *echtra*[77] to woo!), so strong is her character, or her love.

3. As in *AOA*, in *SC* every aspect of the narrative has been advanced by women. First the Ulsterwomen who ask for Cú Chulainn set events in motion, then Emer. Then Fand and Lí Ban do, despite the fact that they are working for their husbands, and despite the catalytic arrival of Óengus. And now, even as Fand and Lí Ban continue to advance the narrative of the space in that world, Emer advances it in this. This indicates another point:

4. Events move in tandem in the two worlds. (As Bill Nicolaisen has written about Irish folktales generally, 'The landscape of otherness is largely a projection of the landscape of home.')[78]

If the Ulaid have deserted him, as Emer says, it is something like the way God deserts Samson when he has used God-given martial abilities not to defeat the tribe's enemy but for the love of an outside-the-tribe woman. He is weak, blinded and out of his own territory because of love of a woman. Cormier sees this parallel here: 'He lay in bed, shorn of his great strength—not unlike some renowned hero sulking in his tent.'[79]

When Emer finally arrives to visit Cú Chulainn she says, 'Shame on you, lying there for love of a woman!'[80] This is the first mention of love in *SC*. Until this point it was at most innuendo, but to Emer it is so clear that she can identify it, name it, and proclaim it on sight. Cú Chulainn himself had said 'Dó duit úaim ... co airm hi tá Emer, & innis condat mna sídi rom thathigset & rom admilset'[81] ('Go to Emer and tell her that women of the *síd* have come and destroyed me'). But when Emer arrives she does not call it destruction but *bangrád*, love for a woman. This does much to confirm that there is an implicit equation in this tale

---

77. This category of tale is usually translated as 'adventure'.

78. W.F.H. Nicolaisen, 'The Past as Place: Names, Stories, and the Remembered Self', *Folklore* 102/1 (1991), pp. 3-15 (7).

79. Cormier, 'Cú Chulainn', p. 127.

80. Gantz, *Early Irish Myths*, p. 164.

81. Dillon, *Serglige*, p. 11. Literally, '(Take yourself) from me to the place where Emer is and tell her that it is the women of the *síd* ...'

and perhaps in early Irish literature generally between love that can knock you flat, and destruction.

In her earlier comments to the Ulstermen Emer does not mention love at all. Instead she says he needs a 'cure' and that the Ulaid should 'heal' him, implying he is gravely wounded. It is notable that she changes her tune so suddenly when she sees him. Is she saving face as long as she is in public chastising the Ulaid, concealing what she knows to be the true embarrassing cause of his wasting-sickness? Or is it that only when she sees him can she diagnose him as love sick?

Cú Chulainn sends for her to save him from destruction, but does not express that feeling when Emer is around. Quite the opposite, he seems to have found a place where everything appeals to him more, and it is for Emer to remind him that 'this' place is very beautiful, too, and to wake him up, where waking up means coming back, full-time.

By going to the world of Lí Ban and Fand he is abandoning the Ulaid and denying his responsibility to them as their defender. At the same time he is going into the arms of a lover and denying his responsibility to his wife (someone who has a special contract with him in the eyes of society).[82] Here, as in the 'exposition', the sexual parallels the martial, in this case sexual and martial duty.

Cú Chulainn may be winning or losing battles, being attracted to or repulsed by women, but the two are always paired. They offer him that chance to prove himself, in both senses, but what attracts him to the situation is the possibility of losing. His aim has failed him for the first time, and women have beaten him into submission for the first time (and he has faced some fierce women). Thus, more than just a chance to redeem himself as a lover and a fighter, they offer him a chance to lose also, and to be free of society's expectations of him as a hero.

Of success or failure, which is it that they promise and deliver? The answer seems to be failure in 'this' world and success in 'that'. To all appearances in this world he misses the birds, is beaten, and lies in a wasting-sickness. In the Otherworld he gets the women and wins the battles. Thus, a strange equation: failure in the world where he is responsible means success in the world where his own will has led him. His luck only fails him in the land of Labraid when he begins to feel responsibility. It is not long afterwards when Emer arrives with knives.

---

82. Emer is not always such a figure. She is in a different position in *TEm*, because she is in a different relation to Cú Chulainn and to that society.

Emer comes with knives and Cú Chulainn offers Fand his protection, although he seems to be unworried by Emer until he starts to talk to her. His gesture of offering Fand protection is much more meaningful than his sleeping with her: he has begun to take responsibility for her. At the same moment, Emer reminds him of his responsibility to herself: 'It is under your protection I have come.' Thus Fand has become comparable to Emer because Fand no longer represents an escape from the world of responsibility but is part of it, and it is at this point that she begins to lose Cú Chulainn. It is apt that Emer should compare herself with Fand saying 'What's new is bright ... what's familiar is stale'.[83] It is when Emer stopped being the new rebellious choice of *TEm* and started being the bearer of Cú Chulainn's guarantee that Cú Chulainn treated her as part of the Ulster contract, and 'by the time' of *SC*, has lost interest in her. So will he lose interest in Fand as she becomes part of his debt to society. 'This' world has followed him into the realm of his interactions with Fand in the form of Emer; the *serglige* is no longer mentioned.

Cú Chulainn says to Emer, 'Not sechnaimsea ... amal sechnas cách a chárait'[84] ('I avoid you as every man avoids the one he loves'). Emer has become his responsibility, and indeed presents herself to him as such. She is therefore part of the Law of the Father, to which he knows he must eventually return. (In this case I am taking loving [*caraid*] very cynically—not as romantic or need-seeking but as part of Cú Chulainn's heavy obligation to the society he must serve and protect.)

The conversation between Emer, Fand, and Cú Chulainn towards the end of *SC*[85] is strange because, among other things, their statements do not obviously respond to each other. Theirs is not the deliberate riddling of a wooing conversation, but one where there are gaps that need to be filled in order for there to be continuity. As an exercise I have rewritten this dialogue with those gaps filled. This is what I understand them to be saying, and how they would say it in twenty-first-century English:

E. I come under your protection because you owe it to me and to a sense of law and order to come back. You will not and cannot leave me!

C. Emer, please. It's not a question of you or vows. It's this woman. Look at her. I need her. I'm her match. She needs me.

83. Gantz, *Early Irish Myths*, p. 175. 'is gel cach núa ... is serb cach gnáth' (Dillon, *Serglige*, p. 25).
84. Dillon, *Serglige*, p. 24.
85. In Dillon, *Serglige*, p. 25; Gantz, *Early Irish Myths*, pp. 174-75.

E.   That's what you think you think. Now. Look: once we needed each
     other like that. We can still, if you still want me.
C.   [A little sad] 'Want' you? God, I'll always want you as long as you
     live.
F.   If you'll just excuse me, I think I'll be going now. Just forget me.
E.   No, he should forget *me*. (I can see he loves you. Why am I tor-
     menting him? If he says he needs you …)
F.   No! Don't you see? I'm the one at risk here, not you. (One day he's
     going to go back to you and I'll be alone, so let it be now.)

This reading has only one uneven response: the 'beat' when Emer shifts
techniques from threatening him to trying to persuade him. (In this case
my adaptation is true to the ambiguity of the original.) As elsewhere,
Emer is flexible, not aligned with an honour code, and can appeal to
authority or true love as the mood demands, and get away with it.

Cú Chulainn feels he has to explain his actions to Emer—and yet he
does not explain them very delicately. He asks her blessing to do what
he has done: 'Emer, will you not permit me to meet this woman?' He
does need her permission, but he finds it a reasonable request to ask his
wife to give her blessing on seeing another woman. The reason Cú
Chulainn cites is that Fand is a perfect match for him.

Even without modern expectations concerning monogamy, but within
the context of this tale, we know from the exposition that women get
jealous and want to look as good as their rivals—if we do not know it
already from other early Irish tales like *Fled Bricrend*. So, does Cú
Chulainn speak specifically to incite Emer, to provoke her into giving
him a real reason to leave her? Or out of sheer stupidity, or a sudden
desire to be honest? His intentions are indeed clear, and it seems that he
means well. In all this he does not come across as a cad, whether or not
we are blinded by his heroic status into forgiving him anything. He is
trapped and is trying to do well by everyone, honestly. Simply by
complying with various demands made on him from conflicting interests he loses everything. We met this earlier in *SC* when Cú Chulainn
runs to meet the demands of the Ulsterwomen and neglects his own
wife's. This is part of the strongman's curse—he is designed to be perfect, but perfection will only upset everyone, especially himself.

Equally remarkably, Fand gives up as soon as she hears Cú Chulainn
say he loves Emer. This response confirms that the all-determining
thing in the narrative is what Cú Chulainn wants. Emer and Fand meanwhile prove each other worthy opponents by their both being willing to
give him up. They are equally judicious and loving in trying to spare

Cú Chulainn (although my interpretation of their dialogue finds self-interest in their responses, too). They would seem to prefer that Cú Chulainn be in one piece with one of them than sliced in half for both—a Solomonic moment.

Cú Chulainn is powerless in all of this. His words are powerless, and the narrative is once again advanced entirely by women's words. He cannot even understand why Fand is going away (and must ask Lóeg). In all, he is slow to react and can only ask his charioteer what is happening, not even claiming Fand for himself, which he would seem to want to do. Lóeg's answer that 'Fand is going away because she did not please you' reminds Cú Chulainn that it is his own power that has caused his suffering. Cú Chulainn learns that his being pleased by someone or not is enough to dictate her location. What he wanted was that Fand's actions continue independently of his feelings, but this cannot be: he is too important, he has the Midas touch. Thus, tortured again by his own will, strength, and fame as a hero he is prevented from satisfying his own desires.

Understatement makes the impact more powerful:

> *'Fand ic dul la Manannán mac Lir ar nocorb álic duitsiu hí.' Is and sin trá ro ling CuChulaind tri ardlémend...*[86]

> 'Fand is going with Manannan mac Lir because she was not desirable to you.' Then Cú Chulainn leaped three high leaps ...

This is mourning and frustration, a pounding of the head against the wall. Does it mean that this was love, between the hero and the woman who beat him up? (The love of a Samson and a Delilah?) Certainly it is a love-sickness that even Emer cannot assuage. It is up to Conchobor to get Cú Chulainn back and up to a magic potion to soothe Cú Chulainn's insurmountable masochism.

Interlude II

There are a few moments in Cú Chulainn's career in the *Táin* that, although not associated with the tales above, offer insights into Cú Chulainn's character. They are also moments that may fruitfully be compared with the portrait of masculinity being developed here, and therefore to Samson. The episodes that struck me concern Cú Chulainn's

---

86. Dillon, *Serglige*, p. 29.

periodic modesty which may be called a fear of women, his night with
Fedelm Noíchride and, briefly, his attitude toward the Morrígan.

> 'I swear by the oath of Ulster's people that if a man isn't found to
> fight me, I'll spill the blood of everyone in this court.'
>
> 'Naked women to him!' Conchobor said.
>
> The women of Emain went forth ... and they stripped their breasts at
> him.
>
> 'These are the warriors you must struggle with today', Mugain said.
>
> He hid his countenance. Immediately the warriors of Emain seized
> him and plunged him in a vat of cold water. The vat burst asunder about
> him.[87]

In this episode from the *Aided Trí Mac Nechta Scéni* ('The Death of
Nechta Scéne's Three Sons'), Cú Chulainn is not a man, but a seven-
year-old child. Women are sent to him to dissolve his rage, and sent by
his 'own' Ulstermen.

As when they look for an (unworthy) mate for him rather than have
him touch their own womenfolk, so here the Ulstermen offer Cú Chulainn no support in dealing with women. Although these women are
sent partly for his own good—to calm him down—the act of dispatch-
ing them is a distancing one.

At the time Cú Chulainn is just a boy, as Connla is when he visits
much later, an equally promising, equally threatening warrior. Cú Chulainn arrived with the same good intentions of supporting the Ulstermen, but when his anger becomes too much for them to contemplate,
his own Ulstermen subdue him with women—women who offer no possibility of intimacy.

If nothing else, this episode may be read to indicate another way that
his relationship with the Ulstermen is fraught—and specifically in ways
which pit his (precocious) masculine desire against his duty to the Law
of the Father. Melia feels this confrontation involved the contrast between warlike and sexual energy.[88] It prefigures Cú Chulainn's own
regret-laden, thwarted attempts at intimacy with women yet to come.

---

87. Kinsella, *The Táin*, pp. 91-92. ' "Tongu do dia toingte Ulaid mani étar fer do
gleó frim-sa, ardáilfe fuil lim cach áein fil isin dún." "Mná ernochta ara chend!" ar
Conchobar. Tothéit iarom bantrocht nEmna ara chend ... & donnochtat a mbruinni
friss. "It é óic inso condricfat frit indiu", or Mugain. Foilgis-[s]eom a gnúis. La
sodain atnethat láith gaile Emna & focherdat i ndabaig n-úarusci. Maitti immi-seom
in dabach hísi" ' (O'Rahilly, *Táin I*, ll. 808-15, p. 25).

88. Melia, *Narrative*, p. 88.

I have already suggested a reading of the Connla episode where Cú Chulainn kills Connla in an attempt to defy the Ulstermen. Perhaps it is not just a way to thwart their demands for an heir, but a belated response to what happened when he himself was seven. Instead of 'Mná ernochta ara chend!' ('Naked women to him!') (a shock of mock-intimacy, the forewarning against any sexual feelings he might have, the Ulaid's breaking of the laws of decorum which they are expected to uphold), Cú Chulainn says: 'Aso mo macsa dúib' ('My son for you!'). This is a shock of intimacy lost, the warning that their chance for future triumph is gone, his own commission of *fingal*, or at least his revealing that in serving them he must destroy what is thought to be closest to him. Finally, he is getting a sort of revenge, proving that the Ulaid must suffer at such moments too, and not just him.

As the Ulstermen are still in their pangs, Fergus sends warning to them that the Connacht armies are advancing. Only Cú Chulainn and his father are able to respond. Cú Chulainn cannot do his work to warn Ulster, however, because he is with his *dormuine*,[89] Fedelm Noíchride. As he retires with her he leaves a riddle-like marking (ogam) for the enemy to guess at in the meantime. He is thus absent from the action, indoors instead of on the battlefield and, like Samson, leaving riddles (or a secret, *rún*) for others:

> Fergus: What is the riddle of the hoop?
>> How many men put it there? …
>
> Druids: It was a great champion made it …[90]

The riddle of the 'spancel-hoop' or 'withe' (*id*) holds the key to who left it and thus the key to Cú Chulainn's identity. This riddle is more thought out and useful than Samson's tearing down of town gates or setting foxes on fire, however: Cú Chulainn is in fact communicating secretly with his friend Fergus and directly affecting Connacht's for-

---

89. 'Concubine'. So is she called in *Táin I* (ll. 222-25), which word means a partner closer in rank to a *prímben* by early Irish law than most concubines. (I am grateful to Próinséas Ní Chatháin for this and other information on women in early Irish society.) For an engaging discussion of this episode, see Dooley, 'Invention', pp. 123-33.

90. Kinsella, *The Táin*, p. 68. ' "Ind id cia fo tá a rún? Cía lín ro lá insé?..." "Crephnas churad caur rod lá" ' (*Táin I*, ll. 274-75; 282 [O'Rahilly (ed.), *Táin*, p.9]).

tune. There is none of the futility that seems to be connected to Samson's actions.

However, Cú Chulainn's passive riddle-leaving is echoed by the passivity he feels on waking up too late, still with the woman.

> But Cú Chulainn did not come early from his tryst; he remained until he had washed and bathed. Then he came onto the trace of the army.[91]
>
> 'I wish we hadn't gone there', Cú Chulainn said, 'and betrayed Ulster...'[92]

In this case he is like Samson, a warrior losing time and energy in the arms of a woman when he should be on the battlefield. Ó Cathasaigh writes with reference to Findabair (in this case, a woman whom Cú Chulainn alone resists) that 'the warrior is single-minded in pursuit of his aims and is not to be distracted by sexual temptation'.[93]

If we pursue a comparison of this episode with Judg. 16.1-3, when Samson spends a night with a Gaza prostitute with the whole town waiting in ambush outside, we must note that Samson, unlike Cú Chulainn, defies them. Samson arises at midnight, which most critics enjoy as a sign of his potency (the Gazites had anticipated his sexual exhaustion; instead he is ready to climb mountains). Cú Chulainn's partner is different, but like the Gaza woman, Fedelm is a distraction from where he ought to be (defending his people). That is, Cú Chulainn has better timing in retiring, but Samson in re-emerging.

Here is the contrast between desire (sexual relations with Fedelm) and political obligation to patriarchy. Cú Chulainn can hide from his heroic responsibility and even from his heroic identity, losing ground in the battle, but only momentarily and regretfully.

Cú Chulainn's interaction with the Morrígan in the *Táin* also deserves mention here. The Morrígan is not a creature whose essence can be captured succinctly, or relative to Cú Chulainn alone; a fair study would have to assess her role in many narratives. Further, this female figure has many manifestations, and because of her very shape-shifting nature it seems inappropriate to compare her strictly either to Cú Chulainn's other women or Samson's. She does represent another threat to

---

91. O'Rahilly, *Táin I*, p. 133. 'Nípo moch didiu dolluid Cú Culaind asa bandáil. Anais co foilc & fothraic. Dotháet íarom for lorg in tslóig.'

92. Kinsella, *The Táin*, p. 72. '"Ní ma lodmar dó", ol Cú Chulainn, "ná mertamar Ultu"' (*Táin I*, ll. 313-35, in O'Rahilly, *Táin I*, p. 70).

93. Ó Cathasaigh, 'Mythology', p. 130.

the warrior in female form, however. She may be too affectionate ('I have come to you. I've loved you from the stories about you')[94] or too ugly ('the Morrígan came to him in the guise of an old hag, one-eyed and half-blind'). [95] Of course, it is not just as the Morrígan that a female threat can take many forms: Findabair's looks are an accessory to dozens of deaths—and old women can rely on their ugliness for immunity.

In the incarnation above, the Morrígan starts as a woman loving him, then promises to destroy him when he rejects her. As she suggests the shape she will take to defeat him, he matches the method of attack to that milieu. This creature may be his match, but she ought no more be discussed here as a woman than as a beast or a god. Her interaction with Cú Chulainn after the initial flirtation is not sexual—it is not even embodied. We may contrast Úathach with this, who is interested in Cú Chulainn and then thwarted by him, but whose sexuality is still exploited by Cú Chulainn. Similarly Aífe is primarily a fierce opponent but her sexuality and child-bearing capacity are crucial to her identity in terms of her interaction with Cú Chulainn.

A final femme fatale who may be mentioned as a sexual woman dangerous to Cú Chulainn is Medb (of Cruachan). She is dangerous to Cú Chulainn not for her sexuality but as leader of the Connacht army. In her relations otherwise, however, her appeal and power have to do with her sexuality. Nagy refers to Medb as attractive not to Cú Chulainn but to the reader for her essentially femme fatale nature and because of 'the universal appeal of tricksterish, subversive, albeit occasionally villainous, figures whose narratological job is to provide the engine that transforms a mass of details into a story, and an interesting one at that'.[96] Further demonstration of Medb's character is to be found in her relationship to Fergus, which has been described as emasculating by Ó Cathasaigh: 'By yielding to Medb's attraction, Fergus is unmanned and betrays his own kith and kin. The unmanning is expressed in terms of the taking of his own sword from its scabbard.'[97]

---

94. 'Dodeochad chucut-su. Rot charus ar th'airscélaib' (O'Rahilly, *Táin I*, l. 1850, p. 57).

95. 'danarraid in Morrígan i ndelb na sentainne caillige & síd cáech losc' (O'Rahilly, *Táin I*, l. 2040, p. 62).

96. J.F. Nagy, review of *Aspects of the Táin*, in *Éigse* 28 (1994–95), pp. 183-88 (185).

97. Ó Cathasaigh, 'Mythology', p. 130.

Without summarizing and dismissing all the intricacies of the *Táin*, it is true that Medb's whims and wiles are behind the death of every man in the book (although Cú Chulainn does much of the killing). Perhaps Medb represents a kingship goddess. Perhaps her power and the ultimate futility of her efforts represents the futility of the whole cattle-raid,[98] and thus the futility of a golden warrior age which is past. Or perhaps she is only a symbol in the *Táin*, but a woman, and a leader. In which case the comment on womankind here is not at all radical, but straightforward and discouraging, as Fergus says at the end: 'That is what usually happens... to a herd of horses led by a mare. Their substance is taken and carried off... as they follow a woman who has misled them'.[99]

5. *The Samson Story*

Like Samson without his hair … my defences are down…
I must confess that I like it: being miserable is going to be fun.
Irving Berlin, *Annie Get Your Gun*

Contrary to what might be remembered about his story, Samson (Judg. 13–16) is not just the poor duped strongman. Delilah is not only not the only woman in his life, she is also not described as being beautiful.

The Samson story is also surprisingly full of repetition. Patterns of telling and not telling emerge, being tricked and tricking, lying and lying again. Cheryl Exum[100] has laid out some of these patterns and Susan Niditch[101] has analysed the folk figure of Samson the trickster. Delilah's predictability is just as striking: she does the same thing every time—and he keeps falling for it.

These are not, however, evaluations of details in Samson's experience, but rather what happens despite those details. If his is such a

98. I am grateful to Patricia Kelly for first mentioning this possibility to me. See also P. O'Leary, 'Choice and Consequence in Irish Heroic Literature', *CMCS* 27 (Summer 1994), pp. 49-59; Radner, ' "Fury" '.

99. O'Rahilly, *Táin I*, p. 237. 'Is bésad …do cach graig remitét láir, rotgata, rotbrata …a moín hi tóin mná misrairleastai' (O'Rahilly, *Táin I*, ll. 4123-24, p. 124).

100. J.C. Exum, 'Aspects of Symmetry and Balance in the Samson Saga', *JSOT* 19 (1981), pp. 3-29.

101. S. Niditch, 'Samson as Culture Hero, Trickster and Bandit', *CBQ* 52/4 (October 1990), pp. 608-24.

predictable pattern, if each woman is going to treat Samson the same way and so obviously, then how does this superhero get himself blinded and killed? I have tried to look at the episodes themselves to find what they tell us about Samson's character, to answer this riddle another way. Who is this seemingly gullible strongman?

Manoah's Wife

> [A]nd the angel of God came to the woman again. She was sitting in the field and her husband Manoah was not with her. The woman ran in haste to tell her husband. She said to him, 'The man who came to me before has just appeared to me.' Manoah promptly followed his wife (Judg. 13.9-11).

A woman stars in each episode in the Samson story. In the first part, Manoah's wife seems to be the main character. Her story is an unusual version of the biblical typescene of the barren wife: she is active where Manoah is passive. In a painting by Rembrandt, *The Angel Ascending in the Flames of Manoah's Sacrifice*, the contrast of their modes is clearly depicted: the woman kneels, praying, her eyes focused and intent while Manoah's face is full of doubt, lower than hers in the scene. In the biblical text, the woman seems to know what is going on at every point while Manoah needs to ask. As the angel repeats the instructions on raising a Nazirite, he addresses the special command-ments to her, making her conduct as precious as Samson's.

This exposition sets the scene for powerful female characters. Manoah's wife also later serves as an example for Samson of what a good wife can do, for even a weak husband. Samson proves to be just such a weak mate to other women who, unlike his mother, do not serve the LORD but other gods. In this exposition, we see the strength of his mother's belief as she worships only the LORD, and knows an angel when she sees one.

Robert Alter has pointed out the pattern of unnamed women in the Samson story.[102] Manoah's wife is referred to in the narrative simply as 'the woman'. The Timnite woman also receives this vague label. One possible reading of Samson involves understanding all the women in his story as milestones in his sexual and martial initiation. In such a scheme, Manoah's wife is the idealized wife, directly connected to

102. Alter, 'Samson without Folklore', pp. 51-52.

Samson's patriarchal society. In order to return to that society he needs first to rebel against it in the arms of foreign women.

Manoah's wife may be the main character here, but the angel's presence and his announcement are the main event. Furthermore, the woman does not have a name (although, it must be said, neither does the angel —they are 'the man' and 'the woman', which has led some critics to conclude that the angel is Samson's father).[103] The woman's significance here highlights her goodness and the strong example set for Samson, as well as the catalytic role of women in divine events.

Being a Nazirite

> For you are going to conceive and bear a son; let no razor touch his head, for the boy is to be a nazirite to God from the womb on. He shall be the first to deliver Israel from the Philistines (Judg. 13.5).

Alter draws attention to the extent to which Samson is in the thrall of God's spirit and the Nazirite vow. Based on a close examination of the Hebrew, Alter finds 'Samson ... is not a judge who is merely taken possession of by the spirit of the LORD but a man in whom it pounds, like the clapper of a bell'.[104] Even Emmanuel Levinas's loving description of the Nazirate leaves room for finding it constraining: '[T]he attachment to the Good precedes the choosing of the Good ... The Good is good precisely because it chooses you before you have had time to raise your eyes to it.'[105]

Phillip Lopate goes even further, saying that Samson is born 'in God's debt. His body itself doesn't quite belong to him. It's a sacred weapon for God to inhabit with His spirit when He so desires.'[106] The Nazirite vow is a dictation of his very nature. It is also contrary to that nature: 'The Nazirite vow was not of his making, and as a human being, Samson chooses to be "ordinary", not "separate" or "dedicated".'[107]

I believe that all of Samson's actions subsequent to the vow and its demand for loyalty are battles between that vow and his own personal

---

103. Margalith ('Samson's Riddle') calls Samson 'a mortal son of a divine father and a Danite woman', p. 397.

104. Alter, 'Samson without Folklore', p. 49.

105. E. Levinas, 'The Youth of Israel', in A. Aronowicz (trans.), *Nine Talmudic Readings* (Bloomington: Indiana University Press, 1990), pp. 120-35 (135).

106. Lopate, 'Samson and Delilah', p. 77.

107. D. Gunn, 'Samson of Sorrows: An Isaiac Gloss on Judges 13–16', in Fewell (ed.), *Reading between Texts*, pp. 225-53 (240).

desire. The conflict of personal and private, desire and law, are also integral parts of masculinity according to Freud's Oedipal model.

Alter goes so far as to say that the force of the LORD within Samson is driving him 'like sexuality itself'. This comment highlights the battle between the two forces, which can be called desire and the Law where the Law means a duty to God, to his parents as representatives of the Jews, to the Nazirite vow itself, to the contract between God and the Jews as well as actual rules from Torah, such as may arise.

A Too Perfect Hero?

In an article to be discussed below, Alan Bruford describes Cú Chulainn as a hero who is too good to be true. Is this also the case with Samson? Is Samson, like Superman, another unbalanced comic-book hero with a special secret? Lopate thinks so: 'For me, Samson was essentially a Superman figure'.[108] Lopate identifies with Superman and Samson and the questions he asks shed light on Samson's actions in a new and personal way: 'Was I good because I chose to be or because I was too timid, too programmed to do otherwise?'[109] The strength, the goodness, the special heroic responsibility of Samson and his vow make his own wishes that much more obscured from view.

Desire and the Law

> His father and mother said to him, 'Is there no one among the daughters of your own kinsmen and among all my people, that you must go and take a wife from the uncircumcised Philistines?' But Samson answered his father, 'Get me that one, for she is the one that pleases me' (Judg. 14.3).

Several scholars have located contrasting obligations in the Samson story, a contrast that may be called one between desire and the Law. Reading Samson for folklore, Susan Niditch sees it in these terms:

> At the heart of the Samson narrative as a whole: nature vs. culture, 'us' vs. 'them'... the confrontation with authority and the issue of empowerment ... The Samson tale deals with the desire to obtain and hold autonomy both personal and political.[110]

108. Lopate, 'Samson and Delilah', p. 74.
109. Lopate, 'Samson and Delilah', p. 76.
110. Niditch, 'Culture Hero', pp. 609-10.

Exum expands on this list, locating these contrasts (which are already so familiar from Cú Chulainn's story):

own kind/ foreign
male /female
...
endogamy/ exogamy
paternal house/ women's houses
...
self/ other
good woman/ bad woman[111]

Crenshaw devotes a book to Samson's riddles, all of which 'examine competing loyalties'[112] which include 'parents v. lovers [and] charisma v. passion'.[113] These themes and this contrast form the core of all tragedy, arguably, and Exum and Crenshaw both explore Samson as tragic hero.

Generally true of famous tragedies, but perhaps especially of each of the two portraits here, is that this contrast goes on inside one man. Women's love both is and symbolizes the other side of loyalty to patriarchy. Women provide the hero with the chance to be whimsical, sexual, id-serving, superego-ignoring.

Freud found his famous psychological model in a character in an ancient Greek play for whom 'the lesson ... is submission to the divine will and the realisation of his own impotence'.[114] Lopate comments on Samson's literal similarity to Oedipus: 'Both men dealt with riddles, both suffered ruin by sleeping with the wrong woman, and both were blinded.'[115] We must wonder with Lopate how much this is Samson's task as well as Oedipus's. Samson's Nazirate is just such a 'lesson': if Samson learns anything by the end of his time in Judges, he learns that the pursuit of his own desires is fruitless, and that he would have been better off submitting to divine will, marrying a nice Jewish girl and settling down. Or conversely, it may be argued that the lesson is that

111. J.C. Exum, *Fragmented Women: Feminist (Sub)versions of Biblical Narratives* (JSOTSup, 163; Sheffield: JSOT Press, 1993), pp. 72-73.

112. Crenshaw, *A Vow Ignored*, p. 65.

113. Crenshaw, *A Vow Ignored*, p. 98.

114. S. Freud, *The Interpretation of Dreams* (London: Penguin Books, 1991), p. 364.

115. Lopate, 'Samson and Delilah', p. 97.

divine will can take many forms, all of which make Samson realize his own impotence.

Summarizing Freud, Frank Krutnik writes that 'the hero is defined in relation both to the legally defined framework of law and to the law of patriarchy which specifies the culturally acceptable positions and the delimitation of masculine identity and desire'.[116]

Samson is introduced specifically as a Nazirite, his very being dictated by the restrictions God puts to his mother ('legally defined framework') and by his duty as a saviour to his people. He does not exist to serve his own desires, and when he tries to pursue them, the Law revolts against him and the spirit of the LORD leaves him. The contract he makes with God and God's people ('the law of patriarchy')—a Nazirite vow—is directly at odds with his instincts ('masculine identity and desires').

His instincts lead him to women around whom he 'cannot help himself': not just any gorgeous women but women who are not Jewish, and women who personally afflict him. Freud offers one explanation for this path in the male psyche: 'In the *amour fou* fantasy, the male "contracts" himself to the woman as a means of directly opposing his post-Oedipal pact to the Law of the Father'.[117] Samson's attraction to the wrong woman is a way for him to counteract God's intentions for him.

Samson has no semblance of an intimate or affectionate relationship with these women by any standards, biblical or psychological. So how do we describe what he is doing by being with them? The question was raised in some sense by Cú Chulainn's actions with Fand and Lí Ban when he first meets them. There I said that Cú Chulainn sought a chance to be weak. With Samson, this can be elaborated on. Women are for Samson a chance to be a masochist where 'male masochism can be seen as manifesting a desire to escape from the regimentation of masculine (cultural) identity effected through the Oedipus complex. The masochist seeks to overthrow the authority of paternal law'.[118]

Here the 'authority of paternal law' is the Nazirite vow and God's authority, God's claim on Samson. Alignment with the patriarchal cultural order would be that much more incumbent upon a Nazirite character than on any other Jew in the Bible. Perhaps this is why Samson is

116. Krutnik, *Lonely Street*, p. 86.
117. Krutnik, *Lonely Street*, p. 84.
118. Krutnik, *Lonely Street*, p. 85.

driven to do the opposite of what is expected of him, committing again and again the cultural sin and severing of exogamy.[119]

Samson is drawn to Delilah not in spite of the fact that she will destroy him but *because* of the fact that she will destroy him. 'He is trying to make a space for his own life inside the one already owed to his parents and God. So he indulges in skirt-chasing ... [This is] why he allows himself so often to be betrayed: it frees him to do what he wants.'[120]

The Lion

> [A] full-grown lion came roaring at him. The spirit of the LORD gripped him, and he tore him asunder with his bare hands as one might tear a kid asunder... (Judg. 14.5-6).

Who tore whom asunder—did Samson tear up the lion? Or did the spirit of the LORD tear Samson? Are these the same? The Hebrew hints at the extent to which his own desire and the LORD's are mixed up in Samson.[121] This allows for the interpretation that the lion is his doppelgänger.

David Bynum admits this possibility when he points out the mythological significance of this scene as it relates to wooings in two Central African stories, 'What a Little Thing Did' and 'Shichinongomunuma and Chilubwelubwe'.[122] In both the African stories and in the Samson story, a lion appears in the story in the middle of a courtship, after the hero has tried to marry outside the tribe (this is also the 'beast like a lion''s place in the narrative of *TEm*).

Bynum calls the lion a honey-trickster because it is a provider of honey and a source for riddling which involves Samson's identity:

119. Perhaps the only other biblical hero who sins so frequently and whose sexuality is equally testament to his conflict with God's high expectations is David. For an exploration of a related idea, see R. Schwartz, 'Adultery in the House of David: The Metanarratives of Biblical Scholarship and the Narratives of the Bible', *Semeia* 54 (1991), pp. 35-56.

120. Lopate, 'Samson and Delilah', pp. 77-78.

121. *wattiṣlaḥ ʿālâw rûaḥ yhwh wayšasʿehû kᵉšassaʿ haggᵉdî* (Judg. 14.6).

122. D. Bynum, *The Daemon in the Wood: A Study of Oral Narrative Patterns* (Cambridge, MA: Center for the Study of Oral Literature, Harvard University, 1978), pp. 42-52.

Posthumously... [the lion is] host to his quest and give[s] him nourish-
ment ... by means of the riddle, which ... effectively transfers to him the
lion's self-contradictory duality as simultaneous consumer and provider
of sustenance ...[123]

The lion not only threatens him and gives him honey but has a secret to
his identity. Samson's lion is the solution to the riddle he asks of the
Timnites, but within the tradition of riddles in Samson, solving it is
tantamount to exposing Samson: 'To overcome Samson his foes have
to overcome the lion in his riddle.'[124]

I would not say, however, that the second part has a parallel in Cú
Chulainn and his 'lion' in *TEm* because it does not represent a threat of
exposure for Cú Chulainn. However, there is an incident in Cú Chulainn's past where a fierce beast threatens him and then becomes the
secret of his identity, then used as a riddle in a courtship scenario. That
is the Hound of Culann, of course, which becomes his own name, and
is then used in place of telling Emer who he is really in *TEm*.

Samson, the lion, and the secret connect to the Superman idea referred to already, where revelation of masculine identity means self-
destruction. Bal calls it this in Samson's case explicitly, finding 'annihilation by revelation' in his identity.[125]

If we are to pursue a reading for masochism where sadism has a
place within it, as Theodor Reik has suggested,[126] this is a significant
example from Samson's story. Samson does not know what to do with
his strength, how to be reckless with it in a way that can counteract his
duty pounding within him. His first victim is his doppelgänger, whose
abuse is an indirect form of self-destruction. His last victim is himself.

Not Telling
When Samson tears into the lion, 'he did not tell his father or his
mother what he had done'. When he goes back the next year he gives
his parents honey but 'he did not tell them that he had taken the honey
out of the carcass of the lion'. At their wedding feast the Timnite
woman says, 'You hate me, you don't love me. You have asked the

123. Bynum, *Daemon*, p. 66.
124. Bynum, *Daemon*, p. 66.
125. M. Bal, *Death and Dissymmetry: The Politics of Coherence in the Book of
Judges* (Chicago: University of Chicago Press, 1988), p. 225.
126. Cf. T. Reik, *Of Love and Lust: On the Psychoanalysis of Romantic and Sexual Emotions* (New York: J. Aronson, 1974) (discussed below).

sons of my people a riddle and you didn't tell me the answer.' Samson says, 'Behold, I have not told my father and my mother, and I should tell you?'

Here Samson is defining his relationship with the Timnite woman as being more revealing than his relationship with his parents (since he does indeed proceed to tell her the answer to the riddle). Crenshaw makes much of the riddling in the Samson story, as does Milton in his *Samson Agonistes*. They have it that Samson wants to keep all the answers to himself, and he comes against the ultimate mystery in woman. All this 'not telling' only highlights Samson's incredible willingness to 'tell' at other points in the narrative, as with his dealings with Delilah.

... and Telling

> ... he told her, because she nagged him so. And she explained the riddle to her countrymen. On the seventh day, before the sunset, the townsmen said to him: 'What is sweeter than honey, And what is stronger than a lion?' (Judg. 14.17-18)

In the episode with the Timnite woman the narrator builds suspense, never revealing the answer to the riddle until the end, but simply describing its transmission to eager ears. His story seems to be revealed triply, filtered through so many ears back to him, with each retelling organized to defy Samson. He seems incapable of knowing when he should trust someone, or he willingly chooses the worst possible people to tell, that is, those who can hurt him the most with the information. 'He proves his love by making himself vulnerable, by furnishing the woman with knowledge that gives her power over him; in other words, by surrendering himself to the woman'.[127]

The stage is set for Samson's sense of timing, more revealing comments, and the ever higher price of Samson's indiscretion.

The test case for telling and not telling comes with Delilah. How can she be asking him the secret to his strength so openly and baiting him so vociferously ('The Philistines are upon you!')? Why does Samson lie so creatively, his lies getting nearer the truth? Finally, why does he tell Delilah the truth?

---

127. J.C. Exum, *Plotted, Shot and Painted: Cultural Representations of Biblical Women* (JSOTSup, 215; GCT, 3; Sheffield: Sheffield Academic Press, 1996), p. 220.

Psychoanalytic theory provides one interpretation of this behaviour, in the portrait of the masochist as defined by Reik. He describes one of the fundamental differences of the masochistic fantasy from normal sexuality as 'the preponderance of the anxiety factor and the tendency to prolong the suspense'.[128] Suspense for the masochistic fantasy is a tension between pleasure and anxiety. This tension can be found in the dialogue between Samson and Delilah at his point:

> So Delilah said to Samson, 'Tell me, what makes you so strong? And how could you be tied up and made helpless?' Samson replied, 'If I were to be tied ...' ... Then she called out to him, 'Samson, the Philistines are upon you!' Whereat he pulled the tendons apart ...
>
> Then Delilah said to Samson, 'Oh, you deceived me; you lied to me! Do tell me now how you could be tied up.' He said, 'If I were to be bound ...' ... And she cried, 'Samson, the Philistines are upon you!' But he tore them off...
>
> Then Delilah said to Samson, '... Tell me, how could you be tied up?' He answered her, 'If you weave seven locks of my head ...' ... 'Samson, the Philistines are upon you!' ... he pulled out the peg, the loom and the web.
>
> Then she said to him, '...This makes three times that you ... haven't told me what makes you so strong.' Finally, after she had nagged him and pressed him constantly, he was wearied to death and he confided everything to her...
>
> '... Samson, the Philistines are upon you!' ... The Philistines seized him and gouged out his eyes (Judg. 16.6-21).

We may compare the widely acknowledged masochism of a hard-boiled hero's experience. In his case, instead of nagging, what he is subject to is usually called 'grilling':

> 'Say that again', he said softly.
> I said it again.
> He hit me across the face with his open hand ...
> 'Say it again', he said softly.
> I said it again. His hand swept and knocked my head to one side again.
> 'Say it again.'
> 'Nope. Third time lucky. You might miss.'[129]

Bal asks of the biblical grilling, 'So, third time lucky? Samson's sur-

---

128. Reik, *Love and Lust*, p. 222.

129. Raymond Chandler, *The Lady in the Lake* (New York: Vintage, 1976), pp. 123-24.

render to women is symbolised as inevitable ...'[130] Significantly, Samson is not at gunpoint when Delilah asks him how she can best torture him, and has therefore made a choice to be there. Indeed he seems more at ease in Delilah's lap than he is anywhere else in the narrative, yet he must also be more anxious than ever as he hands over to her the key to his destruction.

Masochism

Freud finds sadism and masochism in the same realm, both of them 'deviations in respect of the sexual aim' in his 'Three Essays on the Theory of Sexuality'. Thus, the extreme displays both of strength and weakness to which our heroes are prone are not contradictory, psychologically speaking, but complementary. Freud explains:

> Sadism which cannot find employment in actual life is turned round upon the subject's own self and so produces a secondary masochism...
> [I]ts active and passive forms are habitually found to occur in the same individual.[131]

Connecting back to our texts, we may call much of Samson and Cú Chulainn's interaction with women sadomasochism, which other scholars have identified using less psychologically charged words:

> In these trysts isn't the strongman measuring his fortitude against an opponent he recognises as potentially more dangerous than an enemy general?... With a too-docile love slave, there would be no stimulating tension, no edge to the encounter.[132]

David Gunn offers a variation on this: 'Samson may...want to imagine that he is playing the game of love, perhaps an erotic game of reversal, with her strength and weakness as ingredients.'[133] Women are thus pleasurable for the chance to experience loss or pain that they provide, and thereby an antidote to the 'too perfect' hero's heroism.

The hero's desire has him working to try to achieve an intimacy that by its very danger might counteract his planned existence:

> The truth is that self-destruction is actually the only method we have to prove to ourselves our own freedom. If we accept what is comfortable, satisfying and good, how do we convince ourselves that it was our own

130. Bal, *Lethal Love*, p. 55.
131. Freud, *Three Essays*, pp. 71 n. 2, 73.
132. Lopate, 'Samson and Delilah', p. 86.
133. Gunn, 'Samson of Sorrows', p. 244.

will that brought us to such a place? Perhaps we only did what was easiest, let others dictate the course of events, or bowed to cultural pressure to behave thus ...[134]

It may be that the women who can shorten the masculine hero's 'too perfect' life are desirable for just that reason. Exum observes this moment in Samson's experience, too, and acknowledges 'the attraction of losing himself in love, transcending the self through the intimate knowledge of the other, is overwhelming'.[135]

Acting like a Philistine

... Samson declared, 'Now the Philistines can have no claim against me for the harm I shall do them'... He replied, 'As they did to me, so I did to them' (Judg. 15.3, 11).

He says they can have no claim against him for the wrong he will do, but they do have such a claim, and they collect on it. In fact, their claim is valid, so valid that Samson's 'own' Judahites pursue him on the Philistines' behalf and hand him over to them. The Philistines say they want tit for tat. Samson says he wants tit for tat, too, operating according to their credo. Nothing could show more clearly the extent to which he has lowered himself to their level: his idea of justice is based on theirs, he thinks like them. This is even worse, biblically speaking, than taking one of their women: the threat of such proximity is perhaps the core reason against exogamy in Samson's culture—the point is not that one should not have intercourse with Gentiles so much as that intercourse would lead to thinking like one of them (especially towards their gods) and performing acts of idolatry, or worse. Indeed, after Samson is bound he does just this by inspiring others to worship Dagon by his dancing. Finally, he carries this likening to the ultimate extent, actually asking to die with the Philistines in the end.

Tie Me Up, Tie Me Down

'We have come down ... to take you prisoner and to hand you over to the Philistines.' 'But swear to me ... that you yourselves will not attack me.' 'We won't ... We will only take you prisoner and hand you over to them; we will not slay you.' So they bound him with two new ropes ... (Judg. 15.12-13).

134. I am grateful to Kenneth Richter for confirmation of this strain in masculinity (personal correspondence, 6 September 1996).
135. Exum, *Plotted*, p. 221.

The theme of binding begins with the Judahites who take him to Timnah. Then, in the jawbone-of-an-ass episode the ropes melt, as the lion had 'melted' like a kid. Later Samson suggests to Delilah new ways to bind him and she agrees. Is Samson attracted to Delilah because she can bind him?

Corresponding to his reckoning of Samson's masochism, Alter locates sadism in the way the Philistines go after him, especially in the end. They never actually intend to kill him; they only want to bind him so as 'to be their plaything'. Indeed, 'an odd intimation of sadistic fantasy hovers over the whole story'.[136] (It is worth restating Freud's definition of masochism whose 'manifest content is of being gagged, bound, painfully beaten, whipped, in some way maltreated, forced into unconditional obedience ...')[137] Alter points out that Delilah actually uses the language of sadism and masochism to lure the truth out of him because of 'her shrewd intuition of what has impelled Samson all along. The glint of the dagger in the velvet hand of love is what has excited him from Timnah onward.'[138] Part of his relationship with Delilah and the culmination of his self-abuse is the gouging out of his eyes. How much of a masochist is he?

Going Up and Down

> Once Samson went down to Timnah ... Then he went down and spoke to the woman ... He went down to Ashkelon and killed thirty of its men.... Then he went down and stayed in the cave of the rock Etam.... 'We have come down... to take you prisoner ... The Philistines seized him and gouged out his eyes. They brought him down to Gaza ... His brothers and all his father's household came down and carried him up and buried him ... (Judg. 14.1, 17, 19, 15.11, 12; 16.21, 31).

Samson's spiritual decline is marked by Hebrew's *yrd* as he goes down cosmologically and geographically, making it back up only by being carried by Jews. This 'down' also marked Jonah's descent as he defied God.

---

136. Alter, 'Samson without Folklore', p. 53. Alter continues of Delilah, 'The maiming to which she will lead him, the gouging out of his eyes, is, of course, in orthodox Freudian terms an image of castration ...'
137. Freud, 'Masochism', p. 162.
138. Alter, 'Samson without Folklore', p. 53.

Delilah

> After that, he fell in love with a woman in the Wadi Sorek, named Delilah ... She lulled him to sleep on her lap. Then she called in a man, and she had him cut off the seven locks of his head; thus she weakened him and made him helpless: his strength slipped away from him (Judg. 16.4, 19).

Delilah is different and Samson falls in love with her. She is the first woman to have a name. She is not a whore like the woman from Gaza, or defined by her relation to her parents like the Timnite woman. She is independent and her motivation seems not to do with self-preservation but with self-promotion: Delilah is a femme fatale.[139]

Samson sees Delilah, but he does not make the first move. For that matter, neither does she. It is the lords of the Philistines who do: they go up to her offering her money for his secret, and that action determines the subsequent narrative. There is no wooing between them as such, just Delilah's no-nonsense questions and Samson's evasive answers. With her questions begins a new pattern of ties melting in his hand.

Camille Paglia, for whom femmes fatales are so important, gives as good a definition of what one is as anyone:

> Her cool unreproachability beckons, fascinates, and destroys ... She has ... an amoral affectlessness, a serene indifference to the suffering of others, which she invites and dispassionately observes as tests of her power.[140]

It is remarkably easy to diagnose Delilah as such a one, despite the spare Hebrew that describes her actions and the results of her actions. 'Delilah has become a trope for the femme fatale.'[141]

---

139. Since I decided to investigate the femme fatale element in Samson's story (inspired partly by Philip Lopate's article 'Samson and Delilah'), Cheryl Exum has published a chapter in a similar vein ('Why, Why, Why, Delilah?', in Exum, *Plotted*, pp. 175-237). As I do, she calls Delilah a femme fatale, uses film theory, cites Camille Paglia, Rubens's paintings, and even Paul Durcan's poems (below). Finally, though, Exum is more interested in Delilah than in Samson. In this, however, she does femmes fatales a disservice, especially when she comments on how 'normal folk' view certain types of women: 'Just by looking at her we know she is a prostitute and a femme fatale ...' Exum says 'we' have less respect for such women, automatically.

140. C. Paglia, *Sex and Violence, or Nature and Art* (London: Penguin Books, 1995), p. 21.

141. Exum, *Plotted*, p. 176.

Samson never gets angry at Delilah. As opposed to other bouts of anger he has in the narrative, here he has plenty of provocation, but for once he does not respond. Unlike with the other 'warp-spasms', furthermore, his offences here also feature no subsequent yield (as of honey, or sets of clothing), no spirit of the LORD to inspire him, and no return to his parents (as there was with the lion). The trick of his anger, previously a vehicle for the LORD, has been reduced to its effective exploitation in a sexual game. Instead of resisting binding and abuse, he is simply asking to be tied up in new and exciting ways. Each time he answers Delilah as to how he might be afflicted, he is essentially asking for that affliction. His evasions are requests because he knows, as does the reader, that she will try them out in order to sap his strength. So, each time he asks to be bound he lies, and the elaborate form of his lies —since we know they are not a confession at all—comes out sounding like a masochistic fantasy: 'If they bind me with seven fresh bowstrings that are not yet dried, then I will be weak, and be as any other man ...' Each successive scenario is more about him and her as Samson cares less about secret-concealment and approaches the truth in his answers. (This secret is not just the secret of destroying him, or the secret to his Nazirite identity, but it is also a thing sacred to God in itself, the revelation of which or not is a holy matter, not to be chatted glibly about.)

Samson seems relaxed and happy for the first time. In Delilah's company he has found a riddle game he can keep playing, and get to be prey to a beautiful woman (or, as the text has it, a woman he loves) at the same time. For her part, Delilah can do her job because she knows when Samson says the real answer, by no reason disclosed in the text. This is further proof of their intimacy, and it even implies that the questions were song and dance for her as well, she only pretending to believe him the other times. Such intimacy further suggests the mutual nature of whatever kind of relationship they have, and not that one party is stupid and the other evil.

Delilah gets paid. The moment of their most obvious intimacy (when he tells her who he really is) is when the sacrilegious nature of their relationship is clearest: her realization of his identity is commemorated in her getting paid. (Milton's Dalila at least, if not everyone's, is a more loyal citizen than Samson; she is openly working for her state from the beginning.) Meanwhile, when Samson reveals the information, he is more removed from his LORD than ever.

Many artists, composers and authors have interpreted this love story on paper and canvas, despite the fact that the book of Judges never says what Delilah thinks of Samson, or what she looks like. Rubens, however, has a clear idea in *Samson Asleep in Delilah's Lap*, where she has a mixture of love and pity on her face. She is of two minds: she keeps one hand back, and one hand she rests on him. It is over this second hand that a Philistine carefully cuts Samson's hair.

As Bal has shown about other paintings and biblical texts, so does Rubens's work and others about Samson offer insights into how this terse story may be read. Paul Durcan's poem 'Samson and Delilah II',[142] about the same painting, confirms the love game, the 'dagger in the velvet hand of love' (Alter) nature of their relationship. Samson's complicity in the act of his haircut is manifest in Rubens's painting as Durcan rewrites the depicted/ biblical dialogue:

—Am I going to die, Delilah?
—A little dying, silly Samson, a little dying.

Durcan's paraphrase reveals a reading of Samson's absolute submission and again, the give-and-take nature of their intimacy.

Commenting on another depiction of this scene, Mantegna's *Samson and Delilah*, R.H. Wilenski writes, 'considered as an illustration of the savagely human story in the Old Testament, it is timid and comically urbane in concept'.[143] The most common reading of the story holds that there can be no logical explanation for this woman's betrayal and for Samson's foolhardiness in believing her. Mantegna sees something else, something that is not tragic, but 'comically urbane' indeed: a private understanding between the abuser and the abused, a sadomasochistic arrangement, a game. Lopate finds that

> a collaboration or collusion existed between Samson and Delilah. Not that 'she done him wrong' but that together the lovers were able to bring about the desired fatalistic result, which they had been working up to in practice three times.[144]

Durcan sees the deathwish in the Mantegna painting and has his Delilah voice the terms of their relationship:

142. In P. Durcan, *Give Me Your Hand* (London: Macmillan, 1994), pp. 69-70.
143. R.H. Wilenski, *Mantegna and the Paduan School* (London: Faber, 1947), p. 20.
144. Lopate, 'Samson and Delilah', p. 88.

Pity about Samson.
I love him.
But let me not be sentimental.
He got what he wanted—
Got to die in my arms…
Pity about men
All the time pining to die.[145]

In this last couplet Durcan suggests not just the play between the two of them but Delilah's recognition of a generally masculine masochism, by which she is willingly cast as the femme fatale. (The femme fatale is not a vulgar, flashily sexy woman, but a woman whom a man seeks because he knows she can destroy him—irrespective of her looks or taste. Exum misses this when she asks about Cecil B. De Mille's Delilah, 'Who but a femme fatale would have a tiger-skin rug in her boudoir?')

In Mantegna (unlike Rubens and Rembrandt) the scene is outdoors and the Philistines are nowhere to be seen. Perhaps this means that Delilah's motivation for her violence lies not in her desire to be a 'good' Philistine, nor in her greed for the money the Philistines promise her. Her motivation comes from her nature, which brings her satisfaction by means of the deadly game they both like. Unfortunately, she seems to say, all the best players die in the end.

Shave and a Haircut

Thus, it is not just a psychoanalytic reading that reveals the association of Samson's strength and masculinity in his hair and his subjugation/ castration in its removal. There is a folk motif of giant strength in hair[146] suggesting the widespread association of the two in mythology, where cutting is strength-depletion and emasculation, as Niditch notes, among others: 'The shearing of Samson's hair is a sexual stripping and subjugation.'[147]

Aided Conrói maic Dáiri ('The Tragic Death of Cú Rói mac Dári')[148]

---

145. Durcan, 'Samson and Delilah I', in *idem*, *Hand*, pp. 29-30.

146. Cf. Stith Thompson, *Motif-Index of Folk Literature* (Bloomington: Indiana University Press, 1955), D1831.

147. Niditch, 'Culture Hero', p. 620.

148. It is presently available in R.I. Best, 'The Tragic Death of Cúrói mac Dári', *Ériu* 2, pp. 18-355. Maria Tymoczko offers a modern translation in *Two Death Tales from the Ulster Cycle: The Death of CuChulainn and the Death of CuRoi* (Dublin: Dolmen Press, 1981). For an interesting analysis of its structure, see B.K.

must be mentioned at this point for its resonances with this theme, although it has no place in the sexual or martial initiation of Cú Chulainn. In this Ulster Cycle tale, Cú Chulainn is not the hero. In fact, the story presents the opposite of most characterizations of Cú Chulainn from the Ulster Cycle. Here Cú Rói is the hero, and his first act is to humiliate Cú Chulainn by shaving off his hair and rubbing cow dung on his head. Once he has done this Cú Chulainn slinks away to conspire with Cú Rói's woman, Bláthnait, to ambush him. In a flurry of Samson-like motifs, Bláthnait 'betrays' Cú Rói mostly by means of his hair.

'Betrayal'

Betsy Meredith points out that this story of Judges and the apocryphal book of Judith feature the same story with different focalization.[149] Bal's work and others on general trends in the book of Judges also draw attention to the comparability of Delilah with other female biblical characters from 'the other side'.[150] The word betrayal depends on who the reader thinks of as the good guy.

It is finally up to the reader how she wants to understand a book or passage, but the decks are stacked against Delilah. (Feminism like Exum's, which accepts Samson's gaze by dividing bad, cheap women from good, marriageable women further dictates how much the reader expects Delilah to be nasty.) Thus, when exegetes refer to Samson's betrayal, it is not because of Delilah's actions alone: 'One of the most important characteristics that has been given to the actors is nationality, and this, of course, has a great effect on the reader's perception of "hero" and "villain" '.[151] Milton's Dalila makes this point herself, defending her actions not only in terms of acting for her own people's good, but also for acting like 'other' biblical heroines like 'Jael, who with inhospitable guile/ Smote Sisera ...'[152]

Martin, 'Medieval Irish *aitheda* and Todorov's "Narratologie" ', *Studia Celtica* 10/11 (1975–76), pp. 138-51.

149. B. Meredith, 'Desire and Danger: The Drama of Betrayal in Judges and Judith', in M. Bal (ed.), *Anti-Covenant: Counter-Reading Women's Lives in the Hebrew Bible* (JSOTSup, 81; Bible and Literature Series, 22; Sheffield: Almond Press, 1989), pp. 63-77.

150. Bal, *Death and Dissymmetry*, and *Anti-Covenant, passim*.

151. Meredith, 'Desire and Danger', p. 69.

152. John Milton, *Samson Agonistes* (London: Davis-Poynter, 1973).

Furthermore, Delilah is not concealing her intentions, as the term 'betrayal' implies. 'Samson takes too much active pleasure inventing the three lies about his strength for him to be seen as merely a passive moth drawn to the flame.'[153] Thus we have to re-evaluate the logic of 'bad woman tricking man' that goes with a traditional reading of Samson. In fact, here, the man is the focus of action and he is choosing his fate. 'Samson is depicted as being completely informed and aware of what is going on.'[154] We can reasonably shift from a feminist reading to a masculinist one.

Without a knowledge of 'sides', the woman's action in this story can be read in many more neutral ways. Exum assesses Cecil B. De Mille's *Samson and Delilah*, but fails to notice one self/other contrast that the film glosses over, diluting the tribal tension of the story. Typical of American cinema (which mentions the word 'Jew' for the first time in 1947[155]), cinema-goers are presented with a story they already know but featuring two basically anonymous tribes whose identities are only as moralistically charged as 'Leinstermen' and 'Munstermen'. In the film, Samson is not even a 'Hebrew', as Lopate points out.[156] The picture is thus 'defanged', free of any contentious pro-Jewish material, and the audience can focus instead on the love story of its two main characters, the greatest consequence of which drama is their love.

Samson's Passivity ...

Bal points out that Delilah is the one to speak in the Samson story, where Samson only reacts.[157] We see Delilah's point of view and not Samson's (as we saw only Emer's in *TEm*). In a later work,[158] Bal identifies this instinct again, using slightly more subversive language about Judges, and pointing towards the viability of a conclusion of masochism. In other words, she locates intent and not just absent-mindedness in his passive role, and takes the first step in saying why he is

---

153. Lopate, 'Samson and Delilah', p. 85.

154. Meredith, 'Desire and Danger', p. 71.

155. In Elia Kazan's *Gentleman's Agreement*. I am grateful to the Jewish Museum, New York City, for this information.

156. Lopate, 'Samson and Delilah', p. 73.

157. Cf. M. Bal, 'Delilah Decomposed: Samson's Talking Cure and the Rhetoric of Subjectivity', in *idem*, *Lethal Love*, pp. 37-67.

158. Bal, *Death and Dissymmetry*, p. 224.

intentionally putting himself in this position. His actions 'point to a desire to stop being the heroic performer and to let himself pursue his own inclinations'.[159] As with Cú Chulainn in *Serglige Con Culainn*, we see here that the strongman's complicity in his damage provides him with a chance to stop being the culture's hero and to rebel against that by lusting, but also by losing.

... and Femininity?

From here, Bal concludes that Samson is insecure about his sexuality. While I do not think this need be true in order for an understanding of his behaviour to be coherent, some of the points she observes are of interest.[160] They also occasionally resonate with Cú Chulainn's portrait, as noted in brackets.

- The hero is conceived 'without sex' (as Cú Chulainn is by most versions of *Compert Con Culainn*).
- 'He moves into the house of a woman as often as three times' (as Cú Chulainn operates in women's realms in *TEm* and *Serglige*).
- 'He keeps his masculinity a secret' (Cú Chulainn in his opening dialogues with Emer in *TEm*, and to the Ulaid in *Serglige*, although sometimes he tries to broadcast it—but so does Samson).
- 'His sexual power is in his hair, a symbol of female appeal.' (No parallel here, but Cú Chulainn is noted for his beauty, as discussed above.)
- 'He has no children' (—or kills them? [*AOA*]).
- 'His love is defined according to the feminine principle of surrender' (as Cú Chulainn's, according to my reading of *Serglige*).
- 'He ends without woman.'

Milton describes a similar weakness in his *Samson*, and even calls it effeminacy. That is, Milton's Samson is not just prey to women, and a weak man because of that, but feminine himself (Milton also picks up on the willingness of binding here):

---

159. Bal, *Death and Dissymmetry*, p. 225.
160. Bal, *Lethal Love*, p. 63.

> ... a grain of manhood well resolved
> Might easily have shook off all her snares:
> But fool effeminacy held me yoked
> Her Bond-slave ...

Lopate also locates femininity in Samson's dealings, especially in his dealings with Delilah. 'The strongman enters the tent, secretly, to become a woman. Lovemaking allows him to be tender, to loll about in bed, to be playful and "effeminate".'[161] I am not arguing that either Cú Chulainn or Samson is feminine. Rather, I accept the above interpretations as signs of weakness, and direct them back to a conclusion of a peculiarly masculine masochism.

Femininity in Freudian terms is basically equivalent to passivity. He labels one phenomenon 'feminine masochism' (although it is, of course, found also in men), explaining that '[the fantasies] place the subject in a characteristically feminine position'.[162] Here, the waiting in the lap, the concealment of identity, and other features that critics have identified as feminine in Samson can be taken a step further towards a specific kind of male (or female) behaviour: masochism. This masochism, an unconscious or conscious weakness, is a reflex of Samson's conflict with the Nazirate, and of the debt he has to his patriarchy to be strong.

Dying

> Samson cried, 'Let me die with the Philistines!' and he pulled with all his might. The temple came crashing down on the lords, and on all the people in it. Those who were slain by him as he died outnumbered those who had been slain by him when he lived (Judg. 16.30).

Samson's final hour is his best, it is generally admitted. Whether we see these lines as a return to the fold, his only act for his people, his only sign of having learned something, or the proof that he has learned nothing and is just demonstrating his renewed superhuman strength, it is certainly a moment of triumph for Samson (and for the Jews, intentionally or unintentionally on his part). It comes at the end of Samson's passivity with Delilah, his playful submission to her in three tyings-up, his strength-sapping through a haircut, his eyes' having been gouged out, and his public humiliation at a feast to honour a pagan god. In this accumulation, too, we see the definition of the masochist who

161. Lopate, 'Samson and Delilah', p. 86.
162. Freud, 'Masochism', p. 162.

loses all battles except the last ... He lets his opponent, sadism, taste all the pleasure of the hour—he even joins in the feast—but he patiently waits for the moment to bring the great turn ... It is characterised by unconscious defeat and by the secret foretaste and foreknowledge of coming conquest.[163]

The 'foreknowledge of coming conquest' is certainly within Samson's experience. In fact, he conquers in several ways during his temple scene. For one, he has his revenge on the Philistines, killing them all after what they have done to him. But is it inconsistent to suggest that he wants revenge at all when, according to the reading thus far he has been gratified by their abuse? How does his defeating the Philistines connect to the apparent willingness with which he pursued his self-de-structive relations with Delilah and the other Gentile women?

Reik offers a somewhat surrealist description of masochism which is, however, appropriate to the present biblical text:

If not in his lifetime, the masochistic character will assert himself after his death and gain the rights denied to him on this earth. Posterity will judge him better and will take revenge on his enemies ... the masochistic character has expanded his sufferings to cover his whole life.[164]

On a larger level, however, Samson conquers twice, defeating not only the Philistines, but also the law of patriarchy that has thus far informed his existence. How is Samson taking revenge on the LORD and challenging the Law by destroying the Temple? He is 'beating' the LORD because by this act, he has refused to renounce his desire completely. His desire, which takes so many self-destructive turns, takes the ulti-mate self-destructive turn here. We have seen how Samson's masochis-tic drive is a way for him to try to ignore God and his duty to the Law. In bringing down the temple, he has killed not only the Philistines but himself. In destroying himself, he defeats God's plan to 'own' him completely.

Judaism no less than most other religions discourages suicide. How much more of an affront to God it is to destroy his favourite creation, man, and not any man, but a Nazirite, in whom God's spirit not only dwells but throbs. By destroying his own sacred God-created form (by any means) Samson comes as close to destroying God as anyone can come.

163. Reik, *Love and Lust*, p. 363.
164. Reik, *Love and Lust*, p. 363.

Samson's final act has a definite flair: Dagon-worshippers scatter, abandoning half-full glasses of wine, as the walls of their temple crash in on them. Samson is a laughable blind man no more. He is completing his physical destruction, welcoming death while also taking revenge in front of a huge crowd. The masochist needs a witness in his acts which have 'the characteristic of a performance and frequently [do] not dispense with a certain theatrical flavour... Even for the solitary monks ... there was the one and all-important witness: God.'[165]

The submissiveness of Samson towards Delilah is not about Samson and Delilah alone. God's spirit pounds in Samson and he is always acting to escape it, to sully its 'goodness', the goodness that is part of him, working against the other part of him, his desire. Every act of submission to women is an act of rebellion against God.

On some level, however, this is all in God's plan, whether or not Samson's will is taken into account, by means of a method that the God of the book of Jonah also uses. We know when Samson sees the Timnite woman that God has set him up ('His father and mother did not realise that this was the LORD's doing: He was seeking a pretext against the Philistines'). We do not know how many of Samson's adventures are within God's plan, or how far he had wanted Samson to embroil himself in Philistine affairs in order to overturn them. We only know that by the end of Samson's time that spirit is far enough removed that he must beg God to have it back.

Women represent self-destruction by offering Samson the chance to hurt himself *personally* by means of humiliation, as in the episode with the Timnite woman and the riddle. But women are also an occasion for his overall self-destruction, offering him the chance to hurt himself *spiritually* and culturally by exogamy—and therefore helping him to destroy God's spirit within him. It is not just in his sexual dealings that Samson is a masochist, however. His words to God at his death, 'Let me die with the Philistines', would not make sense as part of a system of only sexual masochism—the women are gone now, and he did not appeal to God when they were there. Instead, Samson now asks for God to collaborate in his self-destruction.

If this short story were only about God's conquering all and Samson understanding of his duty at the last, then Samson would not have died. Instead, Samson's line (if he had one) might have been punished, which

165. Reik, *Love and Lust*, pp. 241-42.

might be more in keeping with biblical tradition. God cannot have wanted Samson to end his own life—a life God had devoted his spirit to defending so many times, a life an angel announced—although he supplied him with the strength to take it. Rather, Samson has rigged a situation where both God and his own desire must compromise themselves, and thus fuse within him.

Freud describes the 'end' of a masochistic hero as follows:

> Masochism creates a temptation to perform 'sinful' actions [literally sinful, in this case, seeking exogamous women] which must then be expiated by the reproaches of the sadistic conscience [his frequent sufferings at their hands]... or by chastisement from the great parental power of Destiny. [The LORD] In order to provoke punishment from this last representative of the parents [Samson's parents are openly working with the angel, and thus, the LORD] the masochist must do what is inexpedient, must act against his own interests [seek a Philistine bride, tell Delilah secrets, etc.], must ruin the prospects which open out to him in the real world and must, perhaps, destroy his own real existence.[166]

Samson ends by destroying his own existence. By bringing down the temple he is not just fulfilling the LORD's intended purpose for him, he is also killing himself, and thus directly thwarting God's intentions and any tribal law.

Epitaph
John Vickery writes:

> [O]ne of the most striking things about Samson is precisely the fact that he inspires no confidence in his abilities on the part of others and that he has no followers whatsoever... The net effect of this ambivalence concerning Samson's charismatic qualities is to point up and underscore the significance of ... divine intervention.[167]

That Samson may have had a victory himself does not cast much of a shadow on God's ultimate plan. '[The LORD] takes a bully boy and a muscle man bent on the gratification of his own drives ... and makes him the instrument of a nation's defence and rescue.'[168]

---

166. Freud, 'Masochism', p. 169.

167. J.B. Vickery, 'In Strange Ways: The Story of Samson', in B.O. Long (ed.), *Images of Man and God: Old Testament Short Stories in Literary Focus* (Bible and Literature Series, 1; Sheffield: Almond Press, 1981), pp. 58-73 (60).

168. Vickery, 'In Strange Ways', p. 61.

Samson never acts except in reaction to what God expects of him. We see his interpretation of the Nazirite vow, his straining under its bit, but even his self-destructive acts cannot really shake it. God set out to make someone kill the Philistines; the Philistines are dead: God has succeeded. Samson's brand of weakness becomes another tool in God's plan, much as Jonah's was in the book of Jonah.

6. *Conclusion*

In the following section I hope to sketch some of the attributes that make up the type of masculinity that has been chronicled in the above essays. (More general genre-seeking seems difficult when, as critics have noted, Samson is not typical of biblical heroes, and no picture of the hero could include an accurate portrait of Cú Chulainn. Instead I will offer occasional parallels from other texts that address issues of masculinity. These narratives are useful glosses on these tales where one lone man must pursue his course as a chosen one in a dirty world where women are enemies there to distract and defeat him.)

Krutnik writes about film noir in a way that can be seen to include the masculine hero generally, and our heroes in particular:

> The hero proves his worthiness to take up his place as a man by accomplishing a series of directed tests: a process which will often culminate ... with his integration into the cultural order through marriage ... Indeed, the Oedipal model has a widespread currency in patriarchal fictional forms (from classical mythology to the dime novel).[169]

I have previously referred to the 'Superman' type conflict, in which the hero's excessive goodness is a burden. He is elected to be a people's champion but he is not allowed to participate intimately in the life of that people and is an enemy to other groups.

Alan Bruford addresses this point in his article 'Cú Chulainn—An Ill-Made Hero?'[170] arguing that Cú Chulainn's perfection is cartoonish, and that he is an unlikely folk hero for this reason. The article's subheading 'The Too Perfect Hero' can be seen to connect with what the narrator of *Tochmarc Emire* said about Cú Chulainn's unusual faults: What does it mean for a superhero to be too good at what he does and is?

169. Krutnik, *Lonely Street*, p. 87.
170. A. Bruford, 'Cú Chulainn—An Ill-Made Hero?', in H.L.C. Tristram (ed.), *Text und Zeittiefe* (Tübingen: G. Narr, 1994), pp. 185-215.

Bruford writes a sort of reader-response essay, gauging the response of an audience contemporaneous with the *Táin*, and asking how Cú Chulainn could be taken seriously. He writes with reference to the *Táin* in general that 'It is arguable that an element of the burlesque and self-mockery is built into the story from the first'.[171] He suggests that it is the narrator's intention to 'overdo it', and that what has traditionally been understood as a sincere admiration on the narrator's part for the gore that marks early Irish saga literature is in fact intended as hyperbole.

This mockery, as Bruford sees it, is an intentional distancing of audience from subject, which serves to remind them that the action is not really happening in the narrator's own time (and that of his original audience) and, furthermore, that it could never happen—an early mediaeval *Verfremdung* effect. Elaboration is remembered as exaggeration, and repeated in later centuries as humour.

Bruford feels that Cú Chulainn, as well as most Ulstermen in the Ulster Cycle, is 'too good to be true, a perfect and invincible hero', and that his invincibility makes him an unlikely choice for being an Irish folk hero.[172] Further disqualifying the Ulaid from the role of folk hero-tribe to the Irish is the fact that their enemies are almost always other Irishmen. Bruford feels that such a hero is less sympathetic than one who is remembered for fighting against all of Ireland's enemies.

Bruford compares Cú Chulainn to Superman 'who eliminates the would-be destroyers of his community... has superhuman strength and endurance...'[173] Superman is indeed like Cú Chulainn, but I would take Bruford's analogy even further. These two superheroes are alike, not just for their excessive strength but because of the fact they both do have faults, and inasmuch as they are indeed both folk heroes even if they are sometimes characterized in an 'exaggerated' way. Bruford may have overlooked the crucial appeal of Superman's identity and indeed that of the other strongmen with whose unrealistic strength he would compare Cú Chulainn's: they intrigue us because of their strength despite their weakness. Batman, whom Bruford also invokes, has a great burden: the secret of his identity. The anger he feels about his past (his parents' murder by criminals) serves as a source for his particular warp-

171. Bruford, 'Ill-Made Hero', p. 203.
172. Bruford, 'Ill-Made Hero', p. 202.
173. Bruford, 'Ill-Made Hero', p. 202.

spasm/metamorphosis. And, of course, like Cú Chulainn, he is named
for the animal whose identity he has taken on.

Bruford remembers the indefatigability of Superman and compares it
to the brute strength of Cú Chulainn. We may look past that strength to
the weaknesses also found in both their characters, and the essence
of being a strongman-hero. Seeing himself as Superman and Samson,
Lopate writes, 'I would picture being in the presence of Kryptonite and
the voluptuous surrender to weakness ... this letting go of the effort to
be a little man.'[174]

What are the results of the pressure to be strong, what happens when
the personal desire for weakness and public commitment to honour
codes clash? Early Irish literature in general seems driven to explore
this clash of obligations, as O'Leary has shown, as it does through its
tradition of *gessa*, supernaturally enforced taboos. Dunn notes about the
collection of early Irish stories that he studied that 'an implicit opposition of "self" and "other" structures the action and geography of the
narrative'.[175] O'Leary acknowledges a conflict in the early Irish hero
when he writes that they are all 'enmeshed in a code of expectations
from which they see no... escape'.[176] His language betrays a psycho-

174. (Lopate, 'Samson and Delilah', p. 89). Superman is born on a now-destroyed
planet, Krypton. He comes to earth as an outsider and sees that his strength is
extraordinary by Earth standards. Raised by foster-parents too old to have children
of their own, and under the new name they give him, he shows enormous strength
even as a small boy. Little is known of his boyhood deeds, but while he is still a
young man he sets off on adventures to defend not just his family but his whole country against evil. His successes at this astonish one and all: women fall in love with
him, evil geniuses try to destroy him, and fail. (All this he shares with Cú Chulainn.)

David Mamet discusses Superman's weakness in an essay 'Kryptonite' [in his
Some Freaks (London: Faber & Faber, 1989), pp. 175-80]. In his identity as Clark
Kent, Superman cannot enjoy the fruit of his fame because he must conceal his true
self. At the same time, he cannot remain in the company of the people who admire
him as Superman lest they find out who he really is, and by finding out the secret of
his identity jeopardize his role as saviour. The women who are attracted to him
represent the largest threat, tempting him into revealing who he really is in order to
be closer to them. Thus he can clear buildings in a single bound, but he cannot have
intimacy: 'his power is obtained then, at the expense of any possibility of personal
pleasure' (p. 177).

175. Dunn, *Cattle-Raids*, p. 39.

176. O'Leary, 'Choice and Consequence', p. 50.

analytical sympathy: how do the characters (or people, as he sees them) perceive the situation? They see no escape. Cú Chulainn and others are trapped between what they would like to do ('desire') and what they must do ('the law').

Melia finds that certain Ulster Cycle death-tales reflect this same contrast: 'These stories demonstrate what must be the primary conflict ... that emotional obligations are often in conflict with legal or customary obligations.'[177] But what is 'emotional obligation'? There is only the instinct of breaking the mould, a motion away from society's expectations. No emotions are mentioned in the texts, so the point is that it has to be the wrong woman, not just any woman.

As the Nazirate weighs on Samson and dictates who he may be, so is the weight of expectation on Cú Chulainn great. Cú Chulainn is literally composed of the hopes of the Ulaid, and is their occasion to show off and conquer. The blessing of their fostering is perhaps ambiguous: 'ba cumma no ndamnaigfetar uili etir errid & rig & ollamain' ('let it be thus that all will instruct him—both champion and king and poet').[178] *Damnaigidir* means 'materializes, embodies, shapes, forms, builds',[179] thus stressing the sense of their ownership of Cú Chulainn.

Cú Chulainn has had to assume a strongman identity from the beginning—willingly, perhaps, but as a result of a kind of trick: Conchobor should not have forgotten the little boy he invited home earlier the same day, the dog should not have been released, Cú Chulainn should not have had to save his own life on the way to dinner with friends.

Looking back over some of Cú Chulainn's adventures, we see the conflict of weakness and strength (or desire and the Law) again and again, as illustrated by the chart on p. 180.

---

177. Melia, *Narrative*, p. 117.
178. Van Hamel (ed.), *Compert*, pp. 8, 164.
179. *DIL*, p. 180.

Desire v. Patriarchy

Tale	Masculine Desire	Law of Patriarchy
Macgnímrada ('Boyhood Deeds')	kills recklessly (named Sétantae, his own name)	must defend Ulster, kill according to rules, as named pet (Cú Chulainn)
Tochmarc Emire	chooses exogamous bride, Emer	should go with women chosen by the Ulaid
Aided Óenfir Aífe	acts destructively, kills son (and leaves Ulster without an heir)	must act responsibly, kill boy (and defend Ulster's honour)
Serglige Con Culainn	wants to abandon Ulster, rest, be weak, succumb, go for Otherworld beauties	ought to serve Ulster, wake up, fight, win, go for his wife, Emer
	wants to break contract with patriarchy, dare to fail	must always succeed as hero

Although this has been a reading for masculinity, no single reading covers all the possibilities of a text. Bal's words are too strong if they feminize Samson, but so are mine if I seem to endorse the misogyny of the narrator, and the male character's viewpoint. Certainly the Bible itself is not guilty of such single-mindedness—its agenda is ultimately inclusive, and concerns the coexistence of different kinds of people.

That is, beyond the femme fatale/hard-boiled hero plot-diagnosis, these stories are about human dynamics, social pressures and divided loyalties in general. That enduring theme is what makes connections to twentieth- and twenty-first-century popular literature possible and plausible; it is also what makes the tales good. In some sense, the male–female distinction is useful only in a fabular sense: sexes are relevant only as much as different kinds of animals are in Aesop. As Derek Mahon writes in *The Hudson Letter* about Ovid's *Metamorphoses* and the Philomela episode (another ancient, violent, and sexual text),

> Never mind the hidden agenda, the sub-text;
> It's not really about male arrogance, 'rough sex'
> or vengeful sisterhood, but about art
> and the encoded mysteries of the human heart.[180]

180. Derek Mahon, *The Hudson Letter* (Dublin: The Gallery Press, 1996).

Chapter 5

WEAKNESS AND FOLLY: A READING OF THE BOOK
OF ESTHER AND *TOCHMARC BECFHOLA*

In the preceding readings I hope to have shown that perspective has much to do with what is called good or bad. Much of twentieth-century thinking went towards articulating this—that what some call good is not necessarily intrinsically good. Post-structuralist thought, as I understand it, seeks not only to question the hierarchy of 'good's' and 'not good's', but seeks a way to define X as other than not-Y, to look at something in its own terms.

In my examination of the book of Esther and *Tochmarc Becfhola* I try to understand where lines between categories are drawn in the narrative to determine sides, and what those sides are.[1] The book of Esther becomes an intertext to a reading for the contrasts in *Tochmarc Becfhola*, and its more openly stated sides a provocative scale against which to measure *Tochmarc Becfhola*'s. I try to address such questions as Who has power/who is disempowered? Who belongs to what group/ how is that allegiance established? What are virtues/ how do we know this from the text? Who is weak or strong; is it what we expect?

In *Death and Dissymmetry*, Mieke Bal offers a 'model for narratological analysis' in which she directs the analyst toward questions whose answers point to the balance of power among characters in a narrative.[2] Questions like 'Who never speaks?', 'Who focalises more

---

1. Timothy K. Beal's *The Book of Hiding: Gender, Ethnicity, Annihilation, and Esther* (London: Routledge, 1997) is notable among several important books not available when I wrote this book. Beal explores themes in the book of Esther to which I only allude here, addressing questions of Esther's power, Mordecai's 'borderline' identity and the tribal role of the Jews in the narrative. Beal's enunciation of the theme of Esther's 'coming out' would have been especially useful to me as I tried to illumine some of the book's dark corners and those of its putative parallel, *Tochmarc Becfhola*.

2. Bal, *Death and Dissymmetry*, pp. 248-49.

than he/she speaks?', 'Are actions effective?' characterize this kind of analysis. In the case of *Tochmarc Becfhola* I tried to understand the balance of power by charting the answers to questions like Bal's as well as more mytho-literary questions like 'Is there a boundary being crossed here?' The answers helped me form a more detailed picture of the fabric of this short tale.[3]

In discussing the book of Esther I will refer to the two targums of that book, as well as Midrash Rabbah. (Targums are Aramaic translations of parts of the Hebrew Bible. These two targums have been edited, with commentary, by Bernard Grossfeld, who places them both in the seventh or eight centuries CE.[4] Midrash Rabbah is a collection of rabbinical exegesis from the early mediaeval period. Jacob Neusner dates *Esther Rabbah* to the fifth or sixth centuries CE in his translation.)[5] In Chapter 2, I discussed some of the importance of Midrash. Targumim *Rishon* and *Sheni* of the book of Esther provide an unusual commentary on the book of Esther which can be read alongside more modern critiques.

As John Carey wrote in 1989, *Tochmarc Becfhola* has received 'relatively little scholarly attention'.[6] It was re-edited and translated in 1984, along with historical commentary, by Máire Bhreathnach.[7] This article, along with Carey's, form the foundation of criticism for this small tale. Carney writes that it is a 'peculiar, confused tale'[8] and Carey refers to it as 'rich and significant out of all proportion to its brevity'.[9] Interestingly, James Stephens includes an adaptation of it in his *Irish Fairy Stories*.[10]

3. Some of these details can be found in Appendix III.

4. B. Grossfeld (ed. and trans.), *The Two Targums of Esther* (Collegeville, MN: Liturgical Press, 1991).

5. J. Neusner (ed. and trans.), *Esther Rabbah I: An Analytical Translation* (Atlanta: Scholars Press, 1989), p. xi.

6. J. Carey, 'Otherworlds and Verbal Worlds in Middle Irish Narrative', in William Mahon (ed.), *Proceedings of the Harvard Celtic Colloquium. IX. 1989* (Cambridge, MA: Department of Celtic Languages and Literatures, Harvard University, 1990), pp. 31-39 (35).

7. Details of transmission are discussed in M. Bhreathnach, 'A New Edition of *Tochmarc Becfhola*', *Ériu* 35 (1984), pp. 59-92 (59, 67-71).

8. J. Carney, *Studies in Irish Literature and History* (Dublin: DIAS, 1955), p. 229.

9. Carey, 'Otherworlds', p. 36.

10. J. Stephens, 'The Wooing of Becfola', in *idem*, *Irish Fairy Tales* (London: Macmillan, 1924), pp. 135-56.

Despite its obscurity, it is a very rich tale indeed. Its number of 'disrupted literary themes'[11] can be seen either as a reason to disregard it as a literary piece or as reason to study it more carefully—as Carey has. Bhreathnach follows up a few of its historical leads but comes up mostly empty, despite her thorough analysis.

The story of Esther is perhaps best remembered as the story of Purim. Here a Jewish woman stars and navigates in a world of men, most of them Gentiles. She makes herself a hero partly by virtue of her beauty, but also by her skills in negotiation.

'Outdoing' Jonah and Samson, Esther does not mention God at all, although the Jews and the importance of community are very much at the centre of the book. Like Jonah and Samson, Esther survives in a world where she is alone.[12] Communication to other Jews is available to her only through writing and surreptitious remarks passed out from the royal realm where she must live.

Inside this domain, other characters hold most of the power, notably King Ahasuerus and Haman. It might be expected that the king would be the central figure of the narrative—indeed he would be if it were Persians and not Jews telling the story. The king does indeed play a vital role in the story and it is his weakness that galvanizes the action in the book of Esther.

This is the only book of the Bible for which there is no Dead Sea Scrolls text (although there are two Targums), which means that different early communities felt differently about whether it should be considered part of a canon. Esther is also the only portion of Scripture that can be read in any language in synagogue.

> 1. Ahasuerus is king over a huge area, and likes to give banquets. Drunk one evening, he orders his queen, Vashti, to be brought to him. When she refuses he is enraged and consults his advisors. They draw up a decree dictating that all wives must treat their husbands with respect; it is circulated everywhere.
>
> 2. They advise the king to seek a new queen, and women are assembled for him to choose from, including Esther, daughter of Mordecai, a Jew. She pleases the king. She does not reveal who her people are because Mordecai has told her not to. After she is trained and anointed she

11. Bhreathnach, '*Becfhola*', p. 65.
12. Although Mordecai is her companion in the story, she spends most of the narrated time as the only Jew living among Gentiles.

is brought to the king and he makes her queen. A banquet is held. Meanwhile, Mordecai overhears a plot against the king. He tells Esther and she tells the king—the traitors are caught and killed, the matter recorded.

3. Ahasuerus appoints Haman as his right-hand man. Haman wants respect and gets it from all except Mordecai. Enraged at Mordecai, Haman vows to kill all the Jews, and draws up an edict to this end. The king okays it (absentmindedly?) and the edict is circulated everywhere.

4. Mordecai and all the Jews mourn. Esther sees them but does not know why they are sad, and only finds out by messenger to and from Mordecai. He convinces her to appeal to the king, although she is reluctant. She agrees and tells him to fast for her.

5. Esther approaches the king, charms him, and makes a request: that Haman attend a feast. There, she invites them both to another feast. Haman glows with pride to have been invited, but is still annoyed by the disrespectful Mordecai whom he looks forward to impaling personally.

6. One night the king cannot sleep, and decides to read the royal annals. There he reads that it was Mordecai who found out that plot against him. Seeing Mordecai has received no credit for this, he consults Haman, asking (mysteriously) how Haman thinks a valuable man might best be honoured. Haman swells with pride and answers at length only to find out that this honour is for Mordecai, and that Haman himself must carry it out! Haman and his wife are worried about the future now; he goes off to Esther's banquet.

7. Queen Esther asks the king not to kill her and all her people. The king is horrified that someone has even threatened such a thing—'Who?' 'Haman.' The king storms out and Haman begs Esther for mercy so that when the king comes back in and sees them he thinks Haman is trying to ravish her. The king has Haman impaled on the very stake Haman had set up for Mordecai.

8. The king is introduced to Mordecai and gives him much wealth. The decree (which was still standing) is now rewritten, stamped with the king's mark, and circulated everywhere: the Jews can assemble and fight for their lives. All the Jews everywhere are happy; everyone else wishes they were Jews.

9. The Jews kill everyone who had wanted to kill them. The king says to Esther, 'Anything else?' 'More killing.' These days are to be observed as days of feasting and merrymaking, and called purim, 'lots', as in the intent to kill all the Jews and the reversal of that intent. Every generation is to rejoice. Queen Esther issues another decree asking equality for the Jews; this is recorded.

10. The good deeds of Ahasuerus and Mordecai are recorded.

For its remarkable preoccupation with edicts and decrees, Esther is a text that can be seen to involve all the questions of articulation and writing that concern modern theorists, as well as containing enough information on feasting and fasting to satisfy any anthropologist. Concepts of femininity and feminism as well as nationhood and languages of power come into play here.

Tochmarc Becfhola is an exceptional tale in which some of the most interesting aspects of early Irish literature come together in a bizarre pastiche-like way. The story seems to defy easy categorization: it involves monks, a parallel-time Otherworld, a bold main female character who goes to the Otherworld to woo and then comes back—as well as an Otherworld man who lingers just outside this world, waiting for a woman. Its King Díarmait, putatively the hero of the story, has in fact a more complicated relationship with majesty, and his weakness is proved by his dealings with the other characters in one way or another. This little-known tale has only recently been re-edited in an article in *Ériu*.[13]

> Díarmait is king of Ireland, his foster son Crimthann is in his charge. One day they meet the most beautiful woman. Díarmait lures her back to Tara and since his people want to know who she is, he calls her Becfhola (small bridegift). She, for her part, desires Crimthann and tries to tryst with him.
>
> On Sunday she wakes early to meet Crimthann, but lies about where she is going. Díarmait says not to go anywhere on a Sunday, but she ignores him and sets off with her maid. Wolves come and eat her maid; she escapes up a tree. From there she sees the most handsome man and goes to him, watches him cook and eat a wild boar. Together they row to a perfect palace on a perfect island. They sleep together but he does not touch her.
>
> In the morning he ('Flann') is called to a battle of four against four. He explains to Becfhola afterwards that they were his brothers and cousins and they were fighting for the island. When it is his he says he will claim her for his wife. He produces the maid and walks Becfhola back towards Tara.
>
> [Version 1] Becfhola is lying in Díarmait's bed and Flann lingers outside the window, communicating with her in verse about what has passed between them, and what is to come.
>
> In Tara, Díarmait is still waking up on the same Sunday. Four clerics come in and the king again becomes irritable about this violation of the Sabbath. They explain that they have been at a battle—the same battle (it

---

13. Bhreathnach, '*Tochmarc Becfhola*', 59-92. Two earlier MSS form her Version 1, two later ones, Version 2. Her edition of Version 1 appears in Appendix II.

seems) where Flann fought. They are here to bring the king the booty
from that scene. He refuses to accept it and gives it back to them. The
clerics add that Becfhola was at that battle. In anger he sends Becfhola
away with Flann, to whom she goes happily.

In order to find a new way to guess at all the counterintuitive turns
the story takes, I have tried reading it alongside the book of Esther. In
that text, issues of community and selfhood are to the fore in a way that
resonates with aspects of *Tochmarc Becfhola*, although the former is
a much longer story. Here, as before, a particular sign of weakness is
described, but not on the part of the main characters. Instead, it is the
king in each of these stories who is weak.

In this comparison I am also concerned to show how the heroines are
'other' to the power structures that are set out in the narratives, and yet
manage to negotiate within those power structures. I hope to do this by
a close narratological analysis which focuses on those issues.

Conflating the two stories for a moment, the following narrative
emerges: A king is drawn to a beautiful girl from another 'world'. He
loves her for her beauty and makes her his queen. She acts appealingly
to him but goes beyond what is customary with the king or beyond what
his society expects. Some of the king's advisors or companions are
suspicious of her or her people. At the same time she is drawn to
someone other than the king. As the story develops, we see that her
loyalty is to that person and his people before her loyalty to the king,
either as queen or subject.

The focus, then, seems to be on one woman who has a different
agenda from the people around her—fasting while they feast or living
in another time from the rest. Esther is a Jew living in disguise among
Gentiles, queen to the Persian king Ahasuerus.[14] Becfhola, it seems, is
from the *síd* but has been taken as queen by the high king of Ireland,
Díarmait. She also is in disguise: through to the end the king says he
does not know who she is or where she came from.

They are both elusive women whose true identity is a mystery to the
king. Esther is a mystery, however, only inasmuch as the king does not
know what people she belongs to. While this is true of King Díarmait
and Becfhola too, her 'people' is more obscure, even within the narrative. As Bhreathnach notes, there are 'tags' for the Otherworld which

14. As he is known in most translations of the Masoretic Text. For a discussion
of Ahasuerus's other aliases (e.g. Xerxes), see C.A. Moore, *Esther* (AB; Garden
City, NY: Doubleday, 1971), pp. xli-xliv.

make Becfhola recognizable as a denizen—she appears from nowhere with enviable horsemanship, for example, like Rhiannon in *Pwyll Pendeuic Dyfed*. She is beautiful or, according to Version 1, decked in splendid jewels. But the story does not say that she is from the *síd*; and the intuitive intertextual reading that places her in that tradition is challenged by incongruities in the story, like the fact that she seems to be an Otherworld visitor herself later.

In our two texts, the test of the woman's tie to the other 'world' is in her love for a man from that world. She cannot pursue the course she otherwise would (mourning with Mordecai, being with Flann) and it is not merely her own position in the king's life that prevents her. Ironically, in order to be true to the man's wishes she has to pretend to be someone else living at a distance. The man she loves puts her in the position of waiting and lying. The lies mark her entry into the king's realm.

In early Irish narrative, a woman from the *síd* may appear as a bird, as a shadow in a man's dream, or riding a magically fast horse. She might slip back to the Otherworld at any time—indeed she often operates in another time while 'her' man proceeds at 'this' world's pace. We may think of Nechtan in *Immram Brain* ('The Voyage of Bran') who turns to dust when he reaches his home shore—a shore he had been prevented from returning to by a 'land of women'. Of course, descriptions of the Otherworld vary and any attempt to distil a pattern on their basis is inadequate. By any terms, however, although *TBec* features both a wooing and an Otherworld adventure, it is very unusual both as an Otherworld and as a wooing tale.

We have seen that the casting of 'us' and 'them' can dictate whether someone calls Delilah a heroine or a slut. This kind of polarity is very important to the book of Esther, too. Susan Niditch sees the 'usness' of reader-identification in the Bible as being about 'underdogs' in many cases, and particularly in the book of Esther.

> The underdog tales distinguish between haves and have-nots—those with status and wealth and those without ...—all status issues, to be sure. In Esther, however, the clearest marker of us versus them is whether one is a Jew or not. To be a Jew is to have marginal status. [15]

Esther may be a non-Persian woman in a Persian's palace and in this

---

15. S. Niditch, *Underdogs and Tricksters* (San Francisco: Harper & Row, 1987), p. 136.

sense a minority, but the reader is aware of a larger important community to which she belongs.

Is being of the *síd* like having marginal status? It would be hard to prove, if so, and it is certainly not obvious that there is or was an Irish readership to identify with Becfhola's 'community'. Still, no other party —king, Crimthann, Flann or clergy—is clearly sympathetic either. Indeed, one way to state the strangeness of this tale is that it is not clear with whom one is meant to identify. If Becfhola's is meant to be the portrait of a fickle woman, falling for every man who comes her way, why does she get a verse to herself, why is she so strong as to be able to venture back and forth to the Otherworld, while the reader is enabled to see her point of view? If the king is wise and pious, why does he look so foolish at the end, why does he let the whole story happen while he sleeps? If the king's society are wise, why do they give such bad advice? And if the clerics are well-intentioned, why do they so upset the king—as they do James Stephens who 'translates' one as 'a lank-jawed, thin-browed brother, with uneasy intertwining fingers, and a deep-set, venomous eye'?[16]

It is Flann and Becfhola whom the narrator sends off into the sunset, and thus it is possible to assume a sympathy with them is part of an understanding of the story, as we examine it more closely.

The story begins fairly conventionally: King Díarmait is out riding one day with his foster son and a servant. He sees a beautiful Otherworld woman—but even Stephens is not sure that is where she is from: 'Either she is a woman of this world to be punished, or she is a woman of the Shí to be banished.'[17]

Becfhola is very beautiful, appears mysteriously, and is unknown; by these terms she is *síd* indeed. Version 1 accessorizes her beauty by making much of her specific monetary value. Contrary to her name, her clothes are expensive:

> She wore rounded sandals of white bronze, inset with two jewels of precious stone; a tunic covered with red-gold embroidery about her; a crimson mantle on her; a brooch in fully-wrought gold with shimmering gems of many hues.[18]

The narrator of Version 1 describes her finery but does not commit

16. Stephens, 'Becfola', p. 153.
17. Stephens, 'Becfola', p. 216.
18. Bhreathnach, '*Becfhola*', p. 77.

himself by saying she is, after all, the most beautiful woman in the world—or even beautiful—as Version 2's does.[19]
This is the opening dialogue between Díarmait and Becfhola:

> 'Whence have you come, maiden?' asked Díarmait.
> 'Not from afar', replied the maiden.
> 'What brings you (here) alone?' asked Díarmait.
> 'To seek wheat', replied the woman.
> 'You will find it with me', said Díarmait .
> 'I do not decline it', said the woman.
> After this he brought the woman with him to Temair and she shared his bed.
> 'Whence came the woman, Díarmait?' queried everyone.
> 'I will not tell', answered Díarmait .
> 'Her value is little', they all said.
> 'That will be her name', said the druids, 'Becfhola.'[20]

In nearly each line an exchange of some sort is offered: their relationship appears to be founded on bargaining, lying, sexual promises, money, a change of territory, and mystery. Every word illustrates how they are in a different position in their transactions. 'Cách' (everyone, each person) further evaluates her: her value is measured by money and social acceptance, and society has the ultimate power to name the king's bride. This theme begins here with the question of how much she has, how much she may be paid, how little she is worth, and continues through to the reimbursement that comes to the king in the end. Version 1's insistence on the cost of the wheat Díarmait offers draws further attention to this: 'I shall not refuse ... provided that I get the price.'[21]

Wealth seems to be part of the passage to the Otherworld too: Becfhola sees Flann's beauty, the bronze boat, the palatial house and its bounty (which are also parts of other Otherworld narratives). When Flann enters he is also described in terms of the elaborate wealth he is wearing (which is also not the case in Version 2.) In the end, however, all the Otherworld wealth is reduced to as much as can be stripped off Flann's relatives' bodies in this world. For both Flann and Becfhola value is often measured in terms of wealth—or, more accurately, in what they would be worth if they were exchanged for money.

19. 'Áilliu ná gach ben do mnáibh an betha' (Bhreathnach, '*Becfhola*', p. 81).
20. Bhreathnach, '*Becfhola*', p. 84.
21. Bhreathnach, '*Becfhola*', p. 77.

William McBride has offered a persuasive reading of the book of Esther along similar lines.[22] It is clear from the exposition of the book of Esther that wealth is of major importance in the narrative, but McBride renders visible a pattern of exchange of money and worth (as, for example, Haman and Mordecai's exchanging of position and prosperity). This chiasmus is especially true of Esther's worth. She is

> like an infinitely exchangeable coin [who] first passes from her natural parents ... to her adoptive father/husband/cousin Mordecai. She then passes herself off as a gentile and a virgin ... is deposited for twelve months where she is laundered, homogenised, i.e. purified ... Esther holds in reserve her true racial/religious, familial and hymeneal status, and is rewarded with the crown.[23]

After their dialogue in *Tochmarc Becfhola*, Becfhola goes back with Díarmait to his kingdom and falls in love with his foster son, Crimthann. Bhreathnach discusses parallels with *Scéla Cano Meic Gartnáin* ('The Story of Cano, Son of Gartnán'), *Fingal Rónáin* ('The Death of Mael Fhothartaig'), *Tochmarc Emire* and *Longes Mac n Uislenn*, where there are also difficult triangulations of longing.[24] If this *Fingal Rónáin*/Potiphar's Wife theme continued, we would expect relations between the three characters to deteriorate accordingly. Instead, Crimthann drops out of the narrative when Flann enters. Furthermore, Becfhola leaves her role in that pattern and takes on a role like the king's: she goes out walking one day with only her maid and stumbles, it seems, into the Otherworld, notices a mysterious and very beautiful person and falls in love with him.

Does this mean that she adopts the king's position sexually and cosmologically? If she is the one lured to the Otherworld by Flann, then must not she be the non-*síd* one, within the *echtra* or *immram*[25] idiom? As far as I know this reversal is unusual, if not singular.

22. W.T. McBride, 'Esther Passes: Chiasm, Lex Talio, and Money in the Book of Esther', in J.P. Rosenblatt and J.C. Sitterson (eds.), *Not in Heaven: Coherence and Complexity in Biblical Narrative* (Bloomington: Indiana University Press, 1991), pp. 211-23.

23. McBride, 'Esther Passes', p. 219.

24. Bhreathnach, '*Becfhola*', p. 64. Myles Dillon also comments on this in *The Cycles of the Kings* (Dublin: Four Courts Press, 1994), p. 80.

25. In terms of the tale lists, these two categories are usually translated by 'adventure' and 'voyage', respectively.

Becfhola follows Flann to the Otherworld island. Version 1 builds up the scene: 'This was a fine house with both cubicles and beds ... He reached out his hand as he sat and brought forth a dish of food for them. They both ate and drank and neither of them was drunk.'[26]

He does what pleases him and he sets the tone. She follows him to bed. In bed, he resists her, or 'he did not turn towards her' although, according to Version 1, she 'slipped in beneath his cloak, between him and the wall'.[27] This comment draws attention not just to her sexuality but to the borders that divide everyone in this tale (mirrored in the space between him and the wall). She, however, comes to him even before his clothes, even before his boundary, within his 'zone'. It is also worth noting that while Version 1 includes this sentence, the narrator does not add that this is forward or inappropriate behaviour.

They awake to voices—the first voices heard since Becfhola left Díarmait's side. It is a voice that gives Flann a name, just as strange voices gave Becfhola a name: 'Come out Flann, here come the men.'[28] The voice calls him away from her, but this time she cannot follow him—or will not, going only 'to the door of the house to watch him'. Again, as when she first sees Flann, we see through her eyes, as she watches three others like him and they meet and fight:

> They smote one another until each was red with the blood of the other, then each one went his way, injured.[29]

> The four defeated the other four, but they all fell dead and lifeless.[30]

We do not know what Becfhola makes of the battle. Was her presence instrumental in these people's injury? Are they indeed her people? Has her timidity affected their survival? These are some of the questions that the island-based segment of *TBec* raises.

Flann speaks to Becfhola after the battle. As Cano says to Créd in *Scéla Cano Meic Gartnáin*,[31] Flann says he will come back for Becfhola when it is more appropriate and she will be his only wife.[32] We had

26. Bhreathnach, '*Becfhola*', p. 78.
27. Bhreathnach, '*Becfhola*', p. 78.
28. Bhreathnach, '*Becfhola*', p. 78.
29. Bhreathnach, '*Becfhola*', p. 79.
30. Bhreathnach, '*Becfhola*', p. 85.
31. D.A. Binchy (ed.), *Scéla Cano Meic Gartnáin* (Dublin: DIAS, 1975).
32. Dillon remarks on this similarity in *Cycles*, p. 82 n. 1.

seen the king woo Becfhola and Becfhola woo Crimthann, then Flann.
Now, the counterintuitive courtship continues: who is wooing whom?
Who is being 'womanly' or 'manly'?—Becfhola for following an Other-
world mate, or Flann for promising to come back for her?

Certainly, Becfhola is flexible; she seems to be able to enter this
world at will but must forfeit her 'passport' to the king's world to do so.
Yet she is also from a different world to the king; this is brought home
by his 'sour grapes' rejoinder at her departure (Version 1): 'one knows
not whither she goes nor whence she came'.[33] By the end of the island
segment, it seems clear that Becfhola is both in this world and the other,
and not fully in either.

The verse she utters at this point (§10 in Version 1) seems to hold an
answer to the question of what territory she considers hers. The
metaphor in the poem may be seen to pair her identity with the island's:

> I spent a night in the forest ...
> Although it was with a man, it was no sin,
> It was too soon when we parted ...
> Although [the island] lies close to the road
> Bearded warriors do not find it.[34]

These verses seem to glorify love and the island, its location and en-
chantment. They also suggest her sexuality is like the island in its
purity, underlying her affinity with it.

Like Esther, Becfhola has been invited to stay in both worlds and
must choose. Until she does, Flann will be excluded from her life,
reachable, but at a distance. She can see him and communicate indi-
rectly with him, but he cannot come in yet.

The clerics enter suddenly like an epilogue at this point in *Tochmarc
Becfhola*, much as a religious message enters abruptly at the end of the
book of Esther. With their entrance, Sabbath-breaking becomes an issue
in the narrative, as Carney notes: 'This is a peculiar, confused tale and
it seems to be designed to inculcate Sunday observance.'[35] It is not,
however, the clerics who bring the issue of observance into the tale, but
the king. More accurately put, the king expresses horror at the lack of
such observance (Version 1): ' "What then", cried Díarmait, "the clergy

---

33. Bhreathnach, '*Becfhola*', p. 80.
34. Bhreathnach, '*Becfhola*', pp. 79-80.
35. Carney, *Studies*, p. 229.

travelling on Sunday!" He drew his cloak over his head so that he might not see them at all.'[36]

With the cloak over his head, Díarmait looks weak, passive, frightened and unwise. The clerics only make him seem more so: they are not 'on his side', but rather defend themselves against him, explaining why they are breaking the Sabbath: 'It is the order of our superiors that has brought us ... not wilfulness'.[37] That is, they claim that their action, far from being reckless as the king implies, is a result of obeying authority. There is something of a condoning of Becfhola's actions in their words, and an affirmation of the folly of the king: Flann and Becfhola may have broken the Sabbath, but like the clerics they have acted out of respect for an authority, in this case respect for the island itself.

The clergy explain that they have come to allocate money to the king from a battle fought on his land. The king gives it to the Church. Since this wealth belonged to Flann and his kinsmen, this may seem like a conquest of king and Church over Otherworld, but it can also be read as an equation of the two through the exchange of goods: the clerics embrace the objects that the king thought too dirty for his hands. (This is like McBride's view of the theme of fungibility in Esther.) As elsewhere, the clergy here share a special space with Flann, Becfhola and their world, like the island itself and the time zone they both seem to inhabit. This is one of the points that Carey finds most remarkable about the tale, that the island is a 'magic' one 'identical with the site of a mortal monastery'.[38] The narrator neither condemns nor celebrates their escape together.

After Ahasuerus has Vashti put away, he sets out to find a new queen. Chief among the women he finds is the beautiful Esther, an orphan. Raised by her 'cousin' (see below) Mordecai from a baby, she now lives as a refugee in the acropolis of Susa. She is chosen for the king's harem, but Mordecai forbids her to tell the king who her people really are.

Esther knows how to keep a secret. Like Becfhola she allows herself to be traded on the basis of her beauty. The rabbis elaborate on this, adding that in her wooing dialogues with King Ahasuerus she explicitly conceals her identity and is not merely silent: 'Said she: "I do not know

36. Bhreathnach, '*Becfhola*', p. 80.
37. Bhreathnach, '*Becfhola*', pp. 79-80.
38. Carey, 'Otherworlds', p. 36.

my people or my kinship ...' '[39] Both Esther and Becfhola must wait to make known their identity until it suits a certain male who acts in the interest of a larger community.

Esther's relationship to Mordecai has been variously interpreted by ancient scholars. The Masoretic Text says she is his cousin, others say 'niece', but perhaps because of their closeness and equal partnership, later commentators remember Esther and Mordecai as husband and wife, as in *Esther Rabbah*.[40]

Romantic intimacy, however, is perhaps not the most memorable part of Esther and Mordecai's relationship. The book makes clear that they are both agents for the survival of the Jews and they are to be remembered primarily for this. It is in these terms that the rabbis cherish Esther's loyalty to Mordecai: it served her to save the Jews.

If we look to *Tochmarc Becfhola* for an intertextual reading here, we must examine Flann and Becfhola's short dialogue. After their night together, Becfhola asks Flann what is going on and why he did not sleep with her. In response, he tells her how to act if she wants to be with him. Most of their dialogue, however, is not about their courtship but about the island where they both want to live. It is the first time they speak and yet Becfhola is as interested in the island as she is in him, if not more so:

> 'What have you been fighting about?' asked the woman.
> 'For this island,' he said.
> 'What is the name of the island?' she asked.
> 'The island of Fedach mac in Daill,' he said.
> 'And what is your name?' she asked.[41]

Flann confirms that more than their love is at stake as he says they will be together 'if the island becomes mine and if we are alive', underlining the fact that their fates are connected with the fate of the island. He implies that this is the main reason he is not with her. Furthermore, it is

39. (*Targum Sheni* to Chapter 2) in Grossfeld (ed. and trans.), *Esther*, p. 138.

40. This may also be an attempt to develop Esther's likeness to Sarah. Both *Esther Rabbah* and the Targums insist on their similarity in that each 'wife' is passed off as a sister/niece to save a heroic husband in the domain of a non-Jewish king. (For various readings of Esther's status in rabbinical commentary and the targums, see Grossfeld [ed. and trans.], *Esther*, pp. 43-44 n. 19).

41. Bhreathnach, '*Becfhola*', p. 79. In Version 2, the last line here reads ' "Can duit-se", or seise, "can feis lium-sa?" ' ' "Why have you not slept with me?" he said' (pp. 83, 85).

only after he describes the island that she says, 'Why don't I remain with you?'

When next Flann and Becfhola meet he is hovering just outside the palace, accentuating that they are indeed living in different worlds: 'Díarmait was lying in bed with his wife Becfhola when they saw a man go past the door of the house, and he was severely wounded. It was Flann.' Flann's position makes him visible but unreachable, emphasizing his separation from Becfhola and the choice between worlds that she is faced with.

The border between worlds is significant here, and a reference to such borders in another text may have relevance. Writing about the book of Ruth, Mieke Bal draws attention to the liminality represented by the border of the palace (or 'city') gates, 'the place that separates the female from the male domain. It is the entry point of the city... The trial is at the city gate at the entrance to the female domain, where two men debate the question of who dares to take the woman.'[42]

This may be compared to the role of borders at this point in *Tochmarc Becfhola* as well as gates in the book of Esther. It is Mordecai who hovers outside the palace gates and makes a claim to Esther's attention as her 'husband' and as a representative of her people. Yet he always remains just outside the palace gates, inside which Esther belongs to the king. In the following passage, the artificiality and strain of this arrangement is clear:

> [A]nd then he came as far as the King's Gate (for no one in sackcloth was allowed to enter the King's Gate). And in every province where the king's command was heard there was loud mourning among the Jews...
> [When Esther heard, she] sent clothing for Mordecai to wear so that he could take off his sackcloth, but he would not accept it. So Esther summoned Hatak... So Hatak went out to Mordecai in the city square which was in front of the King's Gate.[43]

This stress on the borderline between worlds galvanizes the action of the narrative. The breakdown of communication forces the heroine in each story to take control in a way she has not before. Esther switches to command position and tells Mordecai what to do for the first time: 'Go and gather all the Jews now in Susa and fast for me... and I... will

42. Bal, *Lethal Love*, p. 83.
43. Moore, *Esther*, p. 45.

fast as you do. In this condition I'll go to the king, even if it's against the law. And if I perish, I perish!'

Becfhola speaks out for herself at an equivalent point in *TBec*, also for the first time: 'I am unable ... to hold out against the fighting of a man when it was Flann that [*sic*] was wounded in the conflict.'[44] With these words she reveals her devotion to Flann in front of the king, not worrying about the consequences. She is free to pursue Flann. Her words are different from Esther's, but like Esther she is illustrating her personal reaction to a crisis involving a group with whom she is coming to identify.

The paucity of love-talk between Flann and Becfhola, her timing in revealing who she is, and the king's recognition of this by throwing her together with Flann all suggest that there is something more to their relationship than romance. Her identification with the fate of the island can be understood in this context as an alternative explanation of their closeness and chastity. We may note the king's reaction to the information that she spent a night on the island accordingly. In the following quote there is no adulterous relationship described and yet the king's reaction is severe, as if he knows much more than he has been told: 'Afterwards the young clerics informed the king that the queen had been at the scene of the battle, at the slaughter of the whole battle. The king's jealousy was aroused because of this and he told Becfhola to go back to Flann.'[45]

When the king condemns her, he is reacting to the fact that she was in two places at once, and not to the fact that she had spent the night with another man; it appears to be her belonging to another people at the same time as being his queen that incenses him. Within the text, Becfhola and her world are not being made to look bad: the king is the one who brings her to bed, while Becfhola and Flann remain pure. Whether this is a sign of approval of the *síd* by a Christian author or the vestiges of an innocent pre-Christian world is ultimately unknowable. The narrator seems to confirm this relative importance of a sense of place ahead of personal relationships in that the island is named by the narrator before Becfhola or Flann is so mentioned.

The reading of the book of Esther with *Tochmarc Becfhola* thus far has drawn attention to themes that the shorter, sketchier Irish tale only hints at. The picture emerging is one that seems to suggest an unusual

44. Bhreathnach, '*Becfhola*', p. 80.
45. Bhreathnach, '*Becfhola*', pp. 86-87.

relationship between characterization of good and bad. The following sections focus on the king as he emerges as a contrast to the couple and their 'community'.

Far from being a royal or stately figure, the king in both stories is weak and naive. Although the tales may seem to be designed to praise their legends, subversive devices in both texts suggest that the kings are ridiculous. In *Tochmarc Becfhola* the first of these devices is the presentation of time in the narrative.

Becfhola leaves on a Sunday morning, spends a day and a night in the Otherworld, and returns to find 'Díarmait was still waking up, on the same Sunday'. That is, Becfhola has been to a world where time moves faster. Flann was also in that time zone and so were the clerics, as it turns out. Thus, time serves in the narrative as another way to measure the distance between the king and the other characters, while suggesting a point of agreement between the clerics and the lovers.

Rees and Rees have said, 'Otherworld "time" is both longer and shorter than the time of our world.'[46] While time has gone faster here, later in this same story, time goes much more slowly. Toward the end of *TBec*, in Version 1, a year has passed in this world since Becfhola saw the battle begin but Flann is still bloody from that battle when he comes back for her. To look at it another way, in this tale time stops whenever Becfhola leaves town. In the quote above, Rees and Rees were referring to qualities of Otherworld passages in several stories. *Tochmarc Becfhola* combines those several qualities in one short narrative much as it conflates idioms for female and male characters, this world and that, ecclesiastical and secular 'good'.

Time continues to conspire against the king on Sunday, the day he seems to want to spend at rest. King Díarmait's strong words (without action, like Ahasuerus's words about Vashti) mark this theme: 'A journey on Sunday is not auspicious.' Stephens caricatures Díarmait's zeal:

> [T]here was one deed entirely hateful to him ... this was, a transgression of the Sunday... Had it been possible he would have tethered the birds to their own green branches on that day, and forbidden the clouds to pack the upper world with stir and colour.[47]

46. Alwyn Rees and Brinley Rees, *Celtic Heritage* (London: Thames & Hudson, 1961), p. 344.

47. Stephens, 'Becfola', p. 143.

Not only is the king's zealotry misplaced here as far as his interaction with Becfhola is concerned, it is unclear whether he is meant to seem like an ideal Christian. In fact, the text does not actually mention Christianity, and while it seems fair to call the king's collection of rules Christianity, they hardly make up a definition of any religion. Within the text, then, the king has two rules: (1) Do not travel on Sundays and (2) Do not take money from spoils of war which could otherwise be given to Molaise. These may overlap with an extratextual knowledge of some facets of religion, but the narrator seems unimpressed with them as kernels of Christian practice.

What causes the king to act so bizarrely as to 'draw his cloak over his head' when he sees the clergy arrive, after they have been to the Otherworld and back with Becfhola on a Sunday morning? The Sabbath, or Christianity, serves in the narrative as another example of the king's weak position relative to the other characters. Just as everyone else in the story can travel to the Otherworld, everyone else can travel in time. He is left clinging to a Sabbath that passed without his knowledge, a time shift that excluded him.

The king's overreaction in *Tochmarc Becfhola* is only one of many moments where he acts foolishly. The stress on the Sabbath as it actually comes through in *Tochmarc Becfhola* does not mean a major shift in the story from the romantic to the religious, an arbitrary 'contamination' of the story's 'information'. In fact, the characters have been constant as their venues changed, from the cosmological to the sexual to politico-religious to chronological.

Some rabbinical commentary on the book of Esther mentions the aspect of time in a related context—that Esther maintained her ties to the Jews by remembering the Sabbath while in the Persian palace. In order to explain how she kept track of time in the king's palace, they suggest that she called the attendants by seven different names—one for each day—'so that she could count the days of the week by them'.[48] Here also, a time link connects Esther and Mordecai despite palace walls, under Ahasuerus's nose and without his knowledge.

We have seen that, although *Tochmarc Becfhola* may appear to exalt King Díarmait's piety, his piety is in fact unflatteringly exaggerated. On the morning of Becfhola's departure on Sunday morning, she wakes up and tells Díarmait a lie, that she is off to fetch some shirts. The reader

---

48. Cf. *b. Meg.* 13a cited in Grossfeld (ed. and trans.), *Esther*, p. 44 n. 26.

knows she intends to meet Crimthann and the narrator plays on that knowledge when, as Díarmait tells her not to go, she says to the king, 'let someone go with me'. If the king went with her then he would find out she means to tryst with Crimthann. She is bluffing, asking to be caught, whereby the reader is invited to think, 'Go on, catch her!' The king does not—and so is cuckolded.

Why does he not manage either to stop her or go with her? The answer is that he is more concerned with the letter than the spirit of his own laws, which is exactly the problem of Ahasuerus (with Vashti). Díarmait saves the penny of not transgressing the Sabbath and loses the pound of having any sort of relationship with his wife.

At the end of *Tochmarc Becfhola*, the king's already vulnerable position in time and space relative to the other characters puts his display of generosity to Molaise at the end in a strange light. He is already naive; is he being wise to give away money which the clerics have come so far to tell him is rightfully his? The moral of the story is not as clearcut as it may have seemed. In the end, for all his earnest strivings and concern for the voice of society and his rules he is left with nothing.

The book of Esther opens with an indulgent king demanding that his wife, Vashti, be brought to him. He does not bother to ask her directly, however, and when she refuses to come he does not reprimand her personally. Rather

> The king became very angry at this, and was quite incensed. The king immediately conferred with the experts, who knew the laws (for that was the king's practise in the presence of all those who knew law and government ...) as to what should be done, from a legal point of view, to Queen Vashti.... Memukan [said] ... 'When all the women hear the rumour about the king, they will look down on their husbands ... So ... let him issue a royal edict'... So the king ... sent dispatches to all the royal provinces ... to the effect that every man should be master in his own home and say whatever suited him.[49]

The focus is no longer on a disobedient wife, but on the king's reaction to her disobedience. Ahasuerus is unable to pick his battles, and in this passage his reaction is excessive. The combination of rage, passivity, and elaborate legislation make this scene laughable. His anger leads him to consult experts, not with a view to taking action but to issuing a decree behind which he can hide. 'That he should have brought into full

49. Moore, *Esther*, pp. 2-3.

play the communications system of the entire Persian empire for such a purpose is ridiculous.'[50]

The rabbis further mock King Ahasuerus's excessive reactions because he gave orders that 'contradicted the normal course of social life'.[51] Certainly it is any king's duty to recognize what the real, social world demands. Thus it is perhaps well to ask for your wife's obedience but it is unreasonable to send out a decree in 127 languages telling all men to yell at their wives. It is this brand of marital/royal stupidity that King Díarmait shares: it is perhaps well to tell your wife to keep the Sabbath but not at the expense of your marriage, and not if you must keep your head in the sand about it when she has broken it.

Although Ahasuerus acts with mercy at some points and although he has been seen by some interpreters as a romantic lead worthy of Esther,[52] he is generally considered weak, specifically for this trait of seeing only his own decrees (especially in his dealings with Vashti). *Targum Sheni* calls him 'that Xerxes, the foolish and presumptuous king (who said): "Let his kingdom be undone rather than let his decree go undone"'.[53]

Ahasuerus seems continually surprised at what has gone on in his own kingdom—as when he reads the annals to learn of an assassination attempt on his own life! He does not have the timing to make good decisions, nor the foresight to see what is of value to him. He may even be said to overdo his devotion to Esther as if to compensate for his loss of Vashti—she has him wrapped around her finger. 'The king, having got rid of one recalcitrant wife ends up with one who controls him completely.'[54]

In *Targum Sheni* of Esther, Ahasuerus is mocked because he 'killed his wife for the sake of his friend; who (then) killed his friend for the sake of his wife'.[55] The 'killing' here is not necessarily death, but his excessive and whimsical dismissals. In other words, he gets rid of a wife (Vashti) because his advisors and 'friends' manipulate him. Then he kills an advisor (Haman) because a wife (Esther) manipulates him.

50. Moore, *Esther*, p. 14.
51. Neusner, *Esther Rabbah*, §1.22.
52. Cf. Racine, 'Esther', in *Œuvres complètes*, I (Paris, 1950), pp. 806-62, and F. Grillparzer, 'Esther', in *Sämtliche Werke*, II (Vienna, 1848).
53. *Targum Sheni* in Grossfeld (ed. and trans.), *Esther*, p. 98.
54. 'Observed by' D.N. Freedman to Moore, *Esther*, p. 14.
55. Grossfeld (ed. and trans.), *Esther*, p. 99.

This is also one of Díarmait's follies: he does not know when to obey his counsellors and when to obey his own instincts. He kills his friend for the sake of his wife, ignores the scathing comments of *cách* and marries an Otherworld maiden, then kills his wife for the sake of his friends, lets his wife run away to the Otherworld, and later dismisses her from his house through a sense of obligation to his set of rules. The narrator drives the point of misplaced zealotry home when we see that even clerics break the commandments for a good reason—and money is a good enough reason.

Society appears in *TBec* like a Greek chorus when matters that concern Díarmait or his foster son Crimthann arise. There is no time when the actions of either of these characters does not depend on what *cách* allows them to do, except the very first scene (which would never have occurred if 'they' had been there to warn the king about Becfhola). Their chief role is to condemn Becfhola, and they name her to commemorate her easily got virtue:

> 'What have you given as her bride-price?' asked everyone.
> 'My little brooch,' said Díarmait.
> 'That is little value,' they all said.
> 'That will be her name then,' said the druid, 'Becfhola.'[56]

The power of advice in *TBec* is also a theme that highlights the king's folly. It is true that in early Irish saga—and by extension, perhaps, society—public humiliation is not something to be sneezed at, so perhaps it behove the king to let his actions be determined by others.[57] Still, in this particular text the voice of society does not seem to do the king much good.

'Everybody' retires from the narrative to leave Díarmait to his mistake, then re-emerges to condemn Becfhola again for Crimthann's sake. They are gone for the entire length of narrative in the Otherworld and return only to be silent when Becfhola recites her verses: 'Everyone wondered at that poem.'[58]

At this point Becfhola is released from the palace and *cách*, as well as from this world in all. The king can say only, 'Let her go... the evil

---

56. Bhreathnach, '*Becfhola*', p. 77.

57. For insights into an early Irish honour code, see any article by Philip O'Leary, including 'Jeers and Judgements: Laughter in Early Irish Literature', *CMCS* 22 (1991), pp. 15-29.

58. Bhreathnach, '*Becfhola*', p. 80.

one, for one knows not [*ní feas*] whither she goes nor whence she came.' This statement confirms not his ignorance, but an impersonal ignorance—society's ignorance—of her identity as the reason why he personally should not be with her.

When the clerics appear, society is again silent and only the weak voice of the self-righteous king comes through: ' "What then…the clergy travelling on Sunday!" He drew his cloak over his head so that he might not see them at all.'

The clerics relate that they saw Becfhola at the battle and do not support or condemn the king when he dismisses her. As discussed above, in Version 1 they do not even mention that she was at the battle; the king has learned that from Becfhola herself. In neither version, in fact, does the king know about her night with Flann.

The news of Becfhola's absence is, in fact, relayed in a way that seems further to highlight the closeness of clerics and *síd*. The story of Becfhola's departure with Flann follows directly on the news of Molaise's crosier. The narrative of Version 1 progresses like this: (1) The king knows of no betrayal. (2) The clergy tell of a battle (3) The gold of the battle is to go to Molaise. (4) The king tells her to go back to Flann (although no one has mentioned Flann to the king!). (5) Flann and Becfhola live happily ever after. The continuity here might even be read to imply causality, that the clergy had somehow aided her escape.

Thus, in *TBec* the voyager (female) goes to the Otherworld, the tempter (male) resides there, the king must stay at home and the clerics can do it all. Their position relative to the Otherworld heroes is strangely intimate: not only can they hear the stories of the Otherworld first hand, but they can go there! They are like half-Otherworld creatures themselves, living in both atmospheres and still breathing comfortably. Carey has noted this of Devenish in *TBec*: 'The island … belongs both to a monastic community and to a band of supernatural warriors residing in an Otherworldly hall.'[59] A chart of all these counterintuitive developments is shown on p. 203.

Naturally Good?

With these points in mind, the main focus of *TBec*, read intertextually with the book of Esther, is the overlap of two worlds in one character's experience. What are those worlds? In Esther's case there is no mystery:

---

59. Carey, 'Location', p. 40.

The Book of Esther and Tochmarc Becfhola

	'Wooing'	Balance of Power	Location
	I. Man → woman	**Establishment has power**	**King's world**
The book of Esther	Ahasuerus finds Esther and takes her home.	Persian government (especially the king), wealth, and society important; upstart Vashti condemned.	Persian world (inside palace).
Tochmarc Becfhola	King Díarmait finds Becfhola and takes her home.	Society's voice and king important.	Tara (inside king's house, in his bed).
	II. Woman → man	**Personal/ familial loyalty important**	**'Other' world**
The book of Esther	Esther communicates with Mordecai.	No government; focus on kinship ties, obligation.	Jewish world (outside palace).
Tochmarc Becfhola	Becfhola seeks Flann.	No society; chaste attraction (kinship tie?).	Otherworld.
	III. Man ↔ woman		
The book of Esther	Esther tells Mordecai what to do, and listens to him, her actions dictated by service to Jews.	Confrontation and resolution (after slaughter) between Persians and Jews; a way of being a Jew within a Persian milieu established; government medium (decrees) used for a Jewish message.	Jews brought into palace.
Tochmarc Becfhola	Flann woos Becfhola, she declares verse, goes away with him.	King vociferous but ignored, present but acting unusually. Flann and Becfhola acknowledged and freed.	Border-crossing (in words): report of Otherworld while in this.

there are Jews and there are Gentiles; the Gentile world here is Aha-suerus's kingdom. The narrative of the book of Esther ends with two emphatic chapters about the political triumph of 'us' over 'them'. But are there comparable sides in the Irish material here, or in early Irish Otherworld tales in general?

This question has been looked at by all manner of Celtic scholars with reference to better-known Otherworld tales. A particular area of interest is not just the overlap of supernatural and natural (or Other-world and 'this' world) but supernatural, natural and ecclesiastical. Nagy has explored the overlapping of worlds in early Irish narrative and the form it takes in several articles, as well as in a recent book.[60] John Carey has also done valuable work on the same topic. They both ad-dress the meeting of the Christian world and the pre-Christian and the form such a meeting may take in a secular narrative.

As discussed in Chapter 1, there are several levels to this Christian–'native' interplay, both historically and as a literary piece. There are narratives exploring the contrasts openly—those that liken the Irish to biblical personages, or that plug them into biblical history—and those that may be said to explore this contrast in a 'concealed' way.

Lebor Gabála Érenn (The Book of the Invasions of Ireland) is an example of the first kind.[61] It provides a history of Ireland from the beginning of time, drawing openly on much of the Bible for its structure and content, and writing the history of Ireland 'into' biblical history. Any of a number of quotes from this text would reveal efforts on the part of the narrators to integrate native Irish lore into biblical legend, as the following:

> 'Which race of the sons of Noah do you belong to?' he said. 'I am older than Noah,' she said, 'I was on this mountain in the Flood. The waves of the Flood went up to this hill here,' she said. 'That is why it is called Tuinde.'[62]

---

60. J.F. Nagy, *Conversing with Angels and Ancients: Literary Myths of Ancient Ireland* (New York: Cornell University Press, 1997).

61. Edited by R.A.S Macalister, *Lebor Gabála Érenn*, I–IV (Dublin: Royal Irish Academy, 1938–42).

62. My translation. I am grateful to Dáibhí Ó Cróinín for checking this. 'Cia ceinél [cen-M] do Macaib Náe duit? ol sé. Am sine-sea nás Náe, ol sí; for ind slébhe ro bhadasa isin dílind; gosa tealsa anois, ol sí, do dhechain tonda dílind. Is dé sin do gairthear Tuinde.' Macalister, *Lebor*, V, p. 76. He translates: 'Of which race of the sons of Noe are thou? said he. I am elder than Noe, said she; upon this

In this fashion, Ireland's 'history' was sometimes read as a footnote to biblical 'history', taking a special place among the 'Ages of the World'. As there are good people without a knowledge of Jesus (because it was their bad luck to have been born before Jesus), there were ('naturally') good Irishmen who were living virtuously all the time while ignorant of the Faith (not yet come to Ireland):

> The national past is viewed ... in terms of a contrast between a gentler order which, though incomplete, could be good, and a Christian order. Such a contrast is implied in references to a *naturale bonum* in Irish ecclesiastical works of a relatively early date.[63]

Lebor Gabála is only one example of this kind of thinking. This section from the prologue to the *Senchas Már* ('Great Tradition', a collection of Old Irish legal texts) is another, where early Irish jurists are like 'Old Testament' prophets:

> For the Holy Spirit spoke and prophesied through the mouths of the righteous men who were the first in the island of Ireland, as He prophesied through the mouths of the chief prophets and patriarchs in the law of the Old Testament.[64]

In our story, *TBec*, Becfhola may not be fashioned after an 'Old Testament' heroine, but her character does seem to have some aspects of the 'natural good' (enunciated here by the reading with the book of Esther). She is loyal to Flann, she is chaste with Flann, and she seems to exist with the approval of the clergy. It is true that she could be more of a model of Judaeo-Christian virtue, perhaps, but it is remarkable that she pursues her course against the king and his Sabbath-observance and is rewarded with a happy ending, in spite of it. It may be her contact with clergy that ensures her success. In this way we can refer to other saga narratives in which Otherworld characters meet with Christian figures to mutual advantage.

In 'Close Encounters of the Traditional Kind', Nagy focuses on the moments of contrast in some early Irish narrative where worlds meet. This meeting goes on in several ways, according to Nagy: 'behind' the

mountain was I in the Flood; to this hill, said she, came the waters of the Flood; thence is it called [Tul] Tuinde' (p. 77).

63. C. Donahue, 'Beowulf, Ireland and the Natural Good', *Traditio* 7 (1949–51), pp. 263-77 (267).

64. J. Carey, 'An Edition of the Pseudo-historical Prologue to the *Senchas Már*', *Ériu* 45 (1994), pp. 1-32 (18).

text, in the overlap of Christianity and pre-Christian times, as well as in the text, with the form of the narrative echoing that surprising continuity. (I understand Nagy to be more concerned with the form this meeting takes in the narrative than the history it may reflect.) What interests him most in this transfer of traditions is the way three meet: pagan, saint, and audience. The meeting also takes place on (at least) three levels. These tales include 'an underlying network of relationships among the three parties, one which is spread out along a continuum encompassing time, space, and the narrative traditions'.[65]

Thus, there are three parallels being evoked (roughly equivalent to 'time', 'space', and 'narrative'):

(historically)	Christian/pre-Christian
(narratologically)	this world/the Otherworld
(compositionally)	literate/oral

In 'Compositional Concerns in the *Acallam na Senórach*' Nagy further discusses that contrast of two world-views meeting and the resultant tension in the telling. The metafictional device[66] he locates is time itself. Time in that story is cyclical (the narrative could begin or end at any point and still follow logically—or as logically as it does in the form we have it) and the narrator's world is the not unhappy meeting of different epochs, thus representing 'almost despite itself a triumph over closure of various kinds'.[67] The task of a narrative combining the story of pre-Christian heroes in a Christian context (the monastic literary milieu) is echoed by the very continuity of the form. Where we would expect opposition in the relating of one tradition to a member of another, there is agreement, Nagy shows. Finally, he finds that 'Caílte's otherworldly renewal and the vindication of his image through the recreation of Fenian heroism is the renewal of his capacity as a storyteller, and the renewal of the Fenian tradition itself within the text.'[68]

Carey has also touched on this contrast in his conference paper 'Varieties of Supernatural Contact in Columban Hagiography'.[69] His focus was on the Middle Irish Life of Adomnán, and he remarked on

---

65. Nagy, 'Close Encounters', p. 149.
66. That is, which addresses that external tension but still within the narrative.
67. Nagy, '*Acallam*', p. 150.
68. Nagy, '*Acallam*', p. 152.
69. J. Carey, 'Varieties of Supernatural Contact in Columban Hagiography' (unpublished paper given at 'Columba and his Churches' Conference, Derry, 1997).

the unusual passing of information between two parties there, also in the presence of a third. He commented on moments like the end of 'The Colloquy of Colum Cille and the Youth at Carn Eolairg' which feature a saintly type (in this case Columba himself) eager to learn from a pre-Christian survivor, but not permitted to relate the information (which reticence is ironically recorded for posterity!):

> When the conversation had come to an end, they suddenly beheld the youth vanishing from them. It is not known whither he went. When his monks asked Colum Cille to make known to them something of the conversation, Colum Cille said to them that he could not tell them even one word of all that he had spoken, and he said it was a proper thing for men not to be told.[70]

Carey sees a comparable tripartite division in *TBec* particularly, without reference to Nagy's: 'The plot is structured around a triple equation *this world: Otherworld: verbal world*.'[71] That is, he feels that there are plays on words in the language of the story that correspond to the content of the story.

Interestingly, it is not known whither Becfhola went. Keeping in mind both perspectives from which narratives may be told, and this unusual strain in early Irish literature, it is possible to understand *TBec* as being within the tradition highlighted by Nagy and Carey, where a holy figure approves of the lore of a 'naturally good' pre-Christian. In this case,

---

70. K. Meyer, 'The Colloquy of Colum Cille and the Youth at Carn Eolairg', *ZCP* 2 (1899), pp. 313-20 (317). A sociological guess at the situation might see it in related terms. Alan Dundes writes that some 'native genre systems distinguish only between true and fictional narratives' ('Introduction', in Dundes [ed.], *Sacred Narrative*, p. 5). If the ancient Irish drew such a distinction, the coming of Christianity may have provoked a sudden reassessment of the categories, with most of the former true ones (those which some might call vestiges of pagan times) relegated to the fictional category because of the 'true', 'historical' nature of the Bible. That this might be the case with Ireland is suggested by the fact that no pre-Christian origin legends remain (if there were any, and there probably were) because in the light of Genesis they were especially and perhaps 'dangerously' untrue. Thus, it might be fair to presume that the pre-Christian system would not have called for much definition of time beyond 'once upon a time'. With Christianity there was a central extra-Hibernian church and official times of the day and year which had to be noted, among other changes. The psychological effect this had may indeed have been something like confusion, as Alfred Nutt suggested in 'The Happy Otherworld' (mentioned in Chapter 1).

71. Carey, 'Otherworlds', p. 37 (his italics).

narrative devices like the portrayal of time could be seen to echo that content, as well as the theme of wealth where the Otherworld gold is made into Molaise's crosier.

It is thus significant that the confrontation in Becfhola between the *síd* and clerical worlds happens at a borderline time for both of them, and maybe this is a reflection of the contrast of time systems mentioned above. It is sunrise, the beginning of day (which moment was presumably observable before Christianity), on Sunday, the beginning of the (Christian) week. The king is the only character who cannot understand the role of time.

In all, the meeting of the worlds of Otherworld and clergy finds a vehicle of sorts in *TBec*. In its unusual form of happy assimilation it can be said to operate in some ways like the plot of the book of Esther ('Esther suggests that you must learn to survive where you are').[72] Although she may seem like an incurable flirt at first, in fact Becfhola demonstrates chastity and loyalty—traits that a Christian might indeed call good. Equally, what might at first seem like an intrusive 'plug' for Sabbath-keeping in a nice pagan story is, on closer reading, a more integrated theme in the tale. If there is a message, that message is that inflexibility in dealing with the unknown is foolish.

72. Fewell, *Reading Between Texts*, p. 13.

CONCLUSION

What drew me to the texts in this book was something about each of them that seemed to me counterintuitive. The hero was not acting like a hero, somehow: he was too hesitant or too masochistic, or too concerned with what his friends thought of him—each trait a sign of weakness. What code or device in the text was forming this impression on me, if anything?

I suggested a coherent and flexible methodology behind the different kinds of interpretation I used. Instead of directly tackling the theme of weakness, I listened for the codes that each text seemed to me to use, and then tied that back into an overarching common point. I have also tried not to insist too much that I am right; I know that my readings are biased, as any reading is. I believe that in bringing the various matrices of the stories to light, other points came up that could be pursued by other scholars to other ends.

When I looked at Jonah and Columba, I looked closely at a few brief episodes, so short that other scholars might have seen them merely as blueprints for actions, their individual words of minor importance. I looked at the structure, attaching weight to the actions in the stories, and even proposing a common myth behind Jonah, a particular hagiographic episode, and Aesop. At the same time, I have tried to leave the conclusion open. Weakness here meant hesitancy, imperfection in the face of divinity, or human frailty before an omnipotent and sometimes cantankerous master.

In comparing Cú Chulainn's stories with Samson, I had a wealth of secondary material to work with, both on the biblical and the Irish side. This meant there was time to 'walk' calmly through many of the scenes in the narrative and debate points that had been raised by others. The Irish texts in question were also longer than the ones I read in the other chapters, so there was more characterization, and more for me to work with by way of character analysis. I found that Cú Chulainn's and Samson's dealings with women revealed similar patterns of strength and weakness resulting from tension with an honour code. They were seen to go weak through a sense of personal desire that overrode their public commitment to strength.

In 'A Reading of the Book of Esther and *Tochmarc Becfhola*', the style of interpretation moved further away from structuralism to a reading that might be called Marxist. Looking for who holds power and money, thereby controlling action, was tough with these two stories, in one sense: the first is long but the second so short that comparisons were hard to sustain. Still, the themes of wealth were there, as well as the importance of selfhood, and, on the part of the king in each story, weakness. I used the longer book of Esther to 'gloss' *TBec* in its brevity, an intertext that shed light on some of the dark corners in the Irish material, which was dense with themes. The process led me to create a language of narratological analysis and ultimately to place *TBec* in a particular tradition within early Irish literature, one that asked questions as sociolgocial as they were literary. Through this process, *TBec* acquired a possible framework for its themes, making them inherently consistent when previously they had been seen as disrupted and arbitrary. I hope to have confirmed that comparisons between biblical and early Irish literature are valid not only on historical grounds but also literary.

Through this reading it has also been shown that the biblical characters have a few things in common themselves. It is true of Samson, Esther and Jonah that, in each of their stories, they are the only Jew alone in a narrative world of Gentiles with very little actual communication with God. Each of these characters is faced with a choice of assimilating, killing them all, judging them as morally inferior, or all three. This theme, as I detect it, says something about why I was drawn to these stories, for the characters' immediate exilic, minority status. It may say more, however, about why they are popular generally, as Niditch's work suggests (cf. *Underdogs and Tricksters*): they are underdog and trickster stories, stories where a main character does things that would seem to be antiheroic, the actions of an outsider.

These stories all also question characterization of 'us' and 'them' in the context of the Bible. If we call Jonah selfish, are we not as bad as Jonah himself? If Delilah is meant to seem manipulative and evil, why isn't Jael? And one of the most poignant 'us-and-them' surprises in the book of Esther happens to Haman when he is asked what he would do to praise a worthy man, a hero; only when he has answered does he learn that the hero is not his 'us', himself, but *our* 'us', Mordecai.

Sides in the narrative are harder to follow, or guess, in the Irish material: is there an us/them in the system of Christian/pre-Christian? It would be interesting to take off from Niditch's folklorist position and investigate the sociology of the early Irish who would have heard and read these stories. These are the question that arise with any discussion of the meeting of supernatural and Christian in a narrative—something that happens literally in *TBec*. (In the Columba episodes there is a big fish who is perhaps commandeered from the supernatural to the Christian, and, in the progression of Cú Chulainn material, Emer herself may be seen as something of a newly naturalized citizen of Ulster.) Was there a specific cultural and sociological need for figures between worlds, such as Becfhola, or are the stories about human nature in general metaphors for the elusiveness of people we love, or something else again?

In each case I was driven by the vividness and subtlety that I saw in the biblical characterization of weakness—so subversive in its way— and I knew I recognized it in the passages from early Irish literature. I suspected at first that the other literature was not capable of the same variety of expression and drama as the Bible's, but I hope to have shown that I was wrong: early Irish texts do indeed hold their own in a literary comparison.

I faced the odd challenge of having to focus my reading of the intricate biblical texts in a way that resonated with the terse early Irish texts (and its almost complete lack of literary-critical material). I could not pursue as full a commentary on Jonah or Esther as I would have liked, for to do so would undermine the aspect of comparison: I had to find a way of making early Irish and biblical texts share the stage without contriving to have them seem identical.

There is no danger of that, of course. Early Irish literature is not comparable even to contemporaneous texts: one can read endlessly about the alterity of mediaeval literature but no book could phrase it in a way that includes the real alterity of Irish early mediaeval literature for its cocktail of abruptness and exaggeration.

To try to customize criticism in a way that makes sense for a canonless literature vast and partly inaccessible was also a strange task. To find a way to do the same for the Bible was a challenge too, of course, but in a very different way (and there, centuries of scholars had paved the way). In the case of the former, even to discuss characterization involves a bracketing of volumes of material; unaccounted for are the

Cú Chulainns lying around in unedited manuscripts, in centuries of Irish writing after the early Irish period, and in folklore. Inevitably, it is the literature of the Bible that is more familiar to me.

I have translated all the texts I have used in this book (except Adomnán's Latin) from their original languages into English to better 'hear' all their words in my own. But they are still different, and different from each other. A banquet such as Ahasuerus would throw, for example, feels like a sign of excess to me in the context of the biblical story, as well as from what I know the rabbis wrote about the story, and the way I heard the story growing up. The same kind of display of wealth in an Ulster Cycle tale may mean something else entirely, and I have had to bracket my impression of the first until I know more about how it comes across in that text, and possibly other related texts. It may turn out that it 'ought to feel like' a sign of a good, wealthy, hospitable host. Thus, the texts demanded looking at again and again for ways to read, not just to reveal 'voices', but to reveal techniques of characterization, methods of exposition.

The early Irish knew much about interpretation that I do not, and they knew how to read and listen to their own texts appreciatively because of this. Unfortunately, we cannot interview them to ask their secrets, and the first step (among many) has to be seeing how the text seems to the present reader, today. For that reason, I tried to work from excerpts and texts that seemed rich to me, even at first glance, such as the excerpt from *Froech* in Chapter 2. Other such moments might include Cú Chulainn's lament for his 'own ardent and adored foster-brother'[1] Ferdia, which reminds me of David and Jonathan.

In both cases the two men meet in the context of war and declare love for each other; Cú Chulainn and Ferdia must actually fight each other. It is particularly in the lament he delivers for Ferdia after he kills him that I am reminded of David's love for Jonathan. Cú Chulainn says,

> I loved the noble way you blushed,
> and loved your fine, perfect form.
> I loved your blue clear eye,
> your way of speech, your skilfulness ...
> Medb's daughter Finnabair,
> whatever beauty she may have,
> was an empty offering ...

---

1.   Kinsella, *The Táin*, p. 168.

> O fair, fine hero
> who shattered armies ...
> golden brooch, I mourn.[2]

And David:

> How have the mighty fallen
> In the thick of battle—
> Jonathan, slain on your heights!
> I grieve for you,
> My brother Jonathan,
> You were most dear to me.
> Your love was wonderful to me
> More than the love of women.[3]

The warrior ethic is here, but also a homosocial, even homoerotic love that is quite a contrast to each of the hero's relationships with women. This is one of the many 'leads' I would have liked to pursue, including the ones that McCone and others provide. Other areas, like kingship narratives and wisdom literature are intriguing: Proverbs and *Tecosca Cormaic* ('The Teaching of Cormac') deserve the attention of a philosopher. Clearly several readers have been drawn to the idea of close comparison, and the range of biblical figures alluded to in the criticism of early Irish texts is enormous, from Nebuchadnezzar and Suibhne to Uriah and Naoise.

In all this, I wish I knew more about each aspect of the study here: if I had an encyclopaedic knowledge of Mishnah and early Irish law, a great many more comparisons could be broached, and as close a reading as I have attempted about tales be performed on law texts and the legal system, as well as such quasi-philosophical issues as the early Irish attitude to litigation.

The ultimate demonstration of such an enquiry would include not just a thorough knowledge of modern techniques, but could combine them with a knowledge of history and an understanding of the degrees of its relevance to each aspect of the comparisons (sometimes it would be irrelevant). Jennifer O'Reilly has shown this kind of thinking with regard to images.[4] She has worked on themes in the illumination of the Book of Kells understood through biblical commentary of the time, but based on a familiarity with contemporary iconography and critical

2. Kinsella, *The Táin*, pp. 200-201.
3. 2 Sam. 1.25-26.
4. Cf. O'Reilly, 'Kells'.

theory. O'Reilly is partly asking, what were native systems of iconography? The answers are not easy, and the issue seems to be one of coming to terms with more of the ancient material while trying hard not to consider it strange, corrupted, or Other. With that approach, a direct line forms from the beginning of the twenty-first century to the beginning of thought.

APPENDIX I

W. Meid (ed.), *Táin Bó Fraích*, ll. 194-219 (Dublin: DIAS, 1967), pp. 8-9.

'Ná tair!' ol Ailill, 'co tuca chroíb dam din chaírthend tall fil i mbruuch na haband. It áildi limm a cháera.' Téitsium ass íarum, & brissis gésca din chrund, & dambeir ria aiss tarsin n-uisci. Ba hed íarum athesc Findabrach, nach álaind atchíd, ba háildiu lee Fróech do acsin tar dublind, in corp do rogili & in folt do roáilli, ind aiged do chumtachtai, int shúil do roglassi, iss hé móethóclach cen locht cen anim, co n-agaid fhocháel forlethain, is é díriuch dianim, in chráeb cosna cáeraib dergaib eter in mbrágit & in n-agid ngil. Iss ed atbered Findabair, nocon fhacca ní rosáissed leth nó trían do chruth.

Íar sain docuirethar na cráeba dóib assind usciu. 'It ségdai & it áildi na cáera. Tuc tórmach dún díb!' Téit ass atherruch co mbuí i mmedón ind usci. Gaibthi in béist assind uisci. 'Domiced claideb úaib!' ol sé. & ní rabai forsin tír fer no lamad a thabairt dó ar omun Ailella & Medba. Íar sin gataid Findabair a hétach dí, & focheird bedg issin n-uisce cossin chlaidiub. Dolléici a hathair sleig cóicrind dí anúas rout n-aurchora co lluid treda triliss, & condo ragaib Fróech inna láim in slig. Fosceirdside issa tír súas in slig, & mmíl inna tháeb. Léciud ón co forgabáil, cenéle n-imberta gaiscid, co lluid tarsin tlacht corcra & tresin léine baí im Ailill. La ssin cotéirget ind claideb i lláim Fhráech, & comben a chend den míl co mbaí fora thóeb, & dobert a mmíl leiss dochum tíre.

Tochmarc Becfhola[1]

§1 Díarmait, son of Áed Sláne, held the kingship of Temair. Crimthann, son of Áed, was in fosterage with him and taken in hostageship by him from the Laigin. He and his foster-son, Crimthann, journeyed one day to Áth Truim in the territory of the Cenél Lóegaire, accompanied by a single attendant. They beheld a woman coming from the west across the ford in a chariot. She wore rounded sandals of white bronze, inset with two jewels of precious stone, a tunic covered with red-gold embroidery about her, a crimson mantle on her, a brooch in fully wrought gold with shimmering gems of many hues fastening the mantle over her breast; necklets of refined gold around her neck; a golden circlet upon her head; two dark-grey horses drew her chariot, (harnessed) with a pair of golden bridles, yokes with animal designs worked in silver upon them.

§2 'Whence have you come, woman?' asked Díarmait.
'It is not from any distance,' she said.
'Why do you come?' asked Díarmait.
'To seek seed-wheat,' said she. 'I have good arable land but lack seed which is suitable for it.'
'If it be the seed of this territory that you desire,' said Díarmait, 'your destiny does not lie beyond me.'
'Indeed, I shall not refuse,' replied she, 'provided that I get the price.'
'You shall have this little brooch,' answered Díarmait.
'It will indeed be accepted,' said she.

§3 And he brings her with him to Temair.
'Who is the woman, Díarmait?' asked everyone.
'Indeed she has not told me who she is,' replied Díarmait.
'What have you given as her bride-price?' asked everyone.
'My little brooch,' said Díarmait.
'That is little value,' they all said.
'That will be her name then,' said the druid, 'Becfhola.'

---

1.   Text by Máire Bhreathnach, based on her edition of Version 1, as published in 'A New Edition of *Tochmarc Becfhola*', *Ériu* 35 (1984), pp. 59-92; Irish, pp. 72-76; English, pp. 77-81.

§4   She, however, had her heart set on his foster son, on Crimthann, son of Áed. She solicited him and yearned for him for a long time. At last the lad was prevailed upon to tryst with her at Cluain Dá Chaileach, at sunrise on Sunday, in order to elope with her. This he mentioned to his people. Thereupon his people forbade him, (saying) that he should not elope with her, the wife of the high-king of Ireland.

§5   However, she arose early on the morning of the Sunday from Díarmait's side.
      'What is this, woman?' asked Díarmait.
      'It is nothing good,' she replied, 'there are possessions of mine at Cluain Dá Chaileach. The servants left them there and fled.'
      'What possessions?' asked Díarmait.
      'Seven embroidered tunics, seven golden brooches, three circlets of gold. It is a pity to have them go astray.'
      'Don't go on Sunday,' said Díarmait, 'a journey on Sunday is not auspicious.'
      'Let someone go forth with me,' she said.
      'He will certainly not come from me,' answered Díarmait.

§6   She and her handmaid set out from Temair southwards, until they reached Dubthor Lagen. There they went astray until nightfall, when wolves came upon them and killed the handmaid. She herself took refuge in a tree. While she was in the tree she saw a fire in the middle of the forest. She went towards the fire and saw a warrior cooking a pig by the fire. He was clad in a silken tunic with a bright border, embroidered with circular designs of gold and silver. A helmet of gold, silver, and crystal was on his head, clusters and loops of gold around every lock of his hair which hung down to his shoulderblade. Two golden balls were at the parting of his braids, each one of them the size of a man's fist. His golden-hilted sword was on his belt. His two five-barbed spears lay on his shield of belly-leather which was embossed in white bronze. A cloak of many hues lay beside him. His two arms were laden to the elbows with gold and silver bracelets.

§7   She went and sat beside him at the fire. He looked and was unconcerned until he had finished cooking the pig. He made a meal of the pig, then washed his hands and left the fire. She followed him as far as the lake. There was a boat of bronze in the middle of the lake. A woven bronze chain from the boat was attached to the shore and another to the island in the middle of the lake. The warrior hauled in the boat. She got into the boat before him. The boat was left in a boathouse of clay in front of the island.

§8   She went before him into the house. This was a fine house with both cubicles and beds. He sat down. Then she sat down beside him. He reached out his hand as he sat and brought forth a dish of food for them. They both ate and drank and neither of them was drunk. There was no one in the house. They did not speak to each other. He went to bed. She slipped in beneath his cloak between him and the wall. However, he did not turn towards her throughout the night until they heard the call in the early morning from the jetty of the island, i.e. 'come out out, Flann, here

come the men.' He arose immediately, donned his armour and strode out. She went
to the door of the house to watch him. He saw three others at the jetty, who re-
sembled him in form, age, and comeliness. She also saw four others at the jetty of
the island, their shields held on guard. Then he and the three others went forth (to
meet them). They smote one another until each was red with blood of the other,
then each one went his way, injured.

§9   He went out to his island again.
     'May you have the victory of your valour,' said she, 'that was an heroic combat.'
     'It would indeed be good if it were against enemies,' said he.
     'Who are the warriors?' she asked.
     'The sons of my father's brother,' he answered, 'the others are my own three
brothers.'
     'What have you been fighting about?' asked the woman.
     'For this island', he said.
     'What is the name of the island?' she asked.
     'The island of Fedach mac in Daill,' he said.
     'And what is your name?' she asked.
     'Flann, grandson of Fedach,' he replied. 'It is the grandsons of Fedach who are
in contention. The island is indeed bountiful. It provides a meal sufficient for a
hundred men, with both food and ale, every evening without human attendants.
Should there be only two people on it, they receive only what can suffice them.'
     'Why don't I remain with you?' she asked.
     'It is indeed a bad union for you,' he answered, 'to stay with me and to forsake
the king of Ireland and to follow me in soldiering and in exile.'
     'Why don't we become lovers?' she asked.
     'Not this time,' he replied coolly. 'However, if the island becomes mine and if
we are alive, I shall go to fetch you and you are the woman who will be with me
always. But go now!'
     'It distresses me to leave my handmaid,' she said.
     'She is alive at the foot of the same tree,' he said, 'because the warriors of the
island protected her, and you will be escorted (home).'
     This was so.

§10 She arrived home to find Díarmait getting up on the same Sunday.
     'That is a wonder, wife,' said Díarmait, 'that you have not made a Sunday
journey in defiance of our prohibition.'
     'I dare not defy your command,' said she, as if she had not gone at all. From
that time onwards the habitual saying of Becfhola was:
     'I spent a night in the forest,
     In the house of the island of Mac in Daill,
     Although it was with a man, it was no sin,
     It was too soon when we parted.

'Inis Fedaich mac in Daill
In Dubthor, in Leinster,
Although it lies close to the road
Bearded warriors do not find it.'

Everyone wondered at that poem.

§11   Now, on that same day one year later, Díarmait was lying in bed with his wife
Becfhola when they saw a man go past the door of the house, and he was severely
wounded. It was Flann. Then Becfhola said:
'I am suspicious about valorous feats of men
At the battle in Daminis,
Was it the four (warriors) who defeated
Four in Daminis?'

Then Flann replied:
'O woman, do not direct reproachful anger
At the warriors concerning their result.
It was not the valorous feats of men that he overcame
But men with charmed spears.'

'I am unable,' said she,
'To hold out against the fighting of a man
When it was Flann that was wounded
In the conflict of the equally matched eight.'
With that he (Díarmait) let her go from them out of the house after him so that
she was not overtaken.
'Let her go,' said Díarmait, 'the evil one, for one knows not whither she goes
nor whence she came.'

§12   While they were saying this, they saw four clerics come into the house.
'What then,' cried Díarmait, 'the clergy travelling on Sunday!'
He drew his cloak over his head so that he might not see them at all.
'It is the order of our superiors that has brought us,' said the clerics, 'not wilfulness. Mo Laise of Daminis has sent us to speak with you. A respected member of
the community of Daminis was rousing his cows this morning and he saw the four
armed warriors with their shields on guard advancing along the island. Then he saw
the other four waiting for them. They smote each other so that the noise of the
shields in battle echoed over the whole island, until they were all slain on both sides
save one man, severely wounded, who alone survived. The other seven were buried
by Mo Laise. However, they left behind as much gold and silver as two of us could
carry, of all that was beneath their cloaks and about their necks and on their shields
and on their spears and about their swords and on their arms and on their tunics.
(We come) that you may know of your share in that gold and silver.'

'Nay,' said Díarmait, 'I will not share in what God has given to him. Let his sacred emblems be made with it.'

This was done. It is from this silver and gold that the sacred reliquaries of Mo Laise were made, that is, his shrine and his travelling service and his crozier. But Becfhola went off with Flann, grandson of Fedach, and has not returned since then. That is the wooing of Becfhola.

APPENDIX III

Notes from my narratological analysis of *Tochmarc Becfhola*

	Version 1: §1	... §3	... §7	... §8	Version 2: §1	... §5
Direct Speech	—	''Everyone' speaks 3 times; Díarmait speaks 2 times; 'The druid' speaks 1 time.	—	(A voice): 1	—	Díarmait: 4; 'Girl': 1; 'Woman': 1
Declaration	—	(Her name is proclaimed.)	—	'Come out, Flann'	—	It is not good to travel on Sunday.
Use of 'Girl' vs. 'Woman'	'Woman':1 time.	'Woman': 1; 'She/Her': 4; 'Becfhola' so named.	'She': 3.	'She': 7.	'Woman': 2.	'She': 2; 'Woman': 2; 'Girl': 2.
Action (Verbs)	Díarmait held the kingship; Crimthann was taken in foster-ship; they journeyed; they saw; she came; she wore; brooches were fastened, etc.	He brings her; they ask; not telling; he replies; she is given as prize; they say; they name	She went beside him; he looked; he finished pig (twice); he washed hands, left fire; she followed him; he hauls in boat; she gets in (first); boat left	She went; he sat; she sat; he reached out and brought forth; they ate and drank; he went to bed; she squeezed in; he did not turn; they heard call; he arose; she went, watched, saw; they looked like, went forth, killed, left.	Díarmait went to Áth Truim; he saw a woman	Becfhola awoke; 'Don't look for shirts'; 'I am going'; 'Come with me'

Notes from my narratological analysis of *Tochmarc Becfhola*

	Version 1: §1	... §3	... §7	... §8	Version 2: §1	... §5
Direction	Díarmait and Crimthann to Áth Truim; she going east	Back (to Tara)	She → fire; he from fire; she follows → lake; boat → shore → island	Into house; out of house; to jetty	(Díarmait saw her) going east	—
Boundary-Crossing	Díarmait and Crimthann to Áth Truim; she crossing ford	Into Tara	To the lake; into boat; to island; out of boat	Into house; into bed; (it is morning); out of house	Díarmait and Crimthann to Áth Truim, she is going east across ford	Breaking Sabbath; disobeying king
Displays of Wealth	—	They ask price; says she is of little value	Bronze boat	Fineness of house	Díarmait's servant	'Left behind brooches, etc.'
Other Notes		Value of women is discussed. Power of advice from 'everyone' established.	Bronze boat is Otherworld sign. He ignores her until after pig (another Otherworld sign). She crosses ahead of him. The boat takes them between worlds (obviously and literally).		Men carry weapons. She is beautiful but has no finery (versus Version 1).	Díarmait calls her 'woman', narrator calls her 'girl', but 'woman' when she says she is going.

GLOSSARY OF IRISH TERMS

I have tried to keep the number of untranslatable terms to a minimum. The following few words either have no straightforward translation or are usually left untranslated in critical texts in early Irish studies:

Gáe Bolga This is Cú Chulainn's mysterious and savage weapon. Gantz calls it his 'ultimate spear-thrusting feat'. He uses it against Connla in *Aided Óenfir Aífe*.

Geis(s) (pl. *gessa/geasa*) Usually translated by 'taboo', this supernatural or religious injunction is often a powerful and elaborate force governing a hero's existence in early Irish literature. Typical *gessa* include not being allowed to spend a night with a woman in your house without sleeping with her, or not eating the meat of dogs. Disobeying one of your *gessa* leads ultimately to your downfall.

Síd This term used to be translated by 'fairy mound' or 'fairies', but since the Irish concept of the Otherworld does not bear close relation to fairies from English or German folk tradition, it is often left untranslated. I have used this term generally to refer to Otherworld characters, usually women.

Ulaid 'Ulster', but literally 'the Ulstermen'.

Warp-spasm This is the customary translation for Cú Chulainn's Incredible Hulk-like metamorphosis preceding intense combat. (Cf. Louis Le Brocquy's illustration in Kinsella's *Táin*, pp. 151-52.)

BIBLIOGRAPHY

Abrams, M.H., *A Glossary of Literary Terms* (New York: Holt, Rinehart & Winston, 5th edn, 1988).

Ackerman, J.A., 'Satire and Symbolism in the Song of Jonah', in B. Halpern and J.D. Levenson (eds.), *Traditions in Transformation: Turning Points in Biblical Faith* (Winona Lake, IN: Eisenbrauns, 1981), pp. 213-46.

Aitchison, N.B., 'The Ulster Cycle: Heroic Image and Historical Reality', *Journal of Medieval History* 13 (1987), pp. 87-116.

Almbladh, Karin, *Studies in the Book of Jonah* (Uppsala: Academia Upsaliensis, 1986).

Alter, Robert, *The Art of Biblical Narrative* (New York: Basic Books, 1981).

—'Samson without Folklore', in Susan Niditch (ed.), *Text and Tradition: The Hebrew Bible and Folklore* (Atlanta: Scholars Press, 1990), pp. 47-56.

Alter, Robert, and Frank Kermode (eds.), *The Literary Guide to the Bible* (Cambridge, MA: Belknap Press at Harvard University Press, 1987).

Anderson, A.O.A., and M.O. Anderson (eds.), *Adomnán's Life of Columba* (London: T. Nelson, 1961).

Auster, Paul, *The Invention of Solitude* (London: Faber & Faber, 1978).

Bakhtin, Mikhail, *Problems of Dostoevsky's Poetics* (Minneapolis: University of Minnesota Press, 1984).

Bal, Mieke (ed.), *Anti-Covenant: Counter-Reading Women's Lives in the Hebrew Bible* (JSOTSup, 81; Bible and Literature Series, 22; Sheffield: Almond Press, 1989).

—'Dealing/With/Women: Daughters in the Book of Judges', in Schwartz (ed.), *The Book and the Text*, pp. 16-39.

—*Death and Dissymmetry: The Politics of Coherence in the Book of Judges* (Chicago: Chicago University Press, 1988).

—*Lethal Love: Feminist Literary Readings of Biblical Love Stories* (Bloomington: Indiana University Press, 1987).

—'Lots of Writing', *Semeia* 54 (1991), pp. 77-102.

Band, A.J., 'Swallowing Jonah: The Eclipse of Parody', *Prooftexts* 10 (1990), pp. 177-95.

Bar-Efrat, Shimon, *Narrative Art in the Bible* (JSOTSup, 70; Bible and Literature Series, 17; Sheffield: Almond Press, 1989).

Barthes, Roland, *Mythologies* (London: Methuen, 1972).

Baudis, Josef, 'On Tochmarc Emere', *Ériu* 9 (1921-23), pp. 98-108.

Baumgarten, Rolf, 'A Hiberno-Isidorian Etymology', *Peritia* 2 (1983), pp. 225-28.

Beal, Tim, 'Ideology and Intertextuality: Surplus of Meaning and Controlling the Means of Production', in Fewell (ed.), *Reading between Texts*, pp. 27-39.

Berlin, Adèle, *The Dynamics of Biblical Parallelism* (Bloomington: Indiana University Press, 1985).

—*Poetics and Interpretation of Biblical Narrative* (Bible and Literature Series, 17; Sheffield: Almond Press, 1983).

—'A Rejoinder to John A. Miles, Jr. with Some Observations on the Nature of Prophecy', *JQR* 66 (1975–76), pp. 227-35.

Best, R.I., *Bibliography of Irish Philology and Manuscript Literature* (Dublin: DIAS, 1969).

Bhreathnach, Máire, 'A New Edition of *Tochmarc Becfhola*', *Ériu* 35 (1984), pp. 59-92.

Bickerman, Elias, *Four Strange Books of the Bible: Jonah, Daniel, Koholeth, Esther* (New York: Schocken Books, 1967).

Binchy, D.A. (ed.), *Críth Gablach* (Dublin: DIAS, 1979).

—*Scéla Cano Meic Gartnáin* (Dublin: DIAS, 1975).

Bischoff, Bernhard, 'Die "Zweite Latinität" des Virgilius Maro Grammaticus und seine jüdische Herkunft', *Mittellateinisches Jahrbuch* 23 (1991), pp. 11-16.

Bitel, Lisa M., ' "Conceived in Sins, Born in Delights": Stories of Procreation from Early Ireland', *Journal of the History of Sexuality* 3/2 (1992), pp. 181-202.

Bloomfield, Morton W., 'Continuities and Discontinuities', *New Literary History* 10/2 (Winter 1979), pp. 409-15.

Borsje, Jacqueline, 'The Monster in the River Ness in *Vita Sancti Columbae*: A Study of a Miracle', *Peritia* 8 (1994), pp. 27-34.

Borsje, Jacqeline and D. Ó Cróinín, 'A Monster in the Indian Ocean', *Nederlands Theologisch Tijdschrift* 49/1 (January 1995), pp. 1-11.

Bové, Paul, 'Discourse', in Lentricchia and McLaughlin (eds.), *Critical Terms*, pp. 50-65.

Bowen, C, 'Great-Bladdered Medb: Mythology and Invention in the *Táin Bó Cuailnge*', *Éire–Ireland* 10/4 (1975), pp. 14-34.

Bray, Dorothy Ann, *A List of Motifs in the Lives of the Early Irish Saints* (Helsinki: Suomalainen Tiedeakatemia, 1992).

Breatnach, Caoimhín, review of *Ulidia*, in *Éigse* 29 (1996), pp. 200-208.

Breatnach, Liam, 'Law', in McCone and Simms, *Progress*, pp. 107-21.

Brenner, A., 'Female Social Behaviour: Two Descriptive Patterns within the "Birth of the Hero" Paradigm', *VT* 36 (1986), pp. 257-73.

Brett, M.G., *Biblical Criticism in Crisis?* (Cambridge: Cambridge University Press, 1991).

Bruford, Alan, 'Cú Chulainn—An Ill-Made Hero?', in H.L.C. Tristram (ed.), *Text und Zeittiefe* (Tübingen: G. Narr, 1994), pp. 185-215.

Brüning, Gertrud, 'Adamnans *Vita Columbae* und ihre Ableitungen', *ZCP* 2 (1917), pp. 213-304.

Burrows, M., 'The Literary Category of the Book of Jonah', in H.T. Frank and W.L. Reed (eds.), *Translating and Understanding the Old Testament* (Nashville: Abingdon Press, 1970), pp. 80-107.

Bynum, David, *The Daemon in the Wood: A Study of Oral Narrative Patterns* (Cambridge, MA: Center for the Study of Oral Literature, Harvard University, 1978).

—'Samson as Biblical φηρ ορεσκωος', in Niditch, *Text and Tradition*, pp. 57-74.

Byrne, F.J., *Irish Kings and High-Kings* (London: Batsford, 1973).

Carey, John, 'An Edition of the Pseudo-historical Prologue to the *Senchas Már*', *Ériu* 45 (1994), pp. 1-32.

—*The Irish National Origin-Legend: Synthetic Pseudohistory* (Cambridge: Institute for Anglo-Saxon, Norse and Celtic, Cambridge University, 1994).

—'The Location of the Otherworld in Irish Tradition', *Éigse* 19 (1982), pp. 36-43.

—'Otherworlds and Verbal Worlds in Middle Irish Narrative', in William Mahon (ed.), *Proceedings of the Harvard Celtic Colloquium. IX. 1989* (Cambridge, MA: Department of Celtic Languages and Literatures, Harvard University, 1990), pp. 31-39.

—review of Kim McCone, *Pagan Past and Christian Present* in *Speculum* 67 (1992), pp. 450-52.

—'The Uses of Tradition in *Serglige Con Culainn*', in Mallory and Stockman (eds.), *Ulidia*, pp. 77-84.

Carney, James, 'The Deeper Level of Early Irish Literature', *Capuchin Annual* 36 (1969), pp. 160-71.

—'The Ecclesiastic Background to Irish Saga', *Artica, Studia Ethnographica Upsaliensia* 11 (1956), pp. 221-27.

—*Studies in Irish Literature and History* (Dublin: DIAS, 1955).

Charles-Edwards, T.M., 'A Contract between King and People in Early Medieval Ireland? *Críth Gablach* on Kingship', *Peritia* 8 (1994), pp. 107-19.

—'Honour and Status in Some Irish and Welsh Prose Tales', *Ériu* 29 (1978), pp. 123-41.

Clancy, Thomas O., 'Saint and Fool: The Image and Function of Cummine Fota and Comgan Mac Da Cherda in Early Irish Literature' (Unpublished PhD, University of Edinburgh, 1992).

Clancy, Thomas O., and Gilbert Márkus, *Iona: The Earliest Poetry of a Celtic Monastery* (Edinburgh: Edinburgh University Press, 1995).

Clines, D.J.A., 'Reading Esther from Left to Right: Contemporary Strategies for Reading a Biblical Text', in D.J.A. Clines, S.E. Fowl and S.E. Porter (eds.), *The Bible in Three Dimensions: Essays in Celebration of Forty Years of Biblical Studies at the University of Sheffield* (JSOTSup, 87; Sheffield: JSOT Press, 1990), pp. 31-52.

Cooper, R, 'Textualizing Determinacy/ Determining Textuality', *Semeia* 62 (1993), pp. 1-27.

Cormier, Raymond, 'Cú Chulainn and Yvain: The Love Hero in Early Irish and Old French Literature', *Studies in Philology* 72/2 (April 1975), pp. 115-39.

Coulter, C.C., 'The "Great Fish" in Ancient and Medieval Story', *TAPA* 57 (1926), pp. 32-50.

Craig, Kenneth, 'Jonah and the Reading Process', *JSOT* 47 (1990), pp. 103-14.

—*A Poetics of Jonah: Art in the Service of Ideology* (Columbia: University of South Carolina Press, 1993).

Crenshaw, James L., *Samson: A Vow Ignored, A Secret Betrayed* (Atlanta: Scholars Press, 1978).

Cross, T.P., 'A Note on "Sohrab and Rustum" in Ireland', *Journal of Celtic Studies* 1 (1950), pp. 176-82.

—*Motif-Index of Early Irish Literature* (Bloomington: Indiana University Press, 1952).

Crouch, W.B., 'Opening the Closure of the Book of Jonah', *JSOT* 62 (1994), pp. 101-12.

Culley, Robert C., *Studies in the Structure of Hebrew Narrative* (Philadelphia: Fortress Press, 1976).

Dan, Joseph, 'Midrash and the Dawn of Kabbalah', in Hartman and Budick (eds.), *Midrash and Literature*, pp. 127-40.

Dauber, Kenneth, 'The Bible as Literature: Reading like the Rabbis', *Semeia* 31 (1985), pp. 27-48.

Davies, Morgan, 'Protocols of Reading in Early Irish Literature: Notes on Some Notes to "Orgain Denna Rig" and "Amra Coluim Cille" ', *CMCS* 32 (Winter 1996), pp. 1-23.

Dentith, Simon, *Bakhtinian Thought* (London: Routledge, 1995).

Derrida, Jacques, 'Des Tours de Babel', *Semeia* 54 (1991), pp. 3-34.

Detweiler, Robert, and Vernon K. Robbins, 'From New Criticism to Poststructuralism: Twentieth-Century Hermeneutics', in Prickett (ed.), *Reading the Text*, pp. 225-80.

DeVries, Jan, *Heroic Song and Heroic Legend* (Oxford: Oxford University Press, 1963).

Dillon, Myles, *The Cycles of the Kings* (Dublin: Four Courts Press, 1994).

—*Early Irish Literature* (Dublin: Four Courts Press, 1994).

Dillon, Myles (ed.), *Early Irish Society* (Dublin: Published for the Public Relations Committee of Ireland for C. Ó Lochlainn, 1954).

—*Serglige Con Culainn* (Dublin: DIAS, 1953).

Doan, J.E., 'A Structural Approach to Celtic Saints' Lives', in Patrick Ford (ed.), *Celtic Folklore and Christianity* (Bloomington: Indiana University Press, 1983), pp. 16-28.

Donahue, Charles, 'Beowulf, Ireland and the Natural Good', *Traditio* 7 (1949–51), pp. 263-77.

Dooley, Ann, 'The Heroic Word: The Reading of Early Irish Sagas', in Robert O'Driscoll (ed.), *The Celtic Consciousness* (New York: Braziller, 1982), pp. 155-59.

—'The Invention of Women in the *Táin*', in Mallory and Stockman (eds.), *Ulidia*, pp. 123-33.

Dumézil, Georges, 'L'idéologie trifonctionelle des Indo-Européans et la Bible', in *idem*, *Mythe et épopée* (Paris: Gallimard, 1968–1973), pp. 338-61.

Dundes, Alan, *Analytic Essays in Folklore* (The Hague: Mouton, 1975).

—*Sacred Narrative: Readings in the Theory of Myth* (Berkeley: University of California Press, 1984).

—'Structuralism and Folklore', *Studia Fennica* 20 (1977), pp. 75-93.

Dunn, Vincent, *Cattle-Raids and Courtships* (New York: Garland Publications, 1989).

Durcan, Paul, *Give Me Your Hand* (London: Macmillan, 1994).

Eagleton, Terry, 'J.L. Austin and the Book of Jonah', in Schwartz (ed.), *The Book and the Text*, pp. 231-36.

—*Literary Theory: An Introduction* (Oxford: Basil Blackwell, 1983).

Eco, Umberto, 'The Return of the Middle Ages', in *idem*, *Travels in Hyperreality* (New York: Harcourt Brace Jovanovich, 1986), pp. 59-86.

Eco, Umberto, and Richard Rorty (eds.), *Interpretation and Overinterpretation* (Cambridge: Cambridge University Press, 1992).

Eliade, Mircea, *The Quest: History and Meaning in Religion* (Chicago: University of Chicago Press, 1969).

Enright, Michael J., *Iona, Tara and Soissons: The Origin of the Royal Anointing Ritual* (Berlin: W. de Gruyter, 1985).

Exum, J. Cheryl, 'Aspects of Symmetry and Balance in the Samson Saga', *JSOT* 19 (1981), pp. 3-29.

—*Fragmented Women: Feminist (Sub)versions of Biblical Narratives* (JSOTSup, 163; Sheffield: JSOT Press, 1993).

—*Plotted, Shot and Painted: Cultural Representations of Biblical Women* (JSOTSup, 215; GCT, 3; Sheffield: Sheffield Academic Press, 1996).

Exum, J. Cheryl and D.J.A. Clines (eds.), *The New Literary Criticism and the Hebrew Bible* (JSOTSup, 143; Sheffield: JSOT Press, 1993).

Exum, J. Cheryl and J.W. Whedbee, 'Isaac, Samson and Saul', *Semeia* 32 (1985), pp. 5-40.

Fewell, Dana Nolan (ed.), *Reading between Texts: Intertextuality and the Hebrew Bible* (Louisville, KY: Westminster/John Knox Press, 1992).

Findon, Joanne, 'A Woman's Words: Emer versus Cú Chulainn in *Aided Óenfir Aífe*', in Mallory and Stockman (eds.), *Ulidia*, pp. 139-48.

—'Emer and the Roles of Female Characters in the Medieval Irish Ulster Cycle', in

R. Black, W. Gillies and R. Ó Maolalaigh (eds.), *Celtic Connections: Proceedings of the 10th International Congress of Celtic Studies* (East Linton: Tuckwell Press, 1999).

—'Negotiating Female Territory: Cú Chulainn's Journeys in Tochmarc Emire' (Unpublished paper given at the 10th ICCS, 1995; proceedings forthcoming).

Fisch, Harold, 'The Hermeneutic Quest in *Robinson Crusoe*', in Hartman and Budick (eds.), *Midrash and Literature*, pp. 213-36.

Ford, Patrick, 'Prolegomena to a Reading of the *Mabinogi*: 'Puryll' and 'Manawydan'', *Studia Celtica* 16/17 (1981–82), pp. 110-25.

—'The Everlasting Fame in the Tain', in Mallory and Stockman (eds.), *Ulidia*, pp. 255-62.

Fournier, P., 'Le *Liber ex Lege Moysi* et les tendences bibliques du droit canonique irlandais', *RC* 30 (1909), pp. 221-34.

Fox, Michael V., *Character and Ideology in the Book of Esther* (Columbia: University of South Carolina, 1991).

Frantzen, Allen J., 'When Women Aren't Enough', in Nancy Partner (ed.), *Studying Medieval Women: Sex, Gender, Feminism* (Cambridge, MA: Medieval Academy of America, 1993), pp. 1-15.

Freud, Sigmund, 'The Economic Problem of Masochism', in *The Standard Edition of the Complete Works of Sigmund Freud. XIX. The Ego and the Id and Other Works* (London: Hogarth Press and The Insitute of Psycho-Analysis, 1961), pp. 157-72.

—*The Interpretation of Dreams* (London: Penguin Books, 1991).

—*On Sexuality: Three Essays on the Theory of Sexuality and Other Works* (London: Penguin Books, 1991).

—*Totem and Taboo* (London: Routledge & Kegan Paul, 1950).

Frye, Northrop, *Anatomy of Criticism* (London: Penguin Books, 1990).

—*The Great Code* (New York: Harcourt Brace Jovanovich, 1982).

Gantz, Jeffrey (trans.), *Early Irish Myths and Sagas* (London: Penguin Books, 1982).

Gaunt, Simon, *Gender and Genre in Medieval French Literature* (Cambridge: Cambridge University Press, 1995).

Goldman, Stan, 'Narrative and Ethical Ironies in Esther', *JSOT* 47 (1990), pp. 15-31.

Goodhart, Sandor, 'Prophecy, Sacrifice and Repentance in the Story of Jonah', *Semeia* 33 (1985), pp. 43-63.

Gottwald, Norman K., *The Hebrew Bible: A Socio-Literary Introduction* (Philadelphia: Fortress Press, 1985).

Graham, Susan Lochrie, 'Intertextual Trekking: Visiting the Iniquity of the Fathers upon "The Next Generation" ', *Semeia* 64 (1995), pp. 195-217.

Gray, Elizabeth, '*Cath Maige Tuired*: Myth and Structure', *Éigse* 18 (1981–82), pp. 183-209; *Éigse* 19 (1982–83), pp. 1-35, 230-62.

—'Lug and CúChulainn: King and Warrior, God and Man', *Studia Celtica* 24/25 (1989/90), pp. 38-52.

Greene, David, 'Tabu in Early Irish Narrative', in Hans Bekker-Nielsen, P. Foote, A. Haarder and P.M. Sørenson (eds.), *Medieval Narrative* (Odense: Odense University Press, 1979), pp. 9-19.

Gros Louis, K.R.R. (ed.), *Literary Interpretations of Biblical Narratives* (Nashville, KY: Abingdon Press, 1974).

Grossfeld, Bernard (ed. and trans.), *The Two Targums of Esther* (Collegeville, MN: Liturgical Press, 1991).

Gunn, David, 'New Directions in the Study of Biblical Hebrew Narrative', *JSOT* 39 (1987), pp. 65-75.

—'Samson of Sorrows: An Isaiac Gloss on Judges 13–16', in Fewell (ed.), *Reading between Texts*, pp. 225-53.

Gunn, David, and D.N. Fewell, *Narrative in the Hebrew Bible* (Oxford: Oxford University Press, 1993).

Hamel, A.G. van (ed.), *Compert Con Culainn and Other Stories* (Dublin: DIAS, 1933, repr. 1978).

Handelman, Susan, *The Slayers of Moses: The Emergence of Rabbinic Interpretation in Modern Literary Theory* (Albany, NY: State University of New York Press, 1982).

Hart, Kevin, 'The Poetics of the Negative', in Prickett (ed.), *Reading the Text*, pp. 281-340.

Hartman, Geoffrey H., and Sanford Budick (eds.), *Midrash and Literature* (New Haven: Yale University Press, 1986).

Hauser, A.J., 'Jonah: In Pursuit of the Dove', *JBL* 104 (1985), pp. 21-37.

Hennig, John, 'The Literary Tradition of Moses in Ireland', *Traditio* 7 (1949–51), pp. 233-61.

Herbert, Máire, 'Celtic Heroine? The Archaeology of the Deirdre Story', in Toni O'Brien Johnson and D. Cairns (eds.), *Gender in Irish Writing* (Milton Keynes: Open University Press, 1991), pp. 13-22.

—'*Fled Dúin na nGéd*: A Reappraisal', *CMCS* 18 (1989), pp. 75-87.

—'Hagiography', in McCone and Simms (eds.), *Progress*, pp. 79-90.

—*Iona, Kells, and Derry: The History and Hagiography of the Monastic Familia of Columba* (Oxford: Oxford University Press, 1988).

—'The Universe of Male and Female: A Reading of the Deirdre Story', in C.J. Byrne, M. Harry and P. Ó Siadhail (eds.), *Celtic Languages and Celtic People: Proceedings of the Second North American Congress of Celtic Studies* (Halifax, Nova Scotia: D'Arcy McGee Chair of Irish Studies, St Mary's University, 1992), pp. 53-64.

Herren, Michael, 'Virgil the Grammarian: A Spanish Jew in Ireland?', *Peritia* 9 (1995), pp. 51-71.

Hillers, Barbara, 'The Heroes of the Ulster Cycle', in Mallory and Stockman (eds.), *Ulidia*, pp. 99-106.

Holbert, J.C., ' "Deliverance Belongs to the Lord": Satire in the Book of Jonah', *JSOT* 21 (1981), pp. 59-81.

Hollo, Kaarina, 'The Feast of Bricriu and the Exile of the Sons of Dóel Dermait', *Emania* 10 (1992), pp. 18-24.

Hughes, Kathleen, *Early Christian Ireland: Introduction to the Sources* (Ithaca, NY: Cornell University Press, 1972).

Hull, Vernam (ed. and trans.), *Longes Mac n-Uislenn: The Exile of the Sons of Uisliu* (New York: Modern Language Association of America, 1949).

Humphreys, W. Lee, 'A Life-Style for Diaspora: A Study of the Tales of Esther and Daniel', *JBL* 92/2 (1973), pp. 211-23.

Jabès, Edmond, *The Book of Margins* (Chicago: University of Chicago Press, 1993).

Jackson, Kenneth H., *A Celtic Miscellany* (London: Penguin Books, 1971).

Jaeger, David Kenneth, 'The Initiatory Trial Theme of the Hero in Hebrew Bible Narrative' (Unpublished PhD thesis, University of Denver, 1992).

Jauss, H.R., 'The Alterity and Modernity of Medieval Literature', *New Literary History* 10/2 (Winter 1979), pp. 181-27.

Jefferson, Ann, and David Robey, 'Introduction', in *idem* (eds.), *Modern Literary Theory* (London: B.T. Batsford, 1986), pp. 7-23.

Jung, C.G., 'The Psychology of the Child Archetype', with introduction by Alan Dundes, in Dundes (ed.), *Sacred Narrative*, pp. 244-55.

Kearney, Richard, 'Myth as the Bearer of Possible Worlds: Interview with Paul Ricoeur', in M.P. Hederman and R. Kearney (eds.), *The Crane Bag Book of Irish Studies, Vol. I* (Dublin: Blackwater Press, 1982), pp. 260-66.

Kelleher, John V., 'Humor in the Ulster Saga', in H. Levin (ed.), *Veins of Humor* (Cambridge, MA: Harvard University Press, 1972), pp. 35-56.

Keller, Carl, 'Jonas. Le portrait d'un prophète', *TZ* 21 (1965), pp. 329-40.

Kelly, Fergus, *A Guide to Early Irish Law* (Dublin: DIAS, 1988).

Kelly, Joseph F.T., 'Christianity and the Latin Tradition in Early Medieval Ireland', *BJRL* 68 (1985–86), pp. 410-33.

Kermode, Frank, 'The Plain Sense of Things', in Hartman and Budick (eds.), *Midrash and Literature*, pp. 179-94.

Kinsella, Thomas (trans.), *The Táin* (Oxford: Oxford University Press, 1969).

Kottje, Raymund, *Studien zum Einfluss des Alten Testamentes auf Recht und Liturgie des frühen Mittelalters* (Bonn: Röhrscheid, 1970).

Krutnik, Frank, *In a Lonely Street: Film Noir, Genre, Masculinity* (London: Routledge, 1991).

Kugel, James L., 'Two Introductions to Midrash', in Hartman and Budick (eds.), *Midrash and Literature*, pp. 77-104.

Lacocque, A., and P-E. Lacocque, *Jonah: A Psycho-Religious Approach to the Prophet* (Columbia: University of South Carolina Press, 1990).

Leach, Edmund, 'Fishing for Men on the Edge of the Wilderness', in Alter and Kermode (eds.), *Literary Guide*, pp. 579-99.

—'The Legitimacy of Solomon: Some Structural Aspects of the Old Testament History', in E. Leach, *Genesis as Myth* (London: Cape, 1969), pp. 25-84.

Leach, Edmund, and D.A. Aycock (eds.), *Structuralist Interpretations of Biblical Myth* (London: Royal Anthropological Institute of Great Britain and Ireland, 1983).

Lechte, John, *Fifty Key Contemporary Thinkers: From Structuralism to Postmodernity* (London: Routledge, 1994).

Lentricchia, Frank, and Thomas McLaughlin (eds.), *Critical Terms for Literary Study* (Chicago: University of Chicago Press, 1995).

Levinas, Emmanuel, 'The Youth of Israel', in *idem, Nine Talmudic Readings* (Bloomington: Indiana University Press, 1990), pp. 120-35.

Lévi-Strauss, Claude, *Myth and Meaning: Cracking the Code of Culture* (New York: Schocken Books, 1995).

—'The Story of Asdiwal', in *idem, Structural Anthropology*, II (Chicago: University of Chicago, 1983), pp. 146-97.

—'The Structural Study of Myth', in *idem, Structural Anthropology*, I (New York: Basic Books, 1972), pp. 206-31.

Lieu, Judith, John North and Tessa Rajak (eds.), *The Jews among Pagans and Christians in the Roman Empire* (London: Routledge, 1992).

Limburg, James, *Jonah* (Louisville, KY: Westminster/John Knox Press, 1993).

—'Jonah and the Whale through the Eyes of Artists', *Bible Review* 6/4 (August 1990), pp. 18-25.

Littleton, C.S., *The New Comparative Mythology: An Assessment of Dumézil* (Berkeley: University of California Press, 1973).

Lopate, Phillip, 'Judges. Samson and Delilah: Tests of Weakness', in Rosenberg (ed.), *Congregation*, pp. 70-97.

Mac Cana, Proinsias, 'The Sinless Otherworld of Immram Brain', *Ériu* 27 (1976), pp. 95-115.

—'Women in Irish Mythology', *The Crane Bag* 4 (1980), pp. 7-11.

Macalister, R.A.S. (ed.), *Lebor Gabála Érenn*, I–V (Dublin: Royal Irish Academy, 1938–42).

Mackey, James, 'Christian Past and Primal Present', in *Etudes Celtiques 9th CIEC, 1991* (Paris: CNRS, 1993), pp. 285-97.

—'Primal Religion and Christianity in Celtic Tradition and Literature', in F.J. Byrne, H. Margaret and P. Ó Síadhail (eds.), *Celtic Languages and Celtic People: Proceedings of the Second North American Congress of Celtic Studies* (Halifax, Nova Scotia: D'Arcy McGee Chair of Irish Studies, St Mary's University, 1992), pp. 39-51.

Mahon, Derek, *The Hudson Letter* (Dublin: The Gallery Press, 1996).

Mailloux, Steven, 'Interpretation', in Lentricchia and McLaughlin (eds.), *Critical Terms*, pp. 121-34.

Mallory, J.P. (ed.), *Aspects of the Táin* (Belfast: December Publications, 1992).

Mallory, J.P., and G. Stockman (eds.), *Ulidia: Proceedings of the First International Conference on the Ulster Cycle of Tales* (Belfast: December Publications, 1994).

Mamet, David, 'Kryptonite', in *idem*, *Some Freaks* (London: Faber & Faber, 1989), pp. 175-80.

Margalith, O., 'Samson's Riddle and Samson's Magic Locks', *VT* 36, pp. 225-34.

Márkus, Gilbert (ed. and trans.), *Cáin Adomnáin: The Law of the Innocents* (Glasgow: Department of Celtic, University of Glasgow, 1997).

Marsden, John, *The Illustrated Life of Columba* (Edinburgh: Floris Books, 1991).

Martin, B.K., 'Medieval Irish *aitheda* and Todorov's "Narratologie" ', *Studia Celtica* 10/11 (1975–76), pp. 138-51.

McBride, William T., 'Esther Passes: Chiasm, Lex Talio, and Money in the Book of Esther', in Rosenblatt and Sitterson (eds.), *Not in Heaven*, pp. 211-23.

McCone, Kim, 'Aided Cheltchair Maic Uthechair: Hounds, Heroes and Hospitallers in Early Irish Myth and Story', *Ériu* 35 (1984), pp. 1-30.

—'Dubthach Maccu Lugair and a Matter of Life and Death in the Pseudo-historical Prologue to the Senchas Már', *Peritia* 5 (1986), pp. 1-35.

—*Pagan Past and Christian Present* (Maynooth: An Sagart, 1990).

—'A Tale of Two Ditties: Poet and Satirist in Cath Maige Tuired', in Ó Corráin, Breatnach and McCone (eds.), *Sages*, pp. 122-43.

McCone, Kim, and Katherine Simms (eds.), *Progress in Medieval Irish Studies* (Maynooth: Department of Old Irish, St Patrick's College, 1996).

McNamara, Martin, 'The Bible in Ireland', *ScrB* 6 (1975–76), pp. 36-39.

—'The Text of the Latin Bible in the Early Irish Church. Some Data and Desiderata', in Ní Chatháin and Richter (eds.), *Irland*, pp. 7-55.

Meid, Wolfgang (ed.), *Táin Bó Fraích* (Dublin: DIAS, 1967).

Melia, Daniel, 'Law and the Shaman-Saint', in Patrick Ford (ed.), *Celtic Folklore and Christianity* (Bloomington: Indiana University Press, 1983), pp. 113-28.

—'Narrative Structure in Irish Saga' (Unpublished PhD dissertation, Harvard University, 1972).

—'Parallel Versions of "The Boyhood Deeds of Cuchulainn" ', in J.J. Duggan (ed.), *Oral Literature* (New York: Barnes & Noble Books, 1975), pp. 25-40.

—'Remarks on the Structure and Composition of the Ulster Death Tales', *Studia Hibernica* 17/18 (1977–78), pp. 36-57.

Meltzer, Françoise, 'Unconscious', in Lentricchia and McLaughlin (eds.), *Critical Terms*, pp. 147-62.

Meredith, B., 'Desire and Danger: The Drama of Betrayal in Judges and Judith', in Bal (ed.), *Anti-Covenant*, pp. 63-77.

Meyer, Kuno (ed.), *The Death Tales of the Ulster Heroes* (Dublin: Hodges, Figgis, & Co., 1906).

Miles, J.A., 'Laughing at the Bible: Jonah as Parody', *JQR* 65 (1974–75), pp. 168-81.

Miller, J. Hillis, 'Narrative', in Lentricchia and McLaughlin (eds.), *Critical Terms*, pp. 66-79.

Milton, John, *Samson Agonistes* (London: Davis-Poynter, 1973).

Moi, Toril, 'Feminist Literary Criticism', in Jefferson and Robey (eds.), *Modern Literary Theory*, pp. 204-21.

Moore, Carey A., *Esther* (AB; Garden City, NY: Doubleday, 1971).

More, Joe, 'The Prophet Jonah: The Story of an Intrapsychic Process', *American Imago* 27 (1970), pp. 3-11.

Mosala, I.J., 'The Implications of the Text of Esther for the African Women's Struggle in South Africa', *Semeia* 59 (1992), pp. 129-38.

Nagy, J.F., 'Close Encounters of the Traditional Kind', in Patrick Ford (ed.), *Celtic Folklore and Christianity* (Santa Barbara, CA: McNally & Loftin, 1983), pp. 129-49.

—'Compositional Concerns in the *Acallam na Senórach*', in Ó Corráin, Breatnach and McCone (eds.), *Sages*, pp. 149-58.

—'Fenian Heroes and their Rites of Passage', in B. Almqvist, S. Ó Catháin and P. Ó Héalaí (eds.), *The Heroic Process: Form, Function and Fantasy in Folk Epic* (Dún Laoghaire: Glendale Press, 1987), pp. 161-82.

—'Heroic Destinies in the Macgnímrada of Finn and Cú Chulainn', *ZCP* 40 (1984), pp. 23-39.

—'Liminality and Knowledge in Irish Traditon', *Studia Celtica* 16/17 (1981–82), pp. 135-42.

—review of J.P. Mallory (ed.), *Aspects of the Táin*, in *Éigse* 28 (1994–95), pp. 183-88.

—'Sword as Audacht', in A.T.E. Matonis and Dan Melia (eds.), *Celtic Language, Celtic Culture* (Van Nuys, CA: Ford & Bailie, 1990), pp. 131-36.

—*The Wisdom of the Outlaw: The Boyhood Deeds of Finn in Gaelic Narrative Tradition* (Berkeley: University of California Press, 1985).

Neusner, Jacob (ed. and trans.), *Esther Rabbah I: An Analytical Translation* (Atlanta: Scholars Press, 1989).

Ní Bhrolcháin, Muireann, 'Re Tóin Mná: In Pursuit of Troublesome Women', in Mallory and Stockman (eds.), *Ulidia*, pp. 115-21.

Ní Chatháin, Próinséas, and Michael Richter (eds.), *Irland und die Christenheit: Bibelstudien und Mission/ Ireland and Christendom: The Bible and the Missions* (Stuttgart: Klett–Cotta, 1987).

Nicolaisen, W.F.H., 'The Past as Place: Names, Stories, and the Remembered Self', *Folklore* 102/1 (1991), pp. 3-15.

Niditch, Susan, 'Samson as Culture Hero, Trickster and Bandit', *CBQ* 52/4 (October 1990), pp. 608-24.

—*Text and Tradition: The Hebrew Bible and Folklore* (Atlanta: Scholars Press, 1990).

—*Underdogs and Tricksters* (San Francisco: Harper & Row, 1987).

Nutt, Alfred, 'The Happy Otherworld in the Mythico-Romantic Literature of the Irish', in Kuno Meyer (ed.), *The Voyage of Bran*, I (London: D. Nutt, 1895), pp. 105-331.

Ó Cathasaigh, Tomás, 'Between God and Man: The Hero of Irish Tradition', in M.P. Hederman and R. Kearney (eds.), *The Crane Bag Book of Irish Studies, I* (Dublin: Blackwater Press, 1982), pp. 220-27.

—'Curse and Satire', *Éigse* 21 (1986), pp. 10-15.

—'Early Irish Narrative Literature', in McCone and Simms (eds.), *Progress*, pp. 55-64.

—*The Heroic Biography of Cormac mac Airt* (Dublin: DIAS, 1977).

—'Mythology in Táin Bó Cuailnge', in H.L.C. Tristram (ed.), *Studien zur Táin Bó Cuailnge* (Tübingen: G. Narr, 1993), pp. 114-32.

—'Reflections on *Compert Conchubuir* and *Serglige Con Culainn*', in Mallory and Stockman (eds.), *Ulidia*, pp. 85-90.

—'The Rhetoric of Fingal Rónáin', *Celtica* 17 (1985), pp. 123-44.

—'The Rhetoric of Scela Cano Meic Gartnain', in Ó Corráin, Breatnach and McCone (eds.), *Sages*, pp. 233-50.

—'The Semantics of Síd', *Éigse* 17 (1977–79), pp. 137-55.

—'The Sister's Son in Early Irish Literature', *Peritia* 5 (1986), pp. 128-60.

—'The Theme of *lommrad* in Cath Maige Mucrama', *Éigse* 18 (1981), pp. 211-24.

—'Varia III: The Trial of Mael Fhothartaig', *Ériu* 36 (1985), pp. 177-80.

Ó Corráin, Donnchadh, 'An dlí agus an sean-tiomna', *Léachtaí Cholm Cille* 20 (1990), pp. 32-48.

—'Irish Vernacular Law and the Old Testament', in Ní Chatháin and Richter (eds.), *Irland*, pp. 284-307.

Ó Corráin, Donnchadh, Liam Breatnach and A. Breen, 'The Laws of the Irish', *Peritia* 3 (1984), pp. 382-48.

Ó Corráin, Donnchadh, Liam Breatnach and Kim McCone (eds.), *Sages, Saints, and Storytellers* (Maynooth: An Sagart, 1989).

Ó Cróinín, Dáibhí, *Early Medieval Ireland 400–1200* (London: Longman, 1995).

Ó hÓgáin, D., *The Hero in Irish Folk History* (Dublin: Gill & Macmillan, 1985).

Ó Riain, Pádraig, 'The Saints and their Amanuenses: Early Models and Later Issues', in S.N. Tranter and H.L.C. Tristram (eds.) *Early Irish Literature—Media and Communication* (Tübingen: G. Narr, 1989), pp. 267-80.

—'Towards a Methodology in early Irish Hagiography', *Peritia* 1 (1982), pp. 146-59.

O'Grady, Standish Hayes, *Silva Gadelica I and II* (London: Williams & Norgate, 1892).

O'Keeffe, J.G., 'Cuchullin and Conlaech', *Ériu* 1 (1904), pp. 123-27.

O'Kelleher, A., and G. Schoepperle (eds. and trans.), *Betha Colaim Chille: Life of St. Colum Cille* (Urbana: University of Illinois under the auspices of the graduate school, 1918).

O'Leary, Philip, 'Choice and Consequence in Irish Heroic Literature', *CMCS* 27 (Summer 1994), pp. 49-59.

—'Contention at Feasts in Early Irish Literature', *Éigse* 20 (1984), pp. 115-27.

—'*Fír Fer*: An Internalized Ethical Concept in Early Irish Literature?', *Éigse* 22 (1987), pp. 1-14.

—'A Foreseeing Driver of an Old Chariot: Regal Moderation in Early Irish Literature', *CMCS* 11 (1986), pp. 1-16.

—'Honour-Bound: The Social Context of Early Irish Heroic Geis', *Celtica* 20 (1988), pp. 85-107.

—'The Honour of Women in Early Irish Literature', *Ériu* 38 (1987), pp. 27-44.

—'Jeers and Judgements: Laughter in Early Irish Literature', *CMCS* 22 (1991), pp. 15-29.

—'Magnanimous Conduct in Irish Heroic Literature', *Éigse* 25 (1991), pp. 28-44.

—'Verbal Deceit in the Ulster Cycle', *Éigse* 21 (1988), pp. 16-26.

O'Loughlin, Thomas, 'The Latin Sources of Medieval Irish Culture: A Partial Status Quaestionis', in McCone and Simms (eds.), *Progress*, pp. 91-106.

O'Meara, J.J. (trans.), *The Voyage of Saint Brendan: Journey to the Promised Land* (Dublin: Colin Smythe, 1991).

O'Rahilly, Cecile, 'Repetition: A Narrative Device in Táin Bó Cualnge', *Ériu* 30 (1979), pp. 67-74.

O'Rahilly, Cecile (ed. and trans.), *Táin Bó Cuailnge. Recension 1* (Dublin: DIAS, 1976).

O'Reilly, Jennifer, 'Exegesis and the Book of Kells: The Lucan Genealogy', in T. Finan and V. Twomey (eds.), *Scriptural Interpretation in the Fathers: Letter and Spirit* (Dublin: Four Courts, 1995), pp. 315-55.

Olmsted, Garrett, 'The Earliest Narrative version of the Táin: 7th-century Poetic References to Táin Bó Cuailnge', *Emania* 10 (1992), pp. 5-17.

Paglia, Camille, *Sex and Violence, or Nature and Art* (London: Penguin Books, 1995).

Pearl, Chaim, *Rashi* (New York: Grove Press, 1988).

Picard, Jean-Michel, 'The Purpose of the Vita Columba', *Peritia* 1 (1982), pp. 160-77.

—'Structural Patterns in Early Hiberno-Latin Hagiography', *Peritia* 4 (1985), pp. 67-82.

Plaut, W. Gunther, B.J. Bamberger and W.W. Hallo (eds., trans., commentary), *The Torah: A Modern Commentary* (New York: Union of American Hebrew Congregations, 1981).

Polzin, Robert, *Biblical Structuralism* (Philadelphia: Fortress Press, 1977).

Prickett, Stephen (ed.), *Reading the Text: Biblical Criticism and Literary Theory* (Oxford: Basil Blackwell, 1991).

Puhvel, Jaan, *Comparative Mythology* (Baltimore: The Johns Hopkins University Press, 1987).

Radner, Joan ' "Fury Destroys the World": Historical Strategy in Ireland's Ulster Epic', *Mankind Quarterly* 23/1 (1982), pp. 41-60.

Raglan, Lord, *The Hero: A Study in Tradition, Myth, and Drama* (London: Cape, 1936).

Rank, Otto, *The Myth of the Birth of the Hero and Other Writings* (New York: Vintage Books, 1959).

Rees, Alwyn, and Brinley Rees, *Celtic Heritage* (London: Thames & Hudson, 1961).

Reif, Stefan, 'Aspects of Medieval Jewish Literacy', in R. McKitterick (ed.), *The Uses of Literacy in Early Medieval Europe* (Cambridge: Cambridge University Press, 1990), pp. 134-55.

Reik, Theodor, *Of Love and Lust: On the Psychoanalysis of Romantic and Sexual Emotions* (New York: J. Aronson, 1974).

Richter, Michael, 'The Introduction of Alphabetic Writing to Ireland: Implications and Consequences', in *idem* (ed.), *Studies in Medieval Language and Culture* (Dublin: Four Courts, 1995), pp. 186-97.

Robinson, R.B., 'Wife and Sister through the Ages: Textual Determinacy and the History of Interpretation', *Semeia* 62 (1993), pp. 53-67.

Rorty, Richard, 'The Pragmatist's Progress', in Eco and Rorty (eds.), *Interpretation*, pp. 89-108.

Rosenberg, David (ed.), *Congregation: Contemporary Writers Read the Jewish Bible* (New York: Harcourt Brace Jovanovich, 1987).

Rosenblatt, J.P., and J.C. Sitterson (eds.), *Not in Heaven: Coherence and Complexity in Biblical Narrative* (Bloomington: Indiana University Press, 1991).

Roth, Marty, *Foul and Fair Play: Reading Genre in Classic Detective Fiction* (Athens: University of Georgia Press, 1995).

Rowley, H.H., 'The Relevance of Biblical Interpretation', *Int* 1/1 (1947), pp. 3-19.

Sasson, Jack, *Jonah* (Garden City, NY: Doubleday, 1990).

—'Esther', in Alter and Kermode (eds.), *Literary Guide*, pp. 335-42.

Sayers, William, 'Fergus and the Cosmogonic Sword', *HR* 25 (1986), pp. 30-56.

—' "Mani maidi an nem..." Ringing Changes on a Cosmic Motif', *Ériu* 37 (1986), pp. 98-117.

—'The Deficient Ruler as Avian Exile: Nebuchadnezzar and Suibhne Geilt', *Ériu* 43 (1992), pp. 217-20.

Schwartz, Regina, 'Adultery in the House of David: The Metanarratives of Biblical Scholarship and the Narratives of the Bible', *Semeia* 54 (1991), pp. 35-56.

Schwartz, Regina, (ed.), *The Book and the Text: The Bible and Literary Theory* (Oxford: Basil Blackwell, 1990), pp. 1-15.

Scowcroft, R., Mark, 'Abstract Narrative in Ireland', *Ériu* 46 (1995), pp. 121-58.

Sessle, Erica, 'Misogyny and Medb: Approaching Medb with Feminist Criticism', in Mallory and Stockman (eds.), *Ulidia*, pp. 135-38.

Sharpe, Richard (ed. and trans.), *Adomnán of Iona's Life of St Columba* (London: Penguin Books, 1995).

Sheehy, M.P., 'The Bible and the *Collectio Canonum Hibernensis*', in Ní Chatháin and Richter (eds.), *Irland*, pp. 277-307.

Silverman, Kaja, *Male Subjectivity at the Margins* (London: Routledge, 1992).

Sims-Williams, Patrick, review of Kim McCone, *Pagan Past and Christian Present*, in *Éigse* 29 (1996), pp. 181-96.

Sjöblom, Tom, 'On the Threshold: The Sacredness of Borders in Early Irish Literature', in Mallory and Stockman (eds.), *Ulidia*, pp. 159-64.

Sjoestedt, Marie-Louise, *Gods and Heroes of the Celts* (London: Methuen, 1949).

Smith, Roland, 'The Six Gifts', *JCS* 1/1 (1949), pp. 98-104.

Stephens, James, *Irish Fairy Stories* (London: Macmillan, 1924).

Sternberg, Meir, *The Poetics of Biblical Narrative: Ideological Literature and the Drama of Reading* (Bloomington: Indiana University Press, 1985).

Stock, Brian, *Listening for the Text: On the Uses of the Past* (Baltimore: The Johns Hopkins University Press, 1990).

Talmon, S., 'Wisdom in the Book of Esther', *VT* 13 (1963), pp. 419-55.

TANAKH: The Holy Scriptures (Philadelphia: Jewish Publication Society of America, 1988).

Thompson, Stith, *Motif-Index of Folk Literature* (Bloomington: Indiana University Press, 1955).

Trible, Phyllis, *God and the Rhetoric of Sexuality* (Philadelphia: Fortress Press, 1978).

Tymoczko, Maria, *Two Death Tales from the Ulster Cycle: The Death of CuChulainn and the Death of CuRoi* (Dublin: Dolmen Press, 1981).

Van Wolde, E, 'A Text–Semantic Study of the Hebrew Bible', *JBL* 113 (1994), pp. 19-35.

Vermes, Geza (ed. and trans.), *The Dead Sea Scrolls in English* (London: Penguin Books, 1993).

Vickery, John B., 'In Strange Ways: The Story of Samson', in B.O. Long (ed.), *Images of Man and God: Old Testament Short Stories in Literary Focus* (Bible and Literature Series, 1; Sheffield: Almond Press, 1981), pp. 58-73.

Wack, Mary, *Lovesickness in the Middle Ages* (Philadelphia: Fortress Press, 1990).

Watson, J.C. (ed.), *Mesca Ulad* (Dublin: DIAS, 1967).

Wharton, James, 'The Secret of [the LORD]: Story and Affirmation in Judges 13–16', *Int* 27/1 (1973), pp. 48-65.

Wilder, D, 'An Experimental Journal', *Semeia* 1/1 (1974), pp. 1-16.

Wilenski, R.H., *Mantegna and the Paduan School* (London: Faber, 1947).

Williams, James G., 'The Beautiful and the Barren: Convention in Biblical Type–Scenes', *JSOT* 17 (1980), pp. 107-19.

Wright, Charles D., 'Hiberno-Latin and Irish-influenced Biblical Commentaries, Florilegia and Homily Collections', in F.M. Biggs, T.D. Hill and P.E. Szarmach (eds.), *The Sources of Anglo-Saxon Literary Culture* (Binghamton, NY: Center for Medieval and Early Renaissance Studies, 1990), pp. 87-90.

—*The Irish Tradition in Old English Literature* (Cambridge: Cambridge University Press, 1993).

Zumthor, Paul, 'Comments on H.R. Jauss' Article', *New Literary History* 10/2 (Winter 1979), pp. 367-76.

INDEXES

INDEX OF BIBLICAL AND ANCIENT REFERENCES

OLD TESTAMENT

INDEX OF EARLY IRISH TEXTS

INDEX OF AUTHORS

JOURNAL FOR THE STUDY OF THE OLD TESTAMENT
SUPPLEMENT SERIES